D0569718

Psychoanalysis and the Unconscious

Fantasia of the Unconscious

BY D. H. LAWRENCE
Published by The Viking Press

NOVELS

- Sons and Lovers
- The Rainbow
- Women in Love
- The Lost Girl
- Aaron's Rod
- Kangaroo

- The Boy In the Bush (with M. L. Skinner)
- Four Short Novels (*Love Among the Haystacks, The Ladybird, The Fox, The Captain's Doll*)
  John Thomas and Lady Jane

NONFICTION

- Psychoanalysis and the Unconscious *and* Fantasia of the Unconscious
- Studies in Classic American Literature

- Apocalypse
- Sex, Literature and Censorship

COLLECTIONS

- Phoenix
  The Portable D. H. Lawrence
- Selected Poems
- The Complete Short Stories of D. H. Lawrence
- Selected Literary Criticism
  The Collected Letters of D. H. Lawrence

- The Complete Poems of D. H. Lawrence
  The Complete Plays of D. H. Lawrence
- Phoenix II
- D. H. Lawrence and Italy: *Twilight in Italy, Sea and Sardinia, Etruscan Places*

VIKING CRITICAL EDITION

Sons and Lovers (*edited by Julian Moynahan*)

- Available in Viking Compass edition.

D. H. LAWRENCE

[handwritten: avid] [handwritten: erbert]

Psychoanalysis
and the Unconscious

and

Fantasia
of the Unconscious

Introduction by Philip Rieff

THE VIKING PRESS · NEW YORK

COPYRIGHT 1921, 1922 BY THOMAS SELTZER, INC.
COPYRIGHT 1949, 1950 BY FRIEDA LAWRENCE
COPYRIGHT © 1960 BY THE VIKING PRESS, INC.

VIKING COMPASS EDITION
ISSUED IN 1960 BY THE VIKING PRESS, INC.
625 MADISON AVENUE, NEW YORK, N.Y. 10022

SBN 670-00060-4

LIBRARY OF CONGRESS CATALOG CARD NUMBER: 60-903

TENTH PRINTING APRIL 1973

DISTRIBUTED IN CANADA BY
THE MACMILLAN COMPANY OF CANADA LIMITED

PRINTED IN THE U.S.A. BY THE COLONIAL PRESS INC.

Contents

Psychoanalysis and the Unconscious

Fantasia of the Unconscious

Introduction

By PHILIP RIEFF

In *Psychoanalysis and the Unconscious* and again in *Fantasia of the Unconscious*, Lawrence made what were to be his main efforts to explain the doctrine otherwise expressed in his creative work. As such, the two books together take on the importance, if not the excellence, of his art.

When *Psychoanalysis and the Unconscious* first appeared in 1921, Lawrence's doctrinal explanations were laughed away by the reviewers, without exception; what scant notice the book received was good-humored, but it was treated as a bizarre and often incomprehensible new testament in the religion of sex, ardent to supersede the then not very old testament of psychoanalysis. In the first few pages Freud does appear to be cast in the role of Judas, putting the finger on the gentle Jesus of the Unconscious for the police forces of civilization. Lawrence himself appears as the good and true disciple; but his attack on Freud is incidental to the presentation of his own doctrine. When he saw how completely his message had been misunderstood, he immediately tried again—belligerently, even somewhat peevishly. "I stick to the solar plexus," he announces, and *Fantasia*, published in 1922, is a restatement and elaboration of his doctrine of the Unconscious as it had been stated in *Psychoanalysis*. Only the "few" will understand, he proclaims, in an unhappy effort to appeal to the snobbishness of his readers.

Apparently very few even pretended to understand, despite the fact that this was their second chance; *Fantasia*, too, had a bad press. To the evident pleasure of his meaner critics, Lawrence the artist had strayed too far from his art and thus exposed the incompetence of the prophet who urged the artist on. Those few critical friends Lawrence had at the time kindly ignored both books, preferring to avoid the embarrassment of defending the artist against his urges toward prophecy. The embarrassment lingers; friendly readers generally assume still that the artist in Lawrence can be distinguished from the prophet, that his fiction can be properly enjoyed without the pathos of learning from it those lessons that Lawrence considered uniquely true to life.

No writer in the twentieth century, except Freud, has been subjected to so much abuse from so many otherwise intelligent people as has Lawrence. Because both Freud and Lawrence did, each in his own way, get down to fundamentals, each has stood accused of being at once irrelevantly eccentric and directly dangerous to the community. To the literary and scientific guardians of mediocrity in our culture, genius is always a thing of the past; it may be discovered in books, but not in the flesh. Freud resented the separation from society that his genius caused him, but Lawrence sought, as well as suffered, his messianic alienation. "Entire separation, that is what must happen to one: not even the nominal shelter left, not even the mere fact of inclusion in the host. One must be entirely cast forth." This alienation he advised his friend Bertrand Russell to seek, if Russell hoped to become something more than an academic philosopher. Lawrence's withdrawal indicates the religious seriousness with which he took himself. As an isolate, desperately seeking community, he self-consciously transformed himself into a representative man of our culture. Deliberately shedding all the devices of a liberal and permissive conformity which he saw coming decades before this insight became commonplace, Lawrence detected in himself the hidden panic of isolation that grips modern man.

Rationalists were bound to oppose a doctrine such as Lawrence's and therefore to criticize with open malice his art. In turn, Lawrence opposed with something less than detachment the doctrine of a rationalist such as Freud. In these two books. the confrontation between Freud and Lawrence recapitulates the historic controversy—on what is the function of reason in the character of man—that divides Western culture still. Lawrence was the most profound spokesman in our century for the irrationalist minority position, defended heretofore by religious mystics living on the emotional and intellectual boundaries of a church civilization. Freud, on the other hand, bequeathed to the rationalist majority position that analytic subtlety in which it had been wanting for more than a century.

Lawrence's two books are rather unevenly divided between analyses of the effects of over-rationalizing our lives and advocacy of the religious mood, which is specifically irrational and erotic. Freud is the object of the Laurentian polemic precisely because he was the genius who took the longest step toward rationalizing even our erotic lives. Lawrence's analytic powers were limited by the passion of his advocacy; Freud remained always supremely analytical because he advocated nothing. For this reason, as Lawrence says early in *Psychoanalysis and the Unconscious*, Freud can never "get down to the rock on which he must build his church."

Because, to Freud no less than to Lawrence, a rational religion is a contradiction in terms, the psychoanalytic movement has no religious potential. No one before Freud had made so precisely for "the origins"; but his purpose in doing so was to tap these religious depths with more powerfully rational controls, distributed, like oil derricks, over the self-conscious surfaces of life. To Lawrence, such controls symbolize the sacrilege against life committed by modern science. Freud, he charges, has forgotten the prayerful attitude that man ought to have toward himself. In fact, Freud dealt most profoundly with the issue of whether man still needs such an attitude, even toward himself—while Lawrence suggests the prayerful attitude, without anyone to whom to pray. Not content with maintaining that religion could be divorced from theology, Lawrence suggests, in these two books written soon after the war that shattered once and for all the Christian moral frame of Western culture, what has become, since the 1920s, the personal position of advanced sensibility: feeling divorced from responsibility.

It is strange to see the novelist who was censored for his literary immoralities defending the "old religious faculty," which is the source of our moral emotions, against a psychologist as widely censored for the immorality of his therapeutic interpretations of that same religious faculty at the end of its strength. It would appear to be a perfect case of the pot calling the kettle black. Lawrence knew what he was about, however, as surely as did Freud. The "debacle" he foresaw really did threaten; the "old world" of Reason was indeed "yielding under us," its thin, dried crust of morality cracking up. But it was just such a debacle that Freud strove to help our civilization avoid, by shoring up Reason against further perverse outbreaks of the religious Unconscious.

The rationalist tradition experienced a chastened culmination in Freud. His is the very opposite of the crude rationalism of the eighteenth century, which rejected all psychic products as somehow fraudulent. Understanding his patient's perceptual and social world as expressions of the percipient's intelligence and emotion, Freud really erases the gap between therapeutic rationalism and self-assertive romanticism. He was aware how little the difference between the mythic and the scientific really mattered, and that his own science in the end came down to myth. This subtle reconciliation Lawrence was too impatient a critic to understand. But genius has a way of not recognizing the character of that genius closest to its own; carried away by the rhetoric of his alienated situation in the twenties, Lawrence marked Freud down as the leader of the enemy rationalist camp. Aiming as he did to liberate the religious impulse in his dogmatically rationalist readers, Lawrence failed to understand how undogmatic was his chosen rationalist opponent.

On the other hand, the fundamentalists of rationalism are still with us; they are frequently to be met among the most highly trained and emancipated people, who, in their yet unspoiled bigotry, fail to realize that everything great and good springs, as Lawrence believed, from man's inner life and not from changes in social and scientific arrangements. This faith in the externals of life has had the effect of making man think less than highly of himself. Such pride was not lacking in the religious epochs of our emotional history. Compare Lawrence's friend Russell's characterization of man as a passing and miserable accident in an indifferent creative universe with Lawrence's own daring not only to place the self at the center of the universe but to imagine it literally as the hot creative stuff from which even the remotest cold stars derive. "It is the [life of the] universe which has resulted from the death of individuals," Lawrence proclaims, proudly anthropomorphic in his opposition to the scientific downgrading of man.

In championing the irrational in a time he considered fatally rationalist, Lawrence may, however, have carried too far his sense of the artist's alienation from his culture. For it was thus that he expressed his uncertainty about the quality and worth of his own participation in the Unconscious. It is questionable, I think, whether any great modern artist can escape the double burden of having to relate himself analytically as well as expressively to his culture. With his sense of blood ties, Shakespeare participated in the unconscious life of his time perhaps more profoundly than any other man who has ever expressed himself in writing. But in that first Elizabethan age—before rationalism moralized as "freedom" and "individualism" the alienation of man from God, community, and finally self—such direct and publicly cognizable transformations as Shakespeare's of the irrational into art were still possible. Lawrence had no such luck; in his time the organic community of extended families had been superseded by societies of mutual manipulation. The family had lost both economic function and emotional authority; the role of the mother had been grotesquely distorted into dominance, and the father's degraded to that of permanent *other*. Only in private erotic relations, thought Lawrence, was it still possible to achieve the silent capacity for "passional communion" once natural in families. Nothing has changed since Lawrence's time, except to become more so.

Lawrence blames the rationalized machine civilization into

which he was born for the progress the disease of alienation has made. But alienation, as he elsewhere sensed, was characteristic of the human condition long before the rationalizing of life by technological science. In its original form, the doctrine was theological and specially Christian: man can cure himself of the disease only by accepting God's forgiveness, through Christ, and thus, in imitation of the divine mood, love not only his neighbor but also himself. When Catholic institutional theology of the Middle Ages had thoroughly rationalized human misery, and made reconciliation a routine, the early Luther recalled Western man to the necessity of leading an inner life, through the doctrine of justification by faith alone. When Luther saw what violence his liberation of the religious faculty had let loose, he hedged, in remorse over the consequences of his own position. But Lawrence, in his polemical enthusiasm for the same liberation, and without that experience of organizational responsibility which is thrust like an object lesson upon every revolutionary, rejects all hedgings. Welcoming as he did the imminent end of a culture created out of the divine ordering word (*Logos*), he is not appalled by the "scream of violence," which to him expresses not death but the birth, in "pain and splendor," of true individuality.

The freedom for which Lawrence argues especially in the later parts of *Fantasia* is not the civil freedom that is at issue for political philosophers. For him, man is everywhere born free; not all the cleverness of constitutional checks and balances, or more equitable distributions of property—the "bread question," as Lawrence says, mocking our politics—can protect this original uncorrupted state of mind. Being a "fearfully religious" man, Lawrence remembered what the post-religious had forgotten: that the human is captive not of political regimes but of his own lust for reasoning. Finally, to Lawrence, freedom in our time consists in the liberation of the inner man from this "idealism"—an idealism that shapes materialist or socialist culture no less than it does Christian or capitalist.

Rid as Lawrence thought he was of all Christian metaphysics, he argued gratuitously with the embarrassed intellectual Russell for just the "opposite principle to Christianity: self-fulfilment and social destruction, instead of self-love and self-sacrifice." That opposite Laurentian principle would, for the sake of immediacy in the expression of the intimate self, admit the scream of violence, as natural to man as the arched and stiffened back of a baby having a temper tantrum and of animals showing their teeth. Our culture has enforced the pretense that every show of teeth is a smile, that love is benevolent in character. There was a period in Lawrence's life when he felt messianic enough to hope for an assembly of men and women to teach us differently—a group that would form the "nucleus of a new belief," launching a "new center of attack" far removed from politics. In this respect, Lawrence shows himself as the most genuine of modern heresiarchs, chief and father—although only long after his death—over all the little heresiarchs: father-killers, ambivalent mother-lovers, culture-breakers, all those professional youngsters who swarm along the literary horizon looking for an older generation with some left-over self-images that might be good for smashing. Lawrence sensed how thoroughly even his elders had constructed their own morals to meet the new criterion of obsolescence. In his rage at the tyrannous permissiveness and publicity of modern life he is truly the revolutionary of the private life.

Perhaps Lawrence would have been a less happy auditor of the scream of violence, which he could not himself learn to utter, had he lived a little longer. He missed hearing the noises from Nuremburg; he did not hear the screams in the neighborhood from which Freud was extricated, despite his reluctance to leave for Lawrence's still idealist England. As it has turned out, no age has been more horrific than this age of science. The Unconscious has revenged itself for the setbacks it has suffered at the hands of rationalist science; repressed as theology, it has manifested itself in all sorts of perverse religions—as we saw in Germany, the great center of rationalism in the nineteenth century.

Lawrence knew intuitively, if not historically, that reason defends mainly against impulse, and against what he considered the legitimate and undeniable power of love. An argument, as he

rightly sensed, is rationalist, or "ideal," when it is pressed against
the possibility of some religious affirmation of our lives. But not
only was his own English community rationalized; all communi-
ties alike are now well along in the same process. It was futile, if
not dangerous, for Lawrence to insist that men ought not to
arbitrate their passions primarily through their analytic intel-
ligences. Analysis can judge not only passion but also itself; as
the common judge of both, it can show itself superior to passion
without killing it, as the Romantics feared. On the other hand,
passion is the common divider of men—in particular when it becomes attached to the world of ideas. A fresh wave of religiosity,
in the form of an indifference to public ideas while teasing out
the *pneuma* of intimate relations, will not of itself either bring
social peace or at last crown the power of love.

Nevertheless the prophet in Lawrence deserves the widest
possible reading; he is, after all, the most talented believer in the
irrational yet to come out of contemporary rationalist culture—
a culture that has survived mainly by taking up religious rejec-
tions, as that represented by the Protestant Reformation, into
itself. It is time again for both the thoughtful and the passionate
of that culture to realize that genuine revolutions are basically
religious in character. The Laurentian criticisms at least go to
fundamentals, however little they may appear to explain them use-
fully. Enseamed as they are in a network of affirmative myths, it
is inevitable that these criticisms should be disputed; but they
cannot, except at our peril, be entirely rejected, let alone ignored.

The "old religious faculty" of which Lawrence writes in advocacy, and in defense against science, is specifically the irrational power of love. It is the religiosity of living, in conjugal
love and with the natural event of children, of which he seeks
to remind us. Lawrence considers the divine as essentially erotic
in character. Though this position has been advanced at least
since the time of Plato, Lawrence is a very modern advocate
of Eros, and therefore very direct: the divine is realized charac-
teristically in the sexual relation between a man and one woman
—and then, in pathos, only fleetingly. Thus, in his great story,

The Man Who Died, he portrayed Jesus himself, upon his resurrection, admitting the error of becoming a Christ. The unnamed man of the story rediscovers his amatory humanity—the true divine in him—in a directly sexual way, taught that much by a blond votary of the Isis cult. Christ is resurrected as Jesus. He has achieved his own innocence of consciousness, understands now that he has misled his poor followers by searching for God the Father in the wrong way. Salvation lies only in the intimate life.

In *Psychoanalysis*, and at greater length in *Fantasia*, Lawrence declares for an innocence of mind that will permit Western man to relocate himself in relation to the rest of natural life. "For heaven's sake," he wrote to Bertrand Russell, "don't think . . . be a baby, and not a savant any more. Don't *do* anything any more—but for heaven's sake begin to *be*—start at the very beginning and be a perfect baby: in the name of courage." The rhetoric of child consciousness, which runs through both these books, must be put in the context of Lawrence's pre-Freudian view of the innocence of the child. Not that he believed the child was innocent of sexuality. Rather, precisely this sexuality is the condition of the innocence of childhood. For in its unconsidered sexual drives—to and from objects—a child cannot abide in any fixed ideals. From this Lawrence makes it follow that little children can, if understood, lead men toward the good life.

From his idealization of the passions as he supposed them to be—fresh in childhood—Lawrence derived, in part, his two main criteria for the living of life: first, the capacity to unite with another in the alternately straining and easing relation of love; second, the special masculine need for a "passionate purpose" in life, beyond meeting the erotic demands in a relation with one woman. The second purpose is in tension, as Freud thought too, with the first. For both Lawrence and Freud, women distract men from the missions in the world upon which they must embark. The feminine is the specifically anti-cultural force. Alone, or in a company of like-minded men, the husband must set out from his home to make something new and better in the world.

Yet, if they are to be effective, passionate purposes must be steady; and if they are steady, they develop inevitably into "fixed ideals." Just this steadiness of purpose, Lawrence considers, needs breaking. This second and higher satisfaction of the religious need through passionate purpose dissolves, under analysis, into mere passion for purpose. A nostalgia—passion once removed from purpose—informs Lawrence's private life. Many of the projections of himself in the male protagonists of his novels, as well as in his exhortatory poetry, reflect his own sterile passion for purpose. Like those for whom faith means mainly a continuing capacity to believe in the possibility of finding themselves, not in finding something beyond themselves, Lawrence's personal religion is all going to church and never getting there. The first criterion, which can be satisfied only in the erotic life, seems more strongly argued. In one respect, this strength compensates for the weakness of his second argument.

Ultimately, Lawrence believed, each self in its destinctiveness has one purpose only: to come into the "fullness of its being." From this fulfillment any fixed direction can only distract. To recognize "the fact of otherness," to accept the good life as an erotic crucible that can, for sacred moments, fuse together self and other—these alone can proximate fulfillment. Thus to take for granted both the distances and proximities of love completes in maturity the innocent eroticism of childhood.

Lawrence's piety toward the possibility of living in continuity with the universe, which he elaborates in his discussion of the alienation from true selfhood that is the burden of the latter half of *Fantasia*, specifies his religious hope for a condition of innocence, a return to that naïveté which can persist beyond the oceanic feelings of identity known at times to mystics and perhaps (Lawrence thought) to life in the womb. Such a state was better known to ages before the emancipation of women—an advance in society which, like the political enfranchisement of the masses, Lawrence bitterly regretted. Limited by their sexuality, both women and the masses have only been made unhappy by the political responsibilities conferred upon them. To Lawrence, not the freedom of self-searching but only a biologically warm family could preserve "the human being all his life fresh and alive, a true individual." Compared to this individual consciousness of continuity with all other selves, our polite social consciousness created individuals in relations of manipulative tension with one another. The modern tolerant, atomized family, educated in the liberal art of togetherness, represented to Lawrence our lowest point of alienation from other selves, and not our harmony with them.

The desire Lawrence built into the uncomplicated having of an *other* is the more pathetic for his irresistible intuitions of the impossibility of such satisfactions. Desires that bring genuine union also bring marriage. Sexual union puts the partners in a family way. Love, when complete, complicates life further; for it involves a group that grows along the line drawn by the original love relation. The final question which tests erotic behavior is whether one can become a good parent. Bad lovers make bad parents. Especially in *Fantasia*, Lawrence concentrates on the consequences of the original love relation for those loved. Without that sense of otherness which balances the capacity for warmth between lovers, they, as parents, kill their children with domineering kindness; on the other hand, alienated from each other, they may use their children as substitute lovers, as Lawrence knew mothers often do.* It is not the child but the parent (and, in particular, the modern mother) who invents the incest problem. Only near the end of his doctrinal volumes will the attack on Freud's idea of the incest taboo, with which Lawrence begins, turn clear and more plausible. To Lawrence the incest taboo represents another of Freud's projections as science of the false standards governing erotic relations in the family. Thus the incest taboo articulates the training in possessive love with which modern mothers, no longer libidinally related to their husbands, manage to keep their sons even after they become mothers-in-law. The sons, when they marry, remain bound to the one true

---

* Or, as an alternative, the alienation of the parents may be expressed in the "freedom" permitted their children. Lawrence noted the decline of immediacy not only in love but in authority. Instead of direct relations of authority, the family is run by oblique manipulations of guilt feelings, which train the child to congenital dishonesty in later life, and often to wearing confusions of sex role.

love they have known, as infants. Freud merely idealized this failure of parental willingness to recognize the child too as an inviolate other, and thus thought the incest taboo into universal existence. The experience of anthropologists and psychologists with pre-modern and un-Christian cultures does not confirm this Laurentian criticism of Freud; nor does it conclusively confirm the Freudian concept. But the weight of evidence inclines to the side of Freud. The ubiquity of the incest taboo, in cultures without our peculiar mother fixations, indicates that the Freudian concept is no mere public projection as science of some occasionally exaggerated notion of the intimacy appropriate across the generations.

Lawrence's practical advice on the conduct of family life seems to me healthy; it is also sad, for in the personal life of this deliberately prophetic figure the love relation with his wife, Frieda, was childless. As a prophet Lawrence drove himself, as much as he was driven, in search of the exemplary life. His rejection of England just equals his acceptance of himself. Yet, in his own private relations, he failed of completion in what was to him a most fundamental way. Not that, viewed from the perspective of prophecy, the personal life of D. H. Lawrence was a failure. Rather, because of his ambition to be an exemplar, his life, more than most, shows up its patches of familiar compromise. He was a second husband. His wife had already had her two children by a man whom she no longer loved—if ever she had. This preacher of family as well as conjugal passion never experienced, in his own childhood, that which he advocated. His own family example could only have taught him what it is he had to criticize, not, except by abstract negation, what to praise. Moreover, while preaching physical exuberance, Lawrence was a sick shell of a man: the gospel of health was carried in a thin hollow vessel. If ever strength of will and intelligence triumphed over weakness of body, this triumph belongs to Lawrence, panegyrist of the body.

Lawrence believed in the ultimacy of means and in the illusoriness of ends. His moral doctrine is of the most modern sort:

neither an ethics of responsibility nor an ethics of conscience, but an ethics of action. In the act of love is, for Lawrence, perfect action; in it we become free of both conscience and responsibility. We merely *are;* we cease to care, consider, reflect. This ecstatic doctrine of erotic action is in no way original with Lawrence; it is a staple of European, and especially German *Lebensphilosophie.* What is new in Lawrence, however, is his hymn-singing attitude toward the physicality of life. His piety toward the body is not vulgar; it is merely gratuitous. The world affirms itself; no religion of assent is needed. Nevertheless, Lawrence's paeans of affirmation are understandable; in modern culture, the emphasis on the sexual, the obsession with the private areas of life, is an implicit criticism of the ugly and deforming thing that our sociability has become.

Lawrence's erotic fiction has the function of critical myth. Those who subscribe narrowly to the rationalist tradition therefore find him a morally subversive writer, for they are inevitably advocates of living on the surface of consciousness, as far away from the religious Unconscious as they can get. It is the purpose of Lawrence's fiction to permit an experience of the divine to be encountered anew. Outside art, the numinous experience is not ordinarily available to modern men of culture. In this sense, all great art is therapeutic. Myth, and an art which expresses the mythic, permit a second level of experience; this time indirectly, the experience of the divine comes to the reader through the imagination of the writer, and is endowed with the form of his own life and special concerns. For this reason the interest in the personal history of the writer is inextricable from an interest in his fiction; the two dimensions live and die together. Lawrence's life is part of his art, for it went obviously into the making of his books. Correspondingly, his art reveals the pathos of his life, for the two—as I have said—are as far apart as an interpretation can be from that which is interpreted.

Lawrence would not have approved the odor of sanctity that now surrounds a work of art. Yet that odor is as inevitable as the odor of churches. The cultured of this era strive to relate themselves to art as a way of recapturing the experience of the divine in which otherwise they no longer believe and in which they cannot feel themselves participants, even indirectly. Through the mediation of a writer, painter, composer, movie director, the work of art is experienced as a thing in itself, bracketed and raised above the ordinary workaday world, yet related to that world as revelation is related to that which is revealed—superior and saving. The work of art becomes that *wholly other*, present and yet inviolate, through which the cultivated may escape, for the time of the relation, their self-isolation. To some, the aesthetic relation may become even more important than directly human contacts, because of the relative frequency with which passional communions occur in confronting the surrogates of life in art.

Such passion is even more likely to occur among the producers of art than among its consumers. A painter may now consider it more important to paint a fine picture than to raise a fine family. With his sense of "vocation," the artist himself becomes the exemplary individualist, justified in his self-isolation by a culture aware of the decline of vocations into jobs. But even an art that preaches life, as Lawrence's did, may perversely sacrifice life to art. For when art becomes invested with religious meaning, it may become the vehicle of nothing other than its own continuance. The cult of the art object in modern society, quite apart from its dynamics of prestige, illustrates just that vicariousness of the erotic which Lawrence opposed. Yet, despite his programmatic statements urging everyone to his own numinous experience of continuity with the other, Lawrence himself has become a major myth-mediator in our time. The continuing excitement about his work and life measures the emotional investment that our culture has made in the invisible church of literary men.

Coming out from behind the fictional mask to speak directly, in his own person, in these two polemics, Lawrence vigorously urges each man to steer toward his own sort of collision with the power of emotions; he considers the very core of religious experience an experience of self. It is this ruthless driving inward, toward the hidden self, rather than outward, toward society, that characterizes both his own fiction and Freud's psycho-therapy. Both, in very different ways and for opposing purposes, encourage as well as express the dominant inward movement of our time.

Despite his heated polemical tone, Lawrence did not exagger-ate the difference between his own and the psychoanalytic en-counter with instinct. In the therapeutic situation, psychological man apparently encounters a variety of that conflict in wills which the religious man must always have experienced. But the Freudian contact with the Unconscious attempts, in effect, to eliminate religious experience by paralleling it, and by subjecting it to the closest intellectual scrutiny and review at decisive stages of its development. In the transference, the sources of erotic feeling are made transparent; every motive, including the in-tellectual one, is seen through and thus put into question. To Lawrence such an approach intellectualizes the genuinely erotic out of life, thus destroying the possibility of achieving that ulti-mate state of "innocence"—as, in fact, Freud intended. In the psychoanalytic situation, Freud brought about a therapeutic col-lision between Reason and that force which religious men have long recognized and agreed to call divine: love, or force in its definitively irrational form.

During the shaping period of Western culture, the encounter with love was critically represented in Christian terms. Augus-tine's *Confessions* explain the encounter as it occurred in one man; but they explain, at the same time, how the Christian myth managed for so long to stabilize the encounter, not as art but as theology. Augustine fully recognized the erotic drive, which comes from below and penetrates upward into every aspect of ordinary life at the surface of consciousness. But in the Christian myth of encounter, the violence of erotic feeling is pierced by the counter-eroticism of God, which descends from above and as-sumes, below, the aspect of authority, through the "Word" or "Reason" or "Logos" incarnate in one man. It was just this ra-tionalizing element in the Christian erotic myth that Lawrence rejected. Love, he said, cannot be identified with reason; this is precisely the "mental consciousness" which Christianity criticizes in the myth of the fall of man from innocence to knowledge.

In Lawrence's view the separation between subject and object which he considers the original sin of "mental consciousness," through which all men daily recapitulate the first fall, led on to more and more self-destructive knowledge by science, can only be healed through love. When, through erotic experience, we repair the damage done by abstract thought, we are in fact loving the divine substance in things. Lawrence's mystical intuitions are, as I have said, post-Christian. In the Christian myth, loving oneself derives from experiencing the fact that one is loved by God. But in the Laurentian version, God having died, nothing remains except self-love. Lawrence is a Trinitarian who has understood that the first two persons of the Trinity have gone the way of all myth figures; the third person—the Holy Ghost, the power of love, will—is all that remains, and upon this third person is founded both the Freudian science and the Laurentian art.

Freud possessed a coherent and conservative imagination—he was the one conservative genius of modern culture, defending only what can possibly be defended. Lawrence's was an incoherent and revolutionary imagination—incoherent because revolutionary. In our own immediate period the incoherence of the revolutionary imagination, as we find it exhibited in art and poetry, is a consequence of the decline of the necessary and permitting condition out of which revolutionary imaginations can develop: the vitality of tradition. The continuity between tradition and revolution having been shattered, the revolutionary imagination has been distorted. Because we really have no churches, we can have no reformations.

What ties the Lawrence of *Psychoanalysis and the Unconscious* and *Fantasia of the Unconscious* to an ancient reforming tradition is his belief that the decisive function in man is will, desire—not intellect. Here, in his polemic against Freud, Lawrence reproduces the great struggle in Western culture between voluntarism and intellectualism. Lawrence, the voluntarist, trusts will; Freud, the intellectualist, trusts reason. To Lawrence, therefore, Freud is the great enemy spokesman, engaged to the analysis but not the advocacy of the Unconscious.

University of California
Berkeley
June 1959

Psychoanalysis
and the Unconscious

I

Psychoanalysis v. Morality

Psychoanalysis has sprung many surprises on us, performed more than one volte-face before our indignant eyes. No sooner had we got used to the psychiatric quack who vehemently demonstrated the serpent of sex coiled round the root of all our actions, no sooner had we begun to feel honestly uneasy about our lurking complexes, than lo and behold the psychoanalytic gentleman reappeared on the stage with a theory of pure psychology. The medical faculty, which was on hot bricks over the therapeutic innovations, heaved a sigh of relief as it watched the ground warming under the feet of the professional psychologists.

This, however, was not the end. The ears of the ethnologist began to tingle, the philosopher felt his gorge rise, and at last the moralist knew he must rush in. By this time psychoanalysis had become a public danger. The mob was on the alert. The Oedipus complex was a household word, the incest motive a commonplace of tea-table chat. Amateur analyses became the vogue. "Wait till you've been analysed," said one man to another, with varying intonation. A sinister look came into the eyes of the initiates—the famous, or infamous, Freud look. You could recognize it everywhere, wherever you went.

Psychoanalysts know what the end will be. They have crept in among us as healers and physicians; growing bolder, they have asserted their authority as scientists; two more minutes and they will appear as apostles. Have we not seen and heard the *ex cathedra* Jung? And does it need a prophet to discern that Freud is on the brink of a Weltanschauung—or at least a Menschenschauung, which is a much more risky affair? What detains him? Two things. First and foremost, the moral issue. And next, but more vital, he can't get down to the rock on which he must build his church.

Let us look to ourselves. This new doctrine—it will be called no less—has been subtly and insidiously suggested to us, gradually inoculated into us. It is true that doctors are the priests, nay worse, the medicine-men of our decadent society. Psychoanalysis has made the most of the opportunity.

First and foremost the issue is a moral issue. It is not here a matter of reform, new moral values. It is the life or death of all morality. The leaders among the psychoanalysts know what they have in hand. Probably most of their followers are ignorant, and therefore pseudo-innocent. But it all amounts to the same thing. Psychoanalysis is out, under a therapeutic disguise, to do away entirely with the moral faculty in man. Let us fling the challenge, and then we can take sides in all fairness.

The psychoanalytic leaders know what they are about, and shrewdly keep quiet, going gently. Yet, however gently they go, they set the moral stones rolling. At every step the most innocent and unsuspecting analyst starts a little landslide. The old world is yielding under us. Without any direct attack, it comes loose under the march of the psychoanalyst, and we hear the dull rumble of the incipient avalanche. We are in for a débâcle.

But at least let us know what we are in for. If we are to rear a serpent against ourselves, let us at least refuse to nurse it in our temples or to call it the cock of Aesculapius. It is time the white garb of the therapeutic cant was stripped off the psychoanalyst. And now that we feel the strange crackling and convulsion in our moral foundations, let us at least look at the house which we are bringing down over our heads so blithely.

Long ago we watched in frightened anticipation when Freud set out on his adventure into the hinterland of human consciousness. He was seeking for the unknown sources of the mysterious stream of consciousness. Immortal phrase of the immortal James! Oh stream of hell which undermined my adolescence! The stream of consciousness! I felt it streaming through my brain, in at one ear and out at the other. And again I was sure it went round in my cranium, like Homer's Ocean, encircling my established mind. And sometimes I felt it must bubble up in the cerebellum and wind its way through all the convolutions of the true brain. Horrid stream! Whence did it come, and whither was it bound? The stream of consciousness!

And so, who could remain unmoved when Freud seemed suddenly to plunge towards the origins? Suddenly he stepped out of the conscious into the unconscious, out of the everywhere into the nowhere, like some supreme explorer. He walks straight through the wall of sleep, and we hear him rumbling in the cavern of dreams. The impenetrable is not impenetrable, unconsciousness is not nothingness. It is sleep, that wall of darkness which limits our day. Walk bang into the wall, and behold the wall isn't there. It is the vast darkness of a cavern's mouth, the cavern of anterior darkness whence issues the stream of consciousness.

With dilated hearts we watched Freud disappearing into the cavern of darkness, which is sleep and unconsciousness to us, darkness which issues in the foam of all our day's consciousness. He was making for the origins. We watched his ideal candle flutter and go small. Then we waited, as men do wait, always expecting the wonder of wonders. He came back with dreams to sell.

But sweet heaven, what merchandise! What dreams, dear heart! What was there in the cave? Alas that we ever looked! Nothing but a huge slimy serpent of sex, and heaps of excrement, and a myriad repulsive little horrors spawned between sex and excrement.

Is it true? Does the great unknown of sleep contain nothing else? No lovely spirits in the anterior regions of our being? None! Imagine the unspeakable horror of the *repressions* Freud brought home to us. Gagged, bound, maniacal repressions, sexual complexes, faecal inhibitions, dream-monsters. We tried to repudiate them. But no, they were there, demonstrable. These were the horrid things that ate our souls and caused our helpless neuroses.

We had felt that perhaps we were wrong inside, but we had never imagined it so bad. However, in the name of healing and medicine we prepared to accept it all. If it was all just a result of illness, we were prepared to go through with it. The analyst promised us that the tangle of complexes would be unravelled, the obsessions would evaporate, the monstrosities would dissolve, sublimate, when brought into the light of day. Once all the dream-horrors were translated into full consciousness, they would sublimate into—well, we don't quite know what. But anyhow, they would sublimate. Such is the charm of a new phrase that we accepted this sublimation process without further question. If our complexes were going to sublimate once they were surgically exposed to full mental consciousness, why, best perform the operation.

Thus analysis set off gaily on its therapeutic course. But, like Hippolytus, we ran too near the sea's edge. After all, if complexes exist only as abnormalities which can be removed, psychoanalysis has not far to go. Our own horses ran away with us. We began to realize that complexes were not just abnormalities. They were part of the stock-in-trade of the normal unconscious. The only abnormality, so far, lies in bringing them into consciousness.

This creates a new issue. Psychoanalysis, the moment it begins to demonstrate the nature of the unconscious, is assuming the role of psychology. Thus the new science of psychology proceeds to inform us that our complexes are not just mere interlockings in the mechanism of the psyche, as was taught by one of the first and most brilliant of the analysts, a man now forgotten. He fully realized that even the psyche itself depends on a certain organic, mechanistic activity, even as life depends on the mechanistic organism of the body. The mechanism of the psyche could have its hitches, certain parts could stop working, even as the parts of the body can stop their functioning. This arrest in some part of the functioning psyche gave rise to a complex, even as the stopping of one little cog-wheel in a machine will arrest a whole section of that machine. This was the origin of the complex-theory, purely mechanistic. Now the analyst found that a complex did not necessarily vanish when brought into consciousness. Why should it? Hence he decided that it did not arise from the stoppage of any little wheel. For it refused to disappear, no matter how many psychic wheels were started. Finally, then, a complex could not be regarded as the result of an inhibition.

Here is the new problem. If a complex is not caused by the inhibition of some so-called normal sex-impulse, what on earth is it caused by? It obviously refuses to sublimate—or to come undone when exposed and prodded. It refuses to answer to the promptings of normal sex-impulse. You can remove all possible inhibitions of the normal sex desire, and still you cannot remove the complex. All you have done is to make conscious a desire which previously was unconscious.

This is the moral dilemma of psychoanalysis. The analyst set out to cure neurotic humanity by removing the cause of the neurosis. He finds that the cause of neurosis lies in some unadmitted sex desire. After all he has said about inhibition of normal sex, he is brought at last to realize that at the root of almost every neurosis lies some incest-craving, and that this incest-craving is *not the result of inhibition of normal sex-craving*. Now see the dilemma—it is a fearful one. If the incest-craving is not the outcome of any inhibition of normal desire, if it actually exists and refuses to give way before any criticism, what then? What remains but to accept it as part of the normal sex-manifestation?

Here is an issue which analysis is perfectly willing to face. Among themselves the analysts are bound to accept the incest-craving as part of the normal sexuality of man, normal, but suppressed, because of moral and perhaps biological fear. Once, however, you accept the incest-craving as part of the normal sexuality of man, you must remove all repression of incest itself. In fact, you must admit incest as you now admit sexual marriage, as a duty even. Since at last it works out that neurosis is not the result of inhibition of so-called *normal* sex, but of inhibition of incest-craving. Any inhibition must be wrong, since inevitably in the end it causes neurosis and insanity. Therefore the inhibition of incest-craving is wrong, and this wrong is the cause of practically all modern neurosis and insanity.

Psychoanalysis will never openly state this conclusion. But it is to this conclusion that every analyst must, willy-nilly, consciously or unconsciously, bring his patient.

Trigant Burrow says that Freud's *unconscious* does but represent our conception of conscious sexual life as this latter exists in a state of repression. Thus Freud's unconscious amounts practically to no more than our repressed incest impulses. Again, Burrow says that it is knowledge of sex that constitutes sin, and not sex itself. It is when the mind turns to consider and *know* the great affective-passional functions and emotions that sin enters. Adam and Eve fell, not because they had sex, or even because they committed the sexual act, but because they became aware of their sex and of the possibility of the act. When sex became to them a mental object—that is, when they discovered that they could deliberately enter upon and enjoy and even provoke sexual activity in themselves, then they were cursed and cast out of Eden. Then man became self-responsible; he entered on his own career.

Both these assertions by Burrow seem to us brilliantly true. But must we inevitably draw the conclusion psychoanalysis draws? Because we discover in the unconscious the repressed body of our incest-craving, and because the recognition of *desire*, the making a mental objective of a certain desire causes the introduction of the sin motive, the desire in itself being beyond criticism or moral judgment, must we therefore accept the incest-craving as part of our natural desire and proceed to put it into practice, as being at any rate a lesser evil than neurosis and insanity?

It is a question. One thing, however, psychoanalysis all along the line fails to determine, and that is the nature of the pristine unconscious in man. The incest-craving is or is not inherent in the pristine psyche. When Adam and Eve became aware of sex in themselves, they became aware of that which was pristine in them, and which preceded all knowing. But when the analyst discovers the incest motive in the unconscious, surely he is only discovering a term of humanity's repressed *idea* of sex. It is not even *suppressed* sex-consciousness, but *repressed*. That is, it is nothing pristine and anterior to mentality. It is in itself the mind's ulterior motive. That is, the incest-craving is propagated in the pristine unconscious by the mind itself, even though unconsciously. The mind acts as incubus and procreator of its own horrors, *deliber-*

ately unconsciously. And the incest motive is in its origin not a pristine impulse, but a logical extension of the existent idea of sex and love. The mind, that is, transfers the idea of incest into the affective-passional psyche, and keeps it there as a repressed motive.

This is as yet a mere assertion. It cannot be made good until we determine the nature of the true, pristine unconscious, in which all our genuine impulse arises—a very different affair from that sack of horrors which psychoanalysts would have us believe is source of motivity. The Freudian unconscious is the cellar in which the mind keeps its own bastard spawn. The true unconscious is the well-head, the fountain of real motivity. The sex of which Adam and Eve became conscious derived from the very God who bade them be not conscious of it—it was not spawn produced by secondary propagation from the mental consciousness itself.

✆ I I ✆

The Incest Motive and Idealism

It is obvious we cannot recover our moral footing until we can in some way determine the true nature of the unconscious. The word unconscious itself is a mere definition by negation and has no positive meaning. Freud no doubt prefers it for this reason. He rejects *subconscious* and *preconscious*, because both these would imply a sort of nascent consciousness, the shadowy half-conciousness which precedes mental realization. And by his unconscious he intends no such thing. He wishes rather to convey, we imagine, that which *recoils from* consciousness, that which reacts in the psyche away from mental consciousness. His unconscious is, we take it, that part of the human consciousness which, though mental, ideal in its nature, yet is unwilling to expose itself to full recognition, and so recoils back into the affective regions and acts there as a secret agent, unconfessed, unadmitted, potent, and usually destructive. The whole body of our repressions makes up our unconscious.

The question lies here: whether a repression is a primal impulse which has been deterred from fulfilment, or whether it is an *idea* which is refused enactment. Is a repression a repressed passional impulse, or is it an idea which we suppress and refuse to put into practice—nay, which we even refuse to own at all, a disowned, outlawed idea, which exists rebelliously outside the pale?

Man can inhibit the true passional impulses and so produce a derangement in the psyche. This is a truism nowadays, and we are grateful to psychoanalysis for helping to make it so. But man can do more than this. Finding himself in a sort of emotional cul-de-sac, he can proceed to deduce from his given emotional and passional premises conclusions which are not emotional or passional at all, but just logical, abstract, ideal. That is, a man finds it impossible to realize himself in marriage. He recognizes the fact that his emotional, even passional, regard for his mother is deeper than it ever could be for a wife. This makes him unhappy, for he knows that passional communion is not complete unless it be also sexual. He has a body of sexual passion which he cannot transfer to a wife. He has a profound love for his mother. Shut in between walls of tortured and increasing passion, he must find some escape or fall down the pit of insanity and death. What is the only possible escape? To seek in the arms of the mother the refuge which offers nowhere else. And so the incest motive is born. All the laboured explanations of the psychoanalysts are unnecessary. The incest motive is a logical deduction of the human reason, which has recourse to this last extremity, to save itself. Why is the human reason in peril? That is another story. At the moment we are merely considering the origin of the incest motive.

The logical conclusion of incest is, of course, a profound decision in the human soul, a decision affecting the deepest passional centres. It rouses the deepest instinctive opposition. And therefore it must be kept secret until this opposition is either worn away or persuaded away. Hence the repression and ultimate disclosure.

Now here we see the secret working of the process of idealism. By idealism we understand the motivizing of the great affective sources by means of ideas mentally derived. As for example the incest motive, which first and foremost is a logical deduction made by the human reason, even if unconsciously made, and secondly is introduced into the affective, passional sphere, where it now proceeds to serve as a principle for action.

This motivizing of the passional sphere from the ideal is the final peril of human consciousness. It is the death of all spontaneous, creative life, and the substituting of the mechanical principle.

It is obvious that the ideal becomes a mechanical principle, if it be applied to the affective soul as a fixed motive. An ideal established in control of the passional soul is no more and no less than a supreme machine-principle. And a machine, as we know, is the active unit of the material world. Thus we see how it is that in the end pure idealism is identical with pure materialism, and the most ideal peoples are the most completely material. Ideal and material are identical. The ideal is but the god in the machine— the little, fixed machine-principle which works the human psyche automatically.

We are now in the last stages of idealism. And psychoanalysis alone has the courage necessary to conduct us through these last stages. The identity of love with sex, the single necessity for fulfilment through love, these are our fixed ideals. We must fulfil these ideals in their extremity. And this brings us finally to incest, even incest-worship. We have no option, whilst our ideals stand.

Why? Because incest is the logical conclusion of our ideals, when these ideals have to be carried into passional effect. And idealism has no escape from logic. And once he has built himself in the shape of any ideal, man will go to any logical length rather than abandon his ideal corpus. Nay, some great cataclysm has to throw him down and destroy the whole fabric of his life before the motor-principle of his dominant ideal is destroyed. Hence psychoanalysis as the advance-guard of science, the evangel of the last *ideal* liberty. For of course there is a great fascination in a completely effected idealism. Man is then undisputed master of his own fate, and captain of his own soul. But better say engine-driver, for in truth he is no more than the little god in the machine, this master of fate. He has invented his own automatic principles, and he works himself according to them, like any little mechanic inside the works.

But, ideal or not, we are all of us between the pit and the pendulum, or the walls of red-hot metal, as may be. If we refuse the Freudian *pis aller* as a means of escape, we have still to find some way out. For there we are, all of us, trapped in a corner where we cannot and simply do not know how to fulfil our own natures, passionally. We don't know in which way fulfilment lies. If psychoanalysis discovers incest, small blame to it.

Yet we do know this much: that the pushing of the ideal to any further lengths will not avail us anything. We have actually to go back to our own unconscious. But not to the unconscious which is the inverted reflection of our ideal consciousness. We must discover, if we can, the true unconscious, where our life bubbles up in us, prior to any mentality. The first bubbling life in us, which is innocent of any mental alteration, this is the unconscious. It is pristine, not in any way ideal. It is the spontaneous origin from which it behooves us to live.

What then is the true unconscious? It is not a shadow cast from the mind. It is the spontaneous life-motive in every organism. Where does it begin? It begins where life begins. But that is too vague. It is no use talking about life and the unconscious in bulk. You can talk about electricity, because electricity is a homogeneous force, conceivable apart from any incorporation. But life is inconceivable as a general thing. It exists only in living creatures. So that life begins, now as always, in an individual living creature. In the beginning of the individual living creature is the beginning of life, every time and always, and life has no beginning apart from this. Any attempt at a further generalization takes us merely beyond the consideration of life into the region of mechanical homogeneous force. This is shown in the cosmologies of eastern religions.

The beginning of life is in the beginning of the first individual creature. You may call the naked, unicellular bit of plasm the first individual, if you like. Mentally, as far as thinkable simplicity goes, it is the first. So that we may say that life begins in the first naked unicellular organism. And where life begins the unconscious also begins. But mark, the first naked unicellular organism is an *individual*. It is a specific individual, not a mathematical unit, like a unit of force.

Where the individual begins, life begins. The two are inseparable, life and individuality. And also, where the individual begins, the unconscious, which is the specific life-motive, also begins. We are trying to trace the unconscious to its source. And we find that this source, in all the higher organisms, is the first ovule cell from which an individual organism arises. At the moment of conception, when a procreative male nucleus fuses with the nucleus of the female germ, at that moment does a new unit of life, of consciousness, arise in the universe. Is it not obvious? The unconscious has no other source than this, this first fused nucleus of the ovule.

Useless to talk about the unconscious as if it were a homogeneous force like electricity. You can only deal with the unconscious when you realize that in every individual organism an individual nature, an individual consciousness, is spontaneously created at the moment of conception. We say *created*. And by *created* we mean spontaneously appearing in the universe, out of nothing. *Ex nihilo nihil fit.* It is true that an individual is also generated. By the fusion of two nuclei, male and female, we understand the process of generation. And from the process of generation we may justly look for a new unit, according to the law of cause and effect. As a natural or automatic result of the process of generation we may look for a new unit of existence. But the nature of this new unit must derive from the natures of the parents, also by law. And this we deny. We deny that the nature of any new creature derives from the natures of its parents. The nature of the infant does *not* follow from the natures of its parents. The nature of the infant is *not* just a new permutation-and-combination of elements contained in the natures of the parents. There is in the nature of the infant that which is utterly unknown in the natures of the parents. Something which could never be derived from the natures of all the existent individuals or previous individuals. There is in the nature of the infant something entirely new, underived, underivable, something which is, and which will forever remain, *causeless*. And this something is the unanalysable, indefinable reality of individuality. Every time at the moment of conception of every higher organism an individual nature incomprehensibly arises in the universe, out of nowhere. Granted the whole cause-and-effect process of generation and evolution, still the individual is not explained. The individual unit of consciousness and being which arises at the conception of every higher organism arises by pure creation, by a process not susceptible to understanding, a process which takes place outside the field of mental comprehension, where mentality, which is definitely limited, cannot and does not exist.

This causeless created nature of the individual being is the same as the old mystery of the divine nature of the soul. Religion was right and science is wrong. Every individual creature has a soul, a specific individual nature the origin of which cannot be found in any cause-and-effect process whatever. Cause and effect will not explain even the individuality of a single dandelion. There is no assignable cause, and no logical reason, for individuality. On the contrary, individuality appears in defiance of all scientific law, in defiance even of reason.

Having established so much, we can really approach the unconscious. By the unconscious we wish to indicate that essential unique nature of every individual creature, which is, by its very nature, unanalysable, undefinable, inconceivable. It cannot be conceived, it can only be experienced, in every single instance. And, being inconceivable, we will call it the unconscious. As a matter of fact, *soul* would be a better word. By the unconscious we do mean the soul. But the word *soul* has been vitiated by the idealistic use, until nowadays it means only that which a man conceives himself to be. And that which a man conceives himself to be is something far different from his true unconscious. So we must relinquish the ideal word soul.

If, however, the unconscious is inconceivable, how do we know it at all? We know it by direct experience. All the best part of knowledge is inconceivable. We know the sun. But we cannot conceive the sun, unless we are willing to accept some theory of burning gases, some cause-and-effect nonsense. And even if we do have a mental conception of the sun as a sphere of blazing gas —which it certainly isn't—we are just as far from knowing what *blaze* is. Knowledge is always a matter of whole experience, what St. Paul calls knowing in full, and never a matter of mental conception merely. This is indeed the point of all full knowledge: that it is contained mainly within the unconscious, its mental or conscious reference being only a sort of extract or shadow.

It is necessary for us to know the unconscious, or we cannot live, just as it is necessary for us to know the sun. But we need not explain the unconscious, any more than we need explain the sun. We can't do either, anyway. We know the sun by beholding him and watching his motions and feeling his changing power. The same with the unconscious. We watch it in all its manifestations, its unfolding incarnations. We watch it in all its processes and its unaccountable evolutions, and these we register.

For though the unconscious is the creative element, and though, like the soul, it is beyond all law of cause and effect in its totality, yet in its processes of self-realization it follows the laws of cause and effect. The processes of cause and effect are indeed part of the working out of this incomprehensible self-realization of the individual unconscious. The great laws of the universe are no more than the fixed habits of the living unconscious.

What we must needs do is to try to trace still further the habits of the true unconscious, and by mental recognition of these habits break the limits which we have imposed on the movement of the unconscious. For the whole point about the true unconscious is that it is all the time moving forward, beyond the range of its own fixed laws or habits. It is no good trying to superimpose an ideal nature upon the unconscious. We have to try to recognize the true nature and then leave the unconscious itself to prompt new movement and new being—the creative progress.

What we are suffering from now is the restriction of the unconscious within certain ideal limits. The more we force the ideal the more we rupture the true movement. Once we can admit the *known*, but incomprehensible, presence of the integral unconscious; once we can trace it home in ourselves and follow its first revealed movements; once we know how it habitually unfolds itself; once we can scientifically determine its laws and processes in ourselves: then at last we can begin to live from the spontaneous initial prompting, instead of from the dead machine-principles of ideas and ideals. There is a whole science of the creative unconscious, the unconscious in its law-abiding activities. And of this science we do not even know the first term. Yes, when we know that the unconscious appears by creation, as a new individual reality in every newly fertilized germ-cell, then we know the very first item of the new science. But it needs a superscientific grace before we can admit this first new item of knowledge. It means that science abandons its intellectualist position and embraces the old religious faculty. But it does not thereby become less scientific, it only becomes at last complete in knowledge.

The Birth of Consciousness

It is useless to try to determine *what is consciousness* or *what is knowledge*. Who cares anyhow, since we know without definitions. But what we fail to know, yet what we must know, is the nature of the pristine consciousness which lies integral and progressive within every functioning organism. The brain is the seat of the ideal consciousness. And ideal consciousness is only the dead end of consciousness, the spun silk. The vast bulk of consciousness is non-cerebral. It is the sap of our life, of all life.

We are forced to attribute to a starfish, or to a nettle, its own peculiar and integral consciousness. This throws us at once out of the ideal castle of the brain into the flux of sap-consciousness. But let us not jump too far in one bound. Let us refrain from taking a sheer leap down the abyss of consciousness, down to the invertebrates and the protococci. Let us cautiously scramble down the human declivities. Or rather let us try to start somewhere near the foot of the calvary of human consciousness. Let us consider the child in the womb. Is the foetus conscious? It must be, since it carries on an independent and progressive self-development. This consciousness obviously cannot be ideal, cannot be cerebral, since it precedes any vestige of cerebration. And yet it is an integral, individual consciousness, having its own single purpose and progression. Where can it be centred, how can it operate, before even nerves are formed? For it does steadily and persistently operate, even spinning the nerves and brain as a web for its own motion, like some subtle spider.

What is the spinning spider of the first human consciousness—or rather, where is the centre at which this consciousness lies and spins? Since there must be a centre of consciousness in the tiny foetus, it must have been there from the very beginning. There it must have been, in the first fused nucleus of the ovule. And if we could but watch this prime nucleus, we should no doubt realize that throughout all the long and incalculable history of the individual it still remains central and prime, the source and clue of the living unconscious, the origin. As in the first moment of conception, so to the end of life in the individual, the first nucleus remains the creative-productive centre, the quick, both of consciousness and of organic development.

And where in the developed foetus shall we look for this creative-productive quick? Shall we expect it in the brain or in the heart? Surely our own subjective wisdom tells us, what science can verify, that it lies beneath the navel of the folded foetus. Surely that prime centre, which is the very first nucleus of the fertilized ovule, lies situated beneath the navel of all womb-born creatures. There, from the beginning, it lay in its mysterious relation to the outer, active universe. There it lay, perfectly associated with the parent body. There it acted on its own peculiar independence, drawing the whole stream of creative blood upon itself, and, spinning within the parental blood-stream, slowly creating or bodying forth its own incarnate amplification. All the time between the quick of life in the foetus and the great outer universe there exists a perfect correspondence, upon which correspondence the astrologers based their science in the days before mental consciousness had arrogated all knowledge unto itself.

The foetus is not *personally* conscious. But then what is personality if not ideal in its origin? The foetus is, however, radically, individually conscious. From the active quick, the nuclear centre, it remains single and integral in its activity. At this centre it distinguishes itself utterly from the surrounding universe, whereby both are modified. From this centre the whole individual arises, and upon this centre the whole universe, by implication, impinges. For the fixed and stable universe of law and matter, even the whole cosmos, would wear out and disintegrate if it did not rest and find renewal in the quick centre of creative life in individual creatures.

And since this centre has absolute location in the first fertilized nucleus, it must have location still in the developed foetus, and in the mature man. And where is this location in the unborn infant? Beneath the burning influx of the navel. Where is it in the adult man? Still beneath the navel. As primal affective centre it lies within the solar plexus of the nervous system.

We do not pretend to use technical language. But surely our meaning is plain even to correct scientists, when we assert that in all mammals the centre of primal, constructive consciousness and activity lies in the middle front of the abdomen, beneath the navel, in the great nerve centre called the solar plexus. How do we know? We feel it, as we feel hunger or love or hate. Once we *know* what we are, science can proceed to analyse our knowledge, demonstrate its truth or its untruth.

We all of us know what it is to handle a newborn or at least a quite young infant. We know what it is to lay the hand on the round little abdomen, the round, pulpy little head. We know where is life, where is pulp. We have seen blind puppies, blind kittens crawling. They give strange little cries. Whence these cries? Are they mental exclamations? As in a ventriloquist, they come from the stomach. There lies the wakeful centre. There speaks the first consciousness, the audible unconscious, in the squeak of these infantile things, which is so curiously and indescribably moving, reacting direct upon the great abdominal centre, the preconscious mind in man.

There at the navel, the first rupture has taken place, the first break in continuity. There is the scar of dehiscence, scar at once of our pain and splendour of individuality. Here is the mark of our isolation in the universe, stigma and seal of our free, perfect singleness. Hence the lotus of the navel. Hence the mystic contemplation of the navel. It is the upper mind losing itself in the lower first-mind, that which is last in consciousness reverting to that which is first.

A mother will realize better than a philosopher. She knows the rupture which has finally separated her child into its own single, free existence. She knows the strange, sensitive rose of the navel: how it quivers conscious; all its pain, its want for the old connection; all its joy and chuckling exultation in sheer organic singleness and individual liberty.

The powerful, active psychic centre in a new child is the great solar plexus of the sympathetic system. From this centre the child is drawn to the mother again, crying, to heal the new wound, to re-establish the old oneness. This centre directs the little mouth which, blind and anticipatory, seeks the breast. How could it find the breast, blind and mindless little mouth? But it needs no eyes nor mind. From the great first-mind of the abdomen it moves direct, with an anterior knowledge almost like magnetic propulsion, as if the little mouth were drawn or propelled to the maternal breast by vital magnetism, whose centre of directive control lies in the solar plexus.

In a measure, this taking of the breast reinstates the old connection with the parent body. It is a strange sinking back to the old unison, the old organic continuum—a recovery of the prenatal state. But at the same time it is a deep, avid gratification in drinking in the sustenance of a new individuality. It is a deep gratification in the exertion of a new, voluntary power. The child acts now separately from its own individual centre and exerts still a control over the adjacent universe, the parent body.

So the warm life-stream passes again from the parent into the aching abdomen of the severed child. Life cannot progress without these ruptures, severances, cataclysms; pain is a living reality, not merely a deathly. Why haven't we the courage for life-pains? If we could depart from our old tenets of the mind, if we could fathom our own *unconscious* sapience, we should find we have courage and to spare. We are too mentally domesticated.

The great magnetic or dynamic centre of first-consciousness acts powerfully at the solar plexus. Here the child knows beyond all knowledge. It does not see with the eyes, it cannot perceive, much less conceive. Nothing can it apprehend; the eyes are a strange plasmic, nascent darkness. Yet from the belly it knows, with a directness of knowledge that frightens us and may even seem abhorrent. The mother, also, from the bowels knows her child—as she can never, never know it from the head. There is no thought nor speech, only direct, ventral gurglings and cooings. From the passional nerve-centre of the solar plexus in the mother passes direct, unspeakable effluence and intercommunication, sheer effluent contact with the palpitating nerve-centre in the belly of the child. Knowledge, unspeakable knowledge interchanged, which must be diluted by eternities of materialization before they can come to expression.

It is like a lovely, suave, fluid, *creative* electricity that flows in a circuit between the great nerve-centres in mother and child. The electricity of the universe is a sundering force. But this lovely polarized vitalism is creative. It passes in a circuit between the two poles of the passional unconscious in the two now separated beings. It establishes in each that first primal consciousness which is the sacred, all-containing head-stream of all our consciousness.

But this is not all. The flux between mother and child is not all sweet unison. There is as well the continually widening gap. A wonderful rich communion, and at the same time a continually increasing cleavage. If only we could realize that all through life these are the two synchronizing activities of love, of creativity. For the end, the goal, is the perfecting of each single individuality, unique in itself—which cannot take place without a perfected harmony between the beloved, a harmony which depends on the at-last-clarified singleness of each being, a singleness equilibrized, polarized in one by the counter-posing singleness of the other.

So the child. In its wonderful unison with the mother it is at the same time extricating itself into single, separate, independent existence. The one process, of unison, cannot go on without the other process, of purified severance. At first the child cleaves back to the old source. It clings and adheres. The sympathetic centre of unification, or at least unison, alone seems awake. The child wails with the strange desolation of severance, wails for the old connection. With joy and peace it returns to the breast, almost as to the womb.

But not quite. Even in sucking it discovers its new identity and *power*. Its own new, separate *power*. It draws itself back suddenly; it waits. It has heard something? No. But another centre has flashed awake. The child stiffens itself and holds back. What is it, wind? Stomach-ache? Not at all. Listen to some of the screams. The ears can hear deeper than eyes can see. The first scream of the ego. The scream of asserted isolation. The scream of revolt from connection, the revolt from union. There is a violent anti-maternal motion, anti-everything. There is a refractory, bad-tempered negation of everything, a hurricane of temper. What then? After such tremendous unison as the womb implies, no wonder there are storms of rage and separation. The child is screaming itself rid of the old womb, kicking itself in a blind paroxysm into freedom, into separate, negative independence.

So be it, there must be paroxysms, since there must be independence. Then the mother gets angry too. It affects her, though perhaps not as badly as it affects outsiders. Nothing acts more direct on the great primal nerve-centres than the screaming of an infant, this blind screaming negation of connections. It is the friction of irritation itself. Everybody is implicated, just as they would be if the air were surcharged with electricity. The mother is perhaps less affected because she understands primarily, or because she is polarized directly with the child. Yet she, too, must be angry, in her measure, inevitably.

It is a blind, almost mechanistic effort on the part of the new organism to extricate itself from cohesion with the circumambient universe. It applies direct to the mother. But it affects everybody. The great centres of response vibrate with a maddening, sometimes unbearable friction. What centres? Not the great sympathetic plexus this time, but its corresponding voluntary ganglion. The great ganglion of the spinal system, the lumbar ganglion, negatively polarizes the solar plexus in the primal psychic activity of a human individual. When a child screams with temper, it sends out from the lumbar ganglion violent waves of frictional repudiation, extraordinary. The little back has an amazing power once it stiffens itself. In the lumbar ganglion the unconscious now vibrates tremendously in the activity of sundering, separation. Mother and child, polarized, are primarily affected. Often the mother is so *sure* of her possession of the child that she is almost unmoved. But the child continues, till the frictional response is roused in the mother, her anger rises, there is a flash, an outburst like lightning. And then the storm subsides. The pure act of sundering is effected. Each being is clarified further into its own single, individual self, further perfected, separated.

Hence a duality, now, in primal consciousness in the infant. The warm rosy abdomen, tender with chuckling unison, and the little back strengthening itself. The child kicks away, into independence. It stiffens its spine in the strength of its own private and separate, inviolable existence. It will admit now of no trespass. It is awake now in a new pride, a new self-assertion. The sense of antagonistic freedom is aroused. Clumsy old adhesions must be ruthlessly fused. And so, from the lumbar ganglion the fiery-tempered infant asserts its new, blind will.

And as the child fights the mother fights. Sometimes she fights to keep her refractory child, and sometimes she fights to kick him off, as a mare kicks off her too-babyish foal. It is the great *voluntary* centre of the unconscious flashing into action. Flashing from the deep lumbar ganglion in the mother to the newly awakened, corresponding centre in the child goes the swift negative current, setting each of them asunder in clean individuality. So long as the force meets its polarized response all is well. When a force flashes and has no response, there is devastation. How weary in the back is the nursing mother whose great centre of repudiation is suppressed or weak; how a child droops if only the sympathetic unison is established.

So, the polarity of the dynamic consciousness, from the very start of life! Direct flowing and flashing of two consciousness-streams, active in the bringing forth of an individual being. The sweet commingling, the sharp clash of opposition. And no possibility of creative development without this polarity, this dual circuit of direct, spontaneous, honest interchange. No hope of life apart from this. The primal unconscious pulsing in its circuits between two beings: love and wrath, cleaving and repulsion, inglutination and excrementation. What is the good of inventing "ideal" behaviour? How order the path of the unconscious? For let us now realize that we cannot, even with the best intentions, proceed to order the path of our own unconscious without vitally deranging the life-flow of those connected with us. If you disturb the current at one pole, it must be disturbed at the other. Here is a new moral aspect to life.

❦ I V ❦

The Child and His Mother

In asserting that the seat of consciousness in a young infant is in the abdomen, we do not pretend to suggest that all the other conscious-centres are utterly dormant. Once a child is born, the whole nervous and cerebral system comes awake, even the brain's memories begin to glimmer, recognition and cognition soon begin to take place. But the spontaneous control and all the prime developing activity derive from the great affective centres of the abdomen. In the solar plexus is the first great fountain and issue of infantile consciousness. There, beneath the navel, lies the active human first-mind, the prime unconscious. From the moment of conception, when the first nucleus is formed, to the moment of death, when this same nucleus breaks again, the first great active centre of human consciousness lies in the solar plexus.

The movement of development in any creature is, however, towards a florescent individuality. The ample, mature, unfolded individual stands perfect, perfect in himself, but also perfect in his harmonious relation to those nearest him and to all the universe. Whilst only the one great centre of consciousness is awake, in the abdomen, the infant has no separate existence, his whole nature is contained in the conjunction with the parent. As soon as the complementary negative pole arouses the voluntary centre of the lumbar ganglion, there is at once a retraction into independence and an assertion of singleness. The back strengthens itself.

But still the circuit of polarity, dual as it is, positive and negative from the positive-sympathetic and the negative-voluntary poles, still depends on the duality of two beings—it is still extra-individual. Each individual is vitally dependent on the other, for the life circuit.

Let us consider for a moment the *kind* of consciousness manifested at the two great primary centres. At the solar plexus the new psyche acts in a mode of attractive vitalism, drawing its objective unto itself as by vital magnetism. Here it drinks in, as it were, the contiguous universe, as during the womb-period it drank from the living continuum of the mother. It is darkly self-centred, exultant and positive in its own existence. It is all-in-all to itself, its own great subject. It knows no objective. It only knows its own vital potency, which potency draws the external object unto itself, subjectively, as the blood-stream was drawn into the foetus, by subjective attraction. Here the psyche is to itself the *All*. Blindly self-positive.

This is the first mode of consciousness for every living thing—fascinating in all young things. The second half of the same mode commences as soon as direct activity sets up in the lumbar ganglion. Then the psyche recoils upon itself, in its first reaction against continuity with the outer universe. It recoils even against its own mode of assimilatory unison. Even it must break off, interrupt the great psychic-assimilation process which goes on at the sympathic centre. It must recoil clean upon itself, break loose from any attachment whatsoever. And then it must try its *power*, often playfully.

This reaction is still subjective. When a child stiffens and draws away, when it screams with pure temper, it takes no note of that from which it recoils. It has no objective consciousness of that from which it reacts, the mother principally. It is like a swimmer endlessly kicking the water away behind him, with strong legs vividly active from the spinal ganglia. Like a man in a boat pushing off from the shore, it merely thrusts away, in order to ride free, ever more free. It is a purely subjective motion, in the negative direction.

After our long training in objectivation, and our epoch of worship of the objective mode, it is perhaps difficult for us to realize the strong, blind power of the unconscious on its first plane of activity. It is something quite different from what we call *egoism* —which is really mentally derived—for the ego is merely the sum total of what we *conceive* ourselves to be. The powerful pristine subjectivity of the unconscious on its first plane is, on the other hand, the root of all our consciousness and being, darkly tenacious. Here we are grounded, say what we may. And if we break the spell of this first subjective mode, we break our own main root and live rootless, shiftless, groundless.

So that the powerful subjectivity of the unconscious, where the self is all-in-all unto itself, active in strong desirous *psychic* assimilation or in direct repudiation of the contiguous universe; this first plane of psychic activity, polarized in the solar plexus and the lumbar ganglion of each individual but established in a circuit with the corresponding poles of another individual: this is the first scope of life and being for every human individual, and is beyond question. But we must again remark that the whole circuit is established between *two* individuals—that neither is a free thing-unto-itself—and that the very fact of established polarity between the two maintains that correspondence between the individual entity and the external universe which is the clue to all growth and development. The pure subjectivity of the first plane of consciousness is no more *selfish* than the pure objectivity of any other plane. How can it be? How can any form of pure, balanced polarity between two vital individuals be in any sense selfish on the part of one individual? We have got our moral values all wrong.

Save for healthy instinct, the moralistic human race would have exterminated itself long ago. And yet man *must* be moral, at the very root moral. The essence of morality is the basic desire to preserve the perfect correspondence between the self and the object, to have no trespass and no breach of integrity, nor yet any refaulture in the vitalistic interchange.

As yet we see the unconscious active on one plane only and entirely dependent on *two* individuals. But immediately following the establishment of the circuit of the powerful, subjective, abdominal plane comes the quivering of the whole system into a new degree of consciousness. And two great upper centres are awake.

The diaphragm really divides the human body, psychically as well as organically. The two centres beneath the diaphragm are centres of dark subjectivity, centripetal, assimilative. Once these are established, in the thorax the two first centres of objective consciousness become active, with ever-increasing intensity. The great thoracic sympathetic plexus rouses like a sun in the breast, the thoracic ganglion fills the shoulders with strength. There are now two planes of primary consciousness—the first, the lower, the subjective unconscious, active beneath the diaphragm, and the second upper, objective plane, active above the diaphragm, in the breast.

Let us realize that the subjective and objective of the unconscious are not the same as the subjective and the objective of the *mind*. Here we have no concepts to deal with, no static objects in the shape of ideas. We have none of that tiresome business of establishing the relation between the mind and its own ideal object, or the discriminating between the ideal thing-in-itself and the mind of which it is the content. We are spared that hateful thing-in-itself, the idea, which is at once so all-important and so *nothing*. We are on straightforward solid ground; there is no abstraction.

The unconscious subjectivity is, in its positive manifestation, a great imbibing, and in its negative, a definite blind rejection. What we call an *unconscious* rejection. This subjectivity embraces alike creative emotion and physical function. It includes alike the sweet and untellable communion of love between the mother and child, the irrational reaction into separation between the two, and also the physical functioning of sucking and urination. Psychic and physical development run parallel, though they are for ever distinct. The child sucking, the child urinating, this is the child acting from the great *subjective* centres, positive and negative. When the child sucks, there is a sympathetic circuit between it and the mother, in which the sympathetic plexus in the mother acts as negative or submissive pole to the corresponding plexus in the child. In urination there is a corresponding circuit in the voluntary centres, so that a mother seems gratified, and *is* gratified, inevitably, by the excremental functioning of her child. She experiences a true polar reaction.

Child and mother have, in the first place, no objective consciousness of each other, and certainly no *idea* of each other. Each is a blind desideratum to the other. The strong love between them is effectual in the great abdominal centres, where all love, real love, is primarily based. Of that reflected or moon-love, derived from the head, that spurious form of love which predominates today, we do not speak here. It has its root in the *idea:* the beloved is a mental objective, endlessly appreciated, criticized, scrutinized, exhausted. This has nothing to do with the active unconscious.

Having realized that the unconscious sparkles, vibrates, travels in a strong subjective stream from the abdominal centres, connecting the child directly with the mother at corresponding poles of vitalism, we realize that the unconscious contains nothing ideal, nothing in the least conceptual, and hence nothing in the least personal, since personality, like the ego, belongs to the conscious or mental-subjective self. So the first analyses are, or should be, so impersonal that the so-called *human* relations are not involved. The first relationship is neither personal nor biological—a fact which psychoanalysis has not succeeded in grasping.

For example. A child screams with terror at the touch of fur; another child loves the touch of fur, and purrs with pleasure. How now? Is it a complex? Did the father have a beard?

It is possible. But all-too-human. The physical result of rubbing fur is to set up a certain amount of frictional electricity. Frictional electricity is one of the sundering forces. It corresponds to the voluntary forces exerted at the lower spinal ganglia, the forces of anger and retraction into independence and power. An over-sympathetic child will scream with fear at the touch of fur; a refractory child will purr with pleasure. It is a reaction which involves even deeper things than sex—the primal constitution of the elementary psyche. A sympathetically over-balanced child has a horror of the electric-frictional force such as is emitted from the fur of a black cat, creature of rapacity. The same delights a fierce-willed child.

But we must admit at the same time that from earliest days a child is subject to the definite *conscious* psychic influences of its surroundings and will react almost automatically to a conscious-passional suggestion from the mother. In this way personal sex is prematurely evoked, and real complexes are set up. But these derive not from the spontaneous unconscious. They are in a way dictated from the deliberate, mental consciousness, even if involuntarily. Again they are a result of *mental* subjectivity, self-consciousness—so different from the primal subjectivity of the unconscious.

To return, however, to the pure unconscious. When the upper centres flash awake, a whole new field of consciousness and spontaneous activity is opened out. The great sympathetic plexus of the breast is the heart's mind. This thoracic plexus corresponds directly in the upper man to the solar plexus in the lower. But it is a correspondence in creative opposition. From the sympathetic centre of the breast as from a window the unconscious goes forth seeking its object, to dwell upon it. When a child leans its breast against its mother it becomes filled with a primal, awareness of *her*—not of itself desiring her or partaking of her—but of her as she is in herself. This is the first great acquisition of primal objective knowledge, the objective content of the unconscious. Such knowledge we call the treasure of the heart. When the ancients located the first seat of consciousness in the heart, they were neither misguided nor playing with metaphor. For by consciousness they meant, as usual, objective consciousness only. And from the cardiac plexus goes forth that strange effluence of the self which seeks and dwells upon the beloved, lovingly roving like the fingers of an infant or a blind man over the face of the treasured object, gathering her mould into itself and transferring her mould forever into its own deep unconscious psyche. This is the first acquiring of objective knowledge, sightless, unspeakably direct. It is a dwelling of the child's unconscious within the form of the mother, the gathering of a pure, eternal impression. So the soul stores itself with dynamic treasures; it verily builds its own tissue of such treasure, the tissue of the developing body, each cell stored with creative dynamic content.

The breasts themselves are as two eyes. We do not know how much the nipples of the breast, both in man and woman, serve primarily as poles of vital *conscious* effluence and connection. We do not know how the nipples of the breast are as fountains leaping into the universe, or as little lamps irradiating the contiguous world, to the soul in quest.

But certainly from the passional conscious-centre of the breast goes forth the first joyous discovery of the beloved, the first objective discovery of the contiguous universe, the first ministration of the self to that which is beyond the self. So, functionally, the mother ministers with the milk of her breast. But this is a yielding to the great *lower* plexus, the basic solar plexus. It is the breast as part also of the alimentary system—a special thing.

In sucking the hands also come awake. It is strange to notice the pictures by the old masters of the Madonna and Child. Sometimes the strange round belly of the Infant seems the predominant mystery-centre, and sometimes from the tiny breast it is as if a delicate light glowed, the light of love. As if the breast should illumine the outer world in its seeking administering love. As if the breast of the Infant glimmered its light of discovery on the adoring Mother, and she bowed, submissive to the revelation.

The little hands and arms wave, circulate, trying to touch, to grasp, to know. To grasp in caress, not to receive. To grasp in order to identify themselves with the cherished discovery, to realize the beloved. To cherish, to realize the beloved. To administer the outward-seeking self to the beloved. We give this the exclusive name of love. But it is indeed only the one direction of love, the outgoing from the lovely centre of the breast—the nipples seeking, the hands delicately, caressively exploring, the eyes at last waking to perception. The eyes, the hands, these wake and are alert from the centre of the breast. But the ears and feet move from the deep lower centres—the recipient ears, imbibing vibrations, the feet which press the resistant earth, controlled from the powerful lower ganglia of the spine. And thus great scope of activity opens, in the hands that wave and explore, the eyes that try to perceive, the legs, the little knees that thrust, thrust away, the small feet that curl and twinkle upon themselves, ready for the obstinate earth.

And so, also a wholeness is established within the individual. The two fields of consciousness, the first upper and the first lower, are based upon a correspondence of polarity. The first great complex circuit is now set up *within the individual*, between the upper and lower centres. The individual consciousness has now its own integral independent existence and activity, apart from external connection. It has its right to be alone.

❦   V   ❦

The Lover and the Beloved

Consciousness develops on successive planes. On each plane there is the dual polarity, positive and negative, of the sympathetic and voluntary nerve centres. The first plane is established between the poles of the sympathetic solar plexus and the voluntary lumbar ganglion. This is the active first plane of the subjective unconscious, from which the whole of consciousness arises.

Immediately succeeding the first plane of subjective dynamic consciousness arises the corresponding first plane of objective consciousness, the objective unconscious, polarized in the cardiac plexus and the thoracic ganglion, in the breast. There is a perfect correspondence in difference between the first abdominal and the first thoracic planes. These two planes polarize each other in a fourfold polarity, which makes the first great field of individual, self-dependent consciousness.

Each pole of the active unconscious manifests a specific activity and gives rise to a specific kind of dynamic or creative consciousness. On each plane, the negative voluntary pole *complements* the positive sympathetic pole, and yet the consciousness originating from the complementary poles is not merely negative versus positive, it is categorically different, opposite. Each is pure and perfect in itself.

But the moment we enter the two planes of corresponding consciousness, lower and upper, we find a whole new range of complements. The upper, dynamic-objective plane is complementary to the lower, dynamic-subjective. The mystery of creative opposition exists all the time between the two planes, and this unison in opposition between the two planes forms the first whole field of consciousness. Within the individual the polarity is fourfold. In a relation between two individuals the polarity is already eight-fold.

Now before we can have any sort of scientific, comprehensive psychology we shall have to establish the *nature* of the conscious-ness at each of the dynamic poles—the nature of the conscious-ness, the direction of the dynamic-vital flow, the resultant physi-cal-organic development and activity. This we must do before we can even begin to consider a genuine system of education. Education now is widely at sea. Having ceased to steer by the pole-star of the mind, having ceased to aim at the cramming of the intellect, it veers hither and thither hopelessly and absurdly. Education can never become a serious science until the human psyche is properly understood. And the human psyche cannot begin to be understood until we enter the dark continent of the unconscious. Having begun to explore the unconscious, we find we must go from centre to centre, chakra to chakra, to use an old esoteric word. We must patiently determine the psychic manifes-tation at each centre, and moreover, as we go, we must discover the psychic results of the interaction, the polarized interaction be-tween the dynamic centres both within and without the indi-vidual.

Here is a real job for the scientist, a job which eternity will never see finished though even tomorrow may see it well begun. It is a job which will at last free us from the most hateful of all shackles, the shackles of ideas and ideals. It is a great task of the liberators, those who work forever for the liberation of the free *spontaneous* psyche, the effective soul.

In these few chapters we hope to hint at the establishment of the first field of the unconscious—at the nature of the conscious-ness manifested at each pole—and at the already complex range of dynamic polarity between the various poles. So far we have given the merest suggestion of the nature of the first plane of the unconscious and have attempted the opening of the second or up-

per plane. We profess no scientific *exactitude*, particularly in ter-
minology. We merely wish intelligibly to open a way.

To balance the solar plexus wakes the great plexus of the
breast. In our era this plexus is the great planet of our psychic universe. In the previous sympathetic era the flower of the universal
blossomed in the navel. But since Egypt the sun of creative activity beams from the breast, the heart of the supreme Man. This is
to us the source of light—the loving heart, the Sacred Heart.
Against this we contrast the devouring darkness of the lower man,
the devouring whirlpool beneath the navel. Even theosophists
don't realize that the universal lotus really blossoms in the abdomen—that our lower man, our dark, devouring whirlpool, was
once the creative source, in human estimation.

But in calling the heart the sun, the source of light, we are biologically correct even. For the roots of vision are in the cardiac
plexus. But if we were to consider the heart itself, not its great
nerve plexus, we should have to go further than the nervous system. If we had to consider the whole lambent blood-stream, we
should have to descend too deep for our unpractised minds. Suffice it here to hint that the solar plexus is the first and main clue
to the great alimentary-sexual activity in man, an activity at once
functional and creatively emotional, whilst the cardiac plexus is
first and main clue to the respiratory system and the active-
productive manifestations. The mouth and nostrils are gates to
each great centre, upper and lower—even the breasts have this
duality. Yet the clue to respiration and hand activity and vision
is in the breast, while the clue to alimentation and passion and sex
is in the lower centres. The duality goes so far and is so profound.
And the polarity! The great organs, as well as the lymphatic
glands, depend each on its own specific centre of the unconscious;
each is derived from a specific *dynamic* conscious-clue, what we
might almost call a soul-cell. The inherent unconscious, or soul,
is the first nucleus subdivided, and from its own subdivisions produced, from its own still-creative constellated nuclei, the organs,
glands, nerve-centres of the human organism. This is our answer
to materialism and idealism alike. The *nuclear unconscious*
brought forth organs and consciousness alike. And the great nu-

clei of the unconscious *still* lie active in the great living nerve-centres, which nerve-centres, from the original solar plexus to the conclusive brain, form one great chain of dual polarity and amplified consciousness.

All this is a mere incoherent stammering, broken first-words. To return to the direct path of our progress. It is not merely a metaphor to call the cardiac plexus the sun, the Light. It is metaphor in the first place because the conscious effluence which proceeds from this first upper centre in the breast goes forth and plays upon its external object, as phosphorescent waves might break upon a ship and reveal its form. The transferring of the objective knowledge to the psyche is almost the same as vision. It is root-vision. It happens before the eyes open. It is the first tremendous mode of *apprehension*, still dark, but moving towards light. It is the eye in the breast. Psychically, it is basic objective apprehension. Dynamically, it is love, devotional, administering love.

Now we make already a discrimination between the two natures, even of this first upper consciousness. First from the breast flows the devotional, self-outpouring of love, love which gives its all to the beloved. And back again returns to the ingathered objective consciousness, the first objective content of the psyche.

This argues the dual polarity. From the positive pole of the cardiac plexus flows out that effluence which we call selfless love. It is really self-devoting love, not self-less. This is the one form of love we recognize. But from the strong ganglion of the shoulders proceeds the negative circuit, which searches and explores the beloved, bringing back pure objective apprehension, not critical, in the mental sense, and yet passionally discriminative.

Let us discriminate between the two upper poles. From the sympathetic heart goes forth pure administering, like sunbeams. But from the strong thoracic centre of the shoulders is exerted a strong rejective force, a force which, pressing upon the object of attention, in the mode of separation, succeeds in transferring to itself the impression of the object to which it has attended. This is the other half of devotional love—perfect *knowledge* of the beloved.

Now this knowledge in itself argues a contradistinction between the lover and the beloved. It is the very mould of the contradistinction. It is the impress upon the lover of that which was separate from him, resistant to him, in the beloved. Objective knowledge is always of this kind—a knowledge based on unchangeable difference, a knowledge truly of the gulf that lies between the two beings nearest to each other.

In two kinds, then, consists the activity of the unconscious on the first upper plane. Primal is the blissful sense of ineffable transfusion with the beloved, which we call love, and of which our era has perhaps enjoyed the full. It is a mode of creative consciousness essentially objective, but yet it preserves no object in the memory, even the dynamic memory. It is a great objective flux, a streaming forth of the self in blissful departure, like sunbeams streaming.

If this activity alone worked, then the self would utterly depart from its own integrity; it would pass out and merge with the beloved—which passing out and merging is the goal of enthusiasts. But living beings are kept integral by the activity of the great negative pole. From the thoracic ganglion also the unconscious goes forth in its quest of the beloved. But what does it go to seek? Real objective knowledge. It goes to find out the wonders which itself does not contain and to transfer these wonders, as by impress, into itself. It goes out to determine the limits of its own existence also.

This is the second half of the activity of upper or self-less or spiritual love. There is a tremendous great joy in exploring and discovering the beloved. For what is the beloved? She is that which I myself am not. Knowing the breach between us, the uncloseable gulf, I in the same breath realize her *features*. In the first mode of the upper consciousness there is perfect surpassing of all sense of division between the self and the beloved. In the second mode the very discovery of the features of the beloved contains the full realization of the irreparable, or unsurpassable, gulf. This is objective knowledge, as distinct from objective emotion. It contains always the element of self-amplification, as if the self were amplified by knowledge in the beloved. It should also contain the knowledge of the *limits* of the self.

So it is with the Infant. Curious indeed is the look on the face of the Holy Child, in Leonardo's pictures, in Botticelli's, even in the beautiful Filippo Lippi. It is the Mother who crosses her hands on her breast, in supreme acquiescence, recipient; it is the Child who gazes, with a kind of *objective*, strangely discerning, deep apprehension of her, startling to northern eyes. It is a gaze by no means of innocence, but of profound, pre-visual discerning. So plainly is the child looking across the gulf and *fixing* the gulf by very intentness of pre-visual apprehension, that instinctively the ordinary northerner finds Him antipathetic. It seems almost a cruel objectivity.

Perhaps between lovers, in the objective way of love, either the voluntary separative mode predominates, or the sympathetic mode of communion—one or the other. In the north we have worshipped the latter mode. But in the south it is different; the objective sapient manner of love seems more natural. Moreover in the face of the Infant lingers nearly always the dark look of the pristine mode of consciousness, the powerful self-centring subjective mode, established in the lower body—the so-called sensual mode.

But take our own children. A small infant, as soon as it really begins to direct its attention. How often it seems to be gazing across a strange distance at the mother; what a curious look is on its face, as if the mother were an object set across a far gulf, distinct however, discernible, even obtrusive in her need to be apprehended. A mother will chase away this look with kisses. But she cannot chase away the inevitable effluence of separatist, objective apprehension. She herself sometimes will fall into a half-trance, and the child on her lap will resolve itself into a strange and separate object. She does not criticize or analyse him. She does not even *perceive* him. But as if rapt, she apprehends him lying there, an unfathomable and inscrutable objective, outside herself, never to be grasped or included in herself. She seizes as it were a sudden and final, objective impression of him. And the conclusive sensation is one of *finality*. Something final has happened to her. She has the strange sensation of unalterable certainty a sensation at once profoundly gratifying and rather ap-

palling. She *possesses* something, a certain entity of primal, preconscious knowledge. Let the child be what he may, her knowledge of him is her own, forever and final. It gives her a sense of
wealth in possession, and of power. It gives her a sense also of fatality. From the very satisfaction of the objective finality derives
the sense of fatality. It is a knowledge of the other being, but a
knowledge which contains at the same time a final assurance of
the eternal and insuperable gulf which lies between beings—the
isolation of the self first.

Thus the first plane of the *upper* consciousness—the outgoing,
the sheer and unspeakable bliss of the sense of union, communion,
at-oneness with the beloved—and then the complementary objective *realization* of the beloved, the realization of that which is
apart, different. This realization is like riches to the objective consciousness. It is, as it were, the adding of another self to the own
self, through the mode of apprehension. Through the mode of
dynamic objective apprehension, which in our day we have gradually come to call *imagination*, a man may in his time add on to
himself the whole of the universe, by increasing pristine realization of the universal. This in mysticism is called the progress to
infinity—that is, in the modern, truly male mysticism. The older
female mysticism means something different by the infinite.

But anyhow there it is. The attaining to the Infinite, about
which the mystics have rhapsodized, is a definite process in the
developing unconscious, but a process in the development only
of the objective-apprehensive centres—an exclusive process, naturally.

A soul cannot come into its own through that love alone which
is unison. If it stress the one mode, the sympathetic mode, beyond
a certain point, it breaks its own integrity, and corruption sets in
in the living organism. On both planes of love, upper and lower,
the two modes must act complementary to one another, the sympathetic and the separatist. It is the absolute failure to see this
that has torn the modern world into two halves, the one half war-
ring for the voluntary, objective, separatist control, the other for
the pure sympathetic. The individual psyche divided against it-

self divides the world against itself, and an unthinkable progress of calamity ensues unless there be a reconciliation.

The goal of life is the coming to perfection of each single individual. This cannot take place without the tremendous interchange of love from all the four great poles of the first, basic field of consciousness. There must be the twofold passionate flux of sympathetic love, subjective-abdominal and objective-devotional, both. And there must be the twofold passional circuit of separatist realization, the lower, vital *self-realization*, and the upper, intense realization of the other, a realization which includes a recognition of abysmal *otherness*. To stress any one mode, any one interchange, is to hinder all, and to cause corruption in the end. The human psyche must have strength and pride to accept the whole fourfold nature of its own creative activity.

VI

Human Relations and the Unconscious

The aim of this little book is merely to establish the smallest foot-hold in the swamp of vagueness which now goes by the name of the unconscious. At last we form some sort of notion what the unconscious actually is. It is that active spontaneity which rouses in each individual organism at the moment of fusion of the parent nuclei, and which, in polarized connection with the external universe, gradually evolves or elaborates its own individual psyche and corpus, bringing both mind and body forth from itself. Thus it would seem that the term *unconscious* is only another word for life. But life is a general force, whereas the unconscious is essentially single and unique in each individual organism; it is the active, self-evolving soul bringing forth its own incarnation and self-manifestation. Which incarnation and self-manifestation seems to be the whole goal of the *unconscious* soul: the whole goal of life. Thus it is that the unconscious brings forth not only consciousness, but tissue and organs also. And all the time the working of each organ depends on the primary spontaneous-conscious centre of which it is the issue—if you like, the soul-centre. And consciousness is like a web woven finally in the mind from the various silken strands spun forth from the primal centre of the unconscious.

But the unconscious is never an abstraction, *never to be abstracted*. It is never an ideal entity. It is always concrete. In the very first instance, it is the glinting nucleus of the ovule. And proceeding from this, it is the chain or constellation of nuclei which derive directly from this first spark. And further still it is the great nerve-centres of the human body, in which the primal and pristine nuclei still act direct. The nuclei are centres of spontaneous consciousness. It seems as if their bright grain were germ-consciousness, consciousness germinating forever. If that is a mystery, it is not my fault. Certainly it is not mysticism. It is obvious, demonstrable scientific fact, to be verified under the microscope and within the human psyche, subjectively and objectively, both. Of course, the subjective verification is what men kick at. Thin-minded idealists cannot bear any appeal to their bowels of comprehension.

We can quite tangibly deal with the human unconscious. We trace its source and centres in the great ganglia and nodes of the nervous system. We establish the nature of the spontaneous consciousness at each of these centres; we determine the polarity and the direction of the polarized flow. And from this we know the motion and individual manifestation of the psyche itself; we also know the motion and rhythm of the great organs of the body. For at every point psyche and functions are so nearly identified that only by holding our breath can we realize their *duality* in identification—a polarized duality once more. But here is no place to enter the great investigation of the duality and polarization of the vital-creative activity and the mechanico-material activity. The two are two in one, a polarized quality. They are unthinkably different.

On the first field of human consciousness—the first plane of the unconscious—we locate four great spontaneous centres, two below the diaphragm, two above. These four centres control the four greatest organs. And they give rise to the whole basis of human consciousness. Functional and psychic at once, this is their first polar duality.

But the polarity is further. The horizontal division of the diaphragm divides man forever into his individual duality, the duality of the upper and lower man, the two great bodies of upper and lower consciousness and function. This is the horizontal line.

The vertical division between the voluntary and the sympathetic systems, the line of division between the spinal system and the great plexus-system of the front of the human body, forms the second distinction into duality. It is the great difference between the soft, recipient front of the body and the wall of the back. The front of the body is the live end of the magnet. The back is the closed opposition. And again there are two parallel streams of function and consciousness, vertically separate now. This is the vertical line of division. And the horizontal line and the vertical line form the cross of all existence and being. And even this is not mysticism—no more than the ancient symbols used in botany or biology.

On the first field of human consciousness, which is the basis of life and consciousness, are the four first poles of spontaneity. These have their fourfold polarity within the individual, again figured by the cross. But the individual is never purely a thing-by-himself. He cannot exist save in polarized relation to the external universe, a relation both functional and psychic-dynamic. Development takes place only from the polarized circuits of the dynamic unconscious, and these circuits must be both individual and extra-individual. There must be the circuit of which the complementary pole is external to the individual.

That is, in the first place there must be the *other individual*. There must be a polarized connection with the other individual —or even other individuals. On the first field there are four poles in each individual. So that the first, the basic field of extra-individual consciousness contains eight poles—an eightfold polarity, a fourfold circuit. It may be that between two individuals, even mother and child, the polarity may be established only fourfold, a dual circuit. It may be that one circuit of spontaneous consciousness may never be fully established. This means, for a child, a certain deficiency in development, a psychic inadequacy.

So we are again face to face with the basic problem of human conduct. No human being can develop save through the polarized connection with other beings. This circuit of polarized unison precedes all mind and all knowing. It is anterior to and ascendant over the human will. And yet the mind and the will can both interfere with the dynamic circuit, an idea, like a stone wedged in a delicate machine, can arrest one whole process of psychic interaction and spontaneous growth.

How then? Man doth not live by bread alone. It is time we made haste to settle the bread question, which after all is only the A B C of social economies, and proceeded to devote our attention to this much more profound and vital question: how to establish and maintain the circuit of vital polarity from which the psyche actually develops, as the body develops from the circuit of alimentation and respiration. We have reached the stage where we can settle the alimentation and respiration problems almost off-hand. But woe betide us, the unspeakable agony we suffer from the failure to establish and maintain the vital circuits between ourselves and the effectual correspondent, the other human being, other human beings, and all the extraneous universe. The tortures of psychic starvation which civilized people proceed to suffer, once they have solved for themselves the bread-and-butter problem of alimentation, will not bear thought. Delicate, creative desire, sending forth its fine vibrations in search of the true pole of magnetic rest in another human being or beings, how it is thwarted, insulated by a whole set of india-rubber ideas and ideals and conventions, till every form of perversion and death-desire sets in! How can we *escape* neuroses? Psychoanalysis won't tell us. But a mere shadow of understanding of the true unconscious will give us the hint.

The amazingly difficult and vital business of human relationship has been almost laughably underestimated in our epoch. All this nonsense about love and unselfishness, more crude and repugnant than savage fetish-worship. Love is a thing to be *learned*, through centuries of patient effort. It is a difficult, complex maintenance of individual integrity throughout the incalculable processes of interhuman-polarity. Even on the first great plane of consciousness, four prime poles in each individual, four powerful circuits possible between two individuals, and each of the four circuits to be established to perfection and yet maintained in pure equilibrium with all the others. Who can do it? Nobody. Yet we have all got to do it, or else suffer ascetic tortures of starvation and privation or of distortion and overstrain and slow collapse into corruption. The whole of life is one long, blind effort at an established polarity with the outer universe, human and non-human; and the whole of modern life is a shrieking failure. It is our own fault.

The actual evolution of the individual psyche is a result of the interaction between the individual and the outer universe. Which means that just as a child in the womb grows as a result of the parental blood-stream which nourishes the vital quick of the foetus, so does every man and woman grow and develop as a result of the polarized flux between the spontaneous self and some other self or selves. It is the circuit of vital flux between itself and another being or beings which brings about the development and evolution of every individual psyche and physique. This is a law of life and creation, from which we cannot escape. Ascetics and voluptuaries both try to dodge this main condition, and both succeed perhaps for a generation. But after two generations all collapses. Man doth not live by bread alone. He lives even more essentially from the nourishing creative flow between himself and another or others.

This is the reality of the extra-individual circuits of polarity, those established between two or more individuals. But a corresponding reality is that of the internal, purely individual polarity —the polarity within a man himself of his upper and lower consciousness, and his own voluntary and sympathetic modes. Here is a fourfold interaction within the self. And from this fourfold reaction within the self results that final manifestation which we know as *mind*, mental consciousness.

The brain is, if we may use the word, the terminal instrument of the dynamic consciousness. It transmutes what is a creative flux into a certain fixed cipher. It prints off, like a telegraph instrument, the glyphs and graphic representations which we call percepts, concepts, ideas. It produces a new reality—the ideal. The idea is another static entity, another unit of the mechanical-active and materio-static universe. It is thrown off from life, as leaves are shed from a tree, or as feathers fall from a bird. Ideas are the dry, unliving, insentient plumage which intervenes between us and the circumambient universe, forming at once an insulator and an instrument for the subduing of the universe. The mind is the instrument of instruments; it is not a creative reality.

Once the mind is awake, being in itself a finality, it feels very assured. "The word became flesh, and began to put on airs," says Norman Douglas wittily. It is exactly what happens. Mentality, being automatic in its principle like the machine, begins to assume life. It begins to affect life, to pretend to make and unmake life. "In the beginning was the Word." This is the presumptuous masquerading of the mind. The Word cannot be the beginning of life. It is the *end* of life, that which falls shed. The mind is the dead end of life. But it has all the mechanical force of the non-vital universe. It is a great dynamo of super-mechanical force. Given the *will* as accomplice, it can even arrogate its machine-motions and automatizations over the whole of life, till every tree becomes a clipped teapot and every man a useful mechanism. So we see the brain, like a great dynamo and accumulator, accumulating *mechanical* force and presuming to apply this mechanical force-control to the living unconscious, subjecting everything spontaneous to certain machine-principles called ideals or ideas.

And the human will assists in this humiliating and sterilizing process. We don't know what the human will is. But we do know that it is a certain faculty belonging to every living organism, the faculty for self-determination. It is a strange faculty of the soul itself, for its own direction. The will is indeed the faculty which every individual possesses from the very moment of conception, for exerting a certain control over the vital and automatic processes of his own evolution. It does not depend originally on mind. Originally it is a purely spontaneous control-factor of the living unconscious. It seems as if, primarily, the will and the conscience were identical, in the premental state. It seems as if the will were given as a great balancing faculty, the faculty whereby automatization is *prevented* in the evolving psyche. The *spontaneous* will reacts at once against the exaggeration of any one particular circuit of polarity. Any vital circuit—a fact known to psychoanalysis. And against this automatism, this degradation from the spontaneous-vital reality into the mechanic-material reality, the human soul must always struggle. And the will is the power which the unique self possesses to right itself from automatism.

Sometimes, however, the free psyche really collapses, and the will *identifies* itself with an automatic circuit. Then a complex is set up, a paranoia. Then incipient madness sets in. If the identification continues, the derangement becomes serious. There may come sudden jolts of dislocation of the whole psychic flow, like epilepsy. Or there may come any of the known forms of primary madness.

The second danger is that the will shall identify itself with the mind and become an instrument of the mind. The same process of automatism sets up, only now it is slower. The mind proceeds to assume control over every organic-psychic circuit. The spontaneous flux is destroyed, and a certain automatic circuit substituted. Now an automatic establishment of the psyche must, like the building of a machine, proceed according to some definite fixed scheme, based upon certain fixed principles. And it is here that ideals and ideas enter. They are the machine-plan and the machine-principles of an automatized psyche.

So, humanity proceeds to derange itself, to automatize itself from the mental consciousness. It is a process of derangement, just as the fixing of the will upon any other primary process is a derangement. It is a long, slow development in madness. Quite justly do the advanced Russian and French writers acclaim madness as a great goal. It is the genuine goal of self-automatism, mental-conscious supremacy.

True, we must all develop into mental consciousness. But mental-consciousness is not a goal; it is a cul-de-sac. It provides us only with endless *appliances* which we can use for the all-too-difficult business of coming to our spontaneous-creative fullness of being. It provides us with means to adjust ourselves to the external universe. It gives us further means for subduing the external, materio-mechanical universe to our great end of creative life. And it gives us plain indications of how to avoid falling into automatism, hints for the *applying* of the will, the loosening of false, automatic fixations, the brave adherence to a profound soul-impulse. This is the use of the mind—a great indicator and instrument. The mind as author and director of life is anathema.

So, the few things we have to say about the unconscious end for the moment. There is almost nothing said. Yet it is a beginning. Still remain to be revealed the other great centres of the unconscious. We know four: two pairs. In all there are seven planes. That is, there are six dual centres of spontaneous polarity, and then the final one. That is, the great upper and lower consciousness is only just broached—the further heights and depths are not even hinted at. Nay, in public it would hardly be allowed us to hint at them. There is so much to know, and every step of the progress in knowledge is a death to the human idealism which governs us now so ruthlessly and vilely. It must die, and we *will* break free. But what tyranny is so hideous as that of an automatically ideal humanity?

Fantasia
of the Unconscious

Foreword

The present book is a continuation from *Psychoanalysis and the Unconscious*. The generality of readers had better just leave it alone. The generality of critics likewise. I really don't want to convince anybody. It is quite in opposition to my whole nature. I don't intend my books for the generality of readers. I count it a mistake of our mistaken democracy, that every man who can read print is allowed to believe that he can read all that is printed. I count it a misfortune that serious books are exposed in the public market, like slaves exposed naked for sale. But there we are, since we live in an age of mistaken democracy, we must go through with it.

I warn the generality of readers that this present book will seem to them only a rather more revolting mass of wordy nonsense than the last. I would warn the generality of critics to throw it in the wastepaper basket without more ado.

As for the limited few, in whom one must perforce find an answerer, I may as well say straight off that I stick to the solar plexus. That statement alone, I hope, will thin their numbers considerably.

Finally, to the remnants of a remainder, in order to apologize for the sudden lurch into cosmology, or cosmogony, in this book, I wish to say that the whole thing hangs inevitably together. I am not a scientist. I am an amateur of amateurs. As one of my critics said, you either believe or you don't.

I am not a proper archaeologist nor an anthropologist nor an ethnologist. I am no "scholar" of any sort. But I am very grateful to scholars for their sound work. I have found hints, suggestions for what I say here in all kinds of scholarly books, from the Yoga and Plato and St. John the Evangel and the early Greek philosophers like Herakleitos down to Frazer and his *Golden Bough*, and even Freud and Frobenius. Even then I only remember hints —and I proceed by intuition. This leaves you quite free to dismiss the whole wordy mass of revolting nonsense, without a qualm.

Only let me say that to my mind there is a great field of science which is as yet quite closed to us. I refer to the science which proceeds in terms of life and is established on data of living experience and of sure intuition. Call it subjective science if you like. Our objective science of modern knowledge concerns itself only with phenomena, and with phenomena as regarded in their cause-and-effect relationship. I have nothing to say against our science. It is perfect as far as it goes. But to regard it as exhausting the whole scope of human possibility in knowledge seems to me just puerile. Our science is a science of the dead world. Even biology never considers life, but only mechanistic functioning and apparatus of life.

I honestly think that the great pagan world of which Egypt and Greece were the last living terms, the great pagan world which preceded our own era, once had a vast and perhaps perfect science of its own, a science in terms of life. In our era this science crumbled into magic and charlatanry. But even wisdom crumbles.

I believe that this great science previous to ours and quite different in constitution and nature from our science once was universal, established all over the then existing globe. I believe it was esoteric, invested in a large priesthood. Just as mathematics and mechanics and physics are defined and expounded in the same way in the universities of China or Bolivia or London or Moscow today, so, it seems to me, in the great world previous to ours a great science and cosmology were taught esoterically in all countries of the globe, Asia, Polynesia, America, Atlantis, and Europe. Belt's suggestion of the geographical nature of this previous world seems to me most interesting. In the period which geologists call the Glacial Period, the waters of the earth must have been gathered up in a vast body on the higher places of our globe, vast worlds of ice. And the sea-beds of today must have been comparatively dry. So that the Azores rose up mountainous from the plain of Atlantis, where the Atlantic now washes, and the Easter Isles and the Marquesas and the rest rose lofty from the marvellous great continent of the Pacific.

In that world men lived and taught and knew, and were in one complete correspondence over all the earth. Men wandered back and forth from Atlantis to the Polynesian Continent as men now sail from Europe to America. The interchange was complete, and knowledge, science was universal over the earth, cosmopolitan as it is today.

Then came the melting of the glaciers, and the world flood. The refugees from the drowned continents fled to the high places of America, Europe, Asia, and the Pacific Isles. And some degenerated naturally into cave men, neolithic and paleolithic creatures, and some retained their marvellous innate beauty and life-perfection, as the South Sea Islanders, and some wandered savage in Africa, and some, like Druids or Etruscans or Chaldeans or Amerindians or Chinese, refused to forget, but taught the old wisdom, only in its half-forgotten, symbolic forms. More or less forgotten, as knowledge: remembered as ritual, gesture, and myth-story.

And so, the intense potency of symbols is part at least memory. And so it is that all the great symbols and myths which dominate the world when our history first begins, are very much the same in every country and every people, the great myths all relate to one another. And so it is that these myths now begin to hypnotize us again, our own impulse towards our own scientific way of understanding being almost spent. And so, besides myths, we find the same mathematic figures, cosmic graphs which remain among the aboriginal peoples in all continents, mystic figures and signs whose true cosmic or scientific significance is lost, yet which continue in use for purposes of conjuring or divining.

If my reader finds this bosh and abracadabra, all right for him. Only I have no more regard for his little crowings on his own little dunghill. Myself, I am not so sure that I am one of the one-and-onlies. I like the wide world of centuries and vast ages—mammoth worlds beyond our day, and mankind so wonderful in his distances, his history that has no beginning yet always the pomp and the magnificence of human splendor unfolding through the earth's changing periods. Floods and fire and convulsions and ice-arrest intervene between the great glamorous civilizations of mankind. But nothing will ever quench humanity and the human potentiality to evolve something magnificent out of a renewed chaos.

I do not believe in evolution, but in the strangeness and rainbow-change of ever-renewed creative civilizations.

So much, then, for my claim to remarkable discoveries. I believe I am only trying to stammer out the first terms of a forgotten knowledge. But I have no desire to revive dead kings, or dead sages. It is not for me to arrange fossils and decipher hieroglyphic phrases. I couldn't do it if I wanted to. But then I can do something else. The soul must take the hint from the relics our scientists have so marvellously gathered out of the forgotten past, and from the hint develop a new living utterance. The spark is from dead wisdom, but the fire is life.

And as an example—a very simple one—of how a scientist of the most innocent modern sort may hint at truths which, when stated, he would laugh at as fantastic nonsense, let us quote a word from the already old-fashioned *Golden Bough*. "It must have appeared to the ancient Aryan that the sun was periodically recruited from the fire which resided in the sacred oak."

Exactly. The fire which resided in the Tree of Life. That is, life itself. So we must read: "It must have appeared to the ancient Aryan that the sun was periodically recruited from life." Which is what the early Greek philosophers were always saying. And which still seems to me the real truth, the clue to the cosmos. Instead of life being drawn from the sun, it is the emanation from life itself, that is, from all the living plants and creatures which nourish the sun.

Of course, my dear critic, the ancient Aryans were just doddering, the old duffers: or babbling, the babes. But as for me, I have some respect for my ancestors, and believe they had more up their sleeve than just the marvel of the unborn me.

One last weary little word. This pseudo-philosophy of mine— "pollyanalytics," as one of my respected critics might say—is deduced from the novels and poems, not the reverse. The novels and poems come unwatched out of one's pen. And then the absolute need which one has for some sort of satisfactory mental attitude towards oneself and things in general makes one try to abstract some definite conclusions from one's experiences as a writer and as a man. The novels and poems are pure passionate experience. These "pollyanalytics" are inferences made afterwards, from the experience.

And finally, it seems to me that even art is utterly dependent on philosophy: or if you prefer it, on a metaphysic. The metaphysic or philosophy may not be anywhere very accurately stated and may be quite unconscious, in the artist, yet it is a metaphysic that governs men at the time, and is by all men more or less comprehended, and lived. Men live and see according to some gradually developing and gradually withering vision. This vision exists also as a dynamic idea or metaphysic—exists first as such. Then it is unfolded into life and art. Our vision, our belief, our metaphysic is wearing woefully thin, and the art is wearing absolutely threadbare. We have no future; neither for our hopes nor our aims nor our art. It has all gone gray and opaque.

We've got to rip the old veil of a vision across, and find what the heart really believes in, after all: and what the heart really wants, for the next future. And we've got to put it down in terms of belief and of knowledge. And then go forward again, to the fulfilment in life and art.

Rip the veil of the old vision across, and walk through the rent. And if I try to do this—well, why not? If I try to write down what I see—why not? If a publisher likes to print the book—all right. And if anybody wants to read it, let him. But why any-

body should read one single word if he doesn't want to, I don't
see. Unless of course he is a critic who needs to scribble a dollar's
worth of words, no matter how.

TAORMINA, October 8, 1921

🔊 I 🔊

Introduction

Let us start by making a little apology to psychoanalysis. It wasn't fair to jeer at the psychoanalytic unconscious; or perhaps it *was* fair to jeer at the psychoanalytic unconscious, which is truly a negative quantity and an unpleasant menagerie. What was really not fair was to jeer at psychoanalysis as if Freud had invented and described nothing but an unconscious, in all his theory.

The unconscious is not, of course, the clue to the Freudian theory. The real clue is sex. A sexual motive is to be attributed to all human activity.

Now this is going too far. We are bound to admit that an element of sex enters into all human activity. But so does an element of greed, and of many other things. We are bound to admit that into all human relationships, particularly adult human relationships, a large element of sex enters. We are thankful that Freud has insisted on this. We are thankful that Freud pulled us somewhat to earth, out of all our clouds of superfineness. What Freud says is always *partly* true. And half a loaf is better than no bread.

But really, there is the other half of the loaf. All is *not* sex. And a sexual motive is *not* to be attributed to all human activities. We know it, without need to argue.

Sex surely has a specific meaning. Sex means the being divided into male and female; and the magnetic desire or impulse which puts male apart from female, in a negative or sundering magnetism, but which also draws male and female together in a long and infinitely varied approach towards the critical act of coition. Sex

59

without the consummating act of coition is never quite sex, in human relationships: just as a eunuch is never quite a man. That is to say, the act of coition is the essential clue to sex.

Now does all life work up to the one consummating act of coition? In one direction, it does, and it would be better if psychoanalysis plainly said so. In one direction, all life works up to the one supreme moment of coition. Let us all admit it, sincerely.

But we are not confined to one direction only, or to one exclusive consummation. Was the building of the cathedrals a working up towards the act of coition? Was the dynamic impulse sexual? No. The sexual element was present, and important. But not predominant. The same in the building of the Panama Canal. The sexual impulse, in its widest form, was a very great impulse towards the building of the Panama Canal. But there was something else, of even higher importance, and greater dynamic power.

And what is this other, greater impulse? It is the desire of the human male to build a world: not "to build a world for you, dear"; but to build up out of his own self and his own belief and his own effort something wonderful. Not merely something useful. Something wonderful. Even the Panama Canal would never have been built *simply* to let ships through. It is the pure disinterested craving of the human male to make something wonderful, out of his own head and his own self, and his own soul's faith and delight, which starts everything going. This is the prime motivity. And the motivity of sex is subsidiary to this: often directly antagonistic.

That is, the essentially religious or creative motive is the first motive for all human activity. The sexual motive comes second. And there is a great conflict between the interests of the two, at all times.

What we want to do is to trace the creative or religious motive to its source in the human being, keeping in mind always the near relationship between the religious motive and the sexual. The two great impulses are like man and wife, or father and son. It is no use putting one under the feet of the other.

The great desire today is to deny the religious impulse altogether, or else to assert its absolute alieniety from the sexual impulse. The orthodox religious world says faugh! to sex. Whereupon we thank Freud for giving them tit for tat. But the orthodox scientific world says fie! to the religious impulse. The scientist wants to discover a cause for everything. And there is no cause for the religious impulse. Freud is with the scientists. Jung dodges from his university gown into a priest's surplice till we don't know where we are. We prefer Freud's *Sex* to Jung's *Libido* or Bergson's *Élan Vital*. Sex has at least *some* definite reference, though when Freud makes sex accountable for everything he as good as makes it accountable for nothing.

We refuse any *Cause*, whether it be Sex or Libido or Élan Vital or ether or unit of force or *perpetuum mobile* or anything else. But also we feel that we cannot, like Moses, perish on the top of our present ideal Pisgah, or take the next step into thin air. There we are, at the top of our Pisgah of ideals, crying *Excelsior* and trying to clamber up into the clouds: that is, if we are idealists with the religious impulse rampant in our breasts. If we are scientists we practise airplane flying or eugenics or disarmament or something equally absurd.

The promised land, if it be anywhere, lies away beneath our feet. No more prancing upwards. No more uplift. No more little Excelsiors crying world-brotherhood and international love and Leagues of Nations. Idealism and materialism amount to the same thing on top of Pisgah, and the space is *very* crowded. We're all cornered on our mountain top, climbing up one another and standing on one another's faces in our scream of Excelsior.

To your tents, O Israel! Brethren, let us go down. We will descend. The way to our precious Canaan lies obviously downhill. An end of uplift. Downhill to the land of milk and honey. The blood will soon be flowing faster than either, but we can't help that. We can't help it if Canaan has blood in its veins, instead of pure milk and honey.

If it is a question of origins, the origin is always the same, whatever we say about it. So is the cause. Let that be a comfort to us. If we want to talk about God, well, we can please ourselves. God has been talked about quite a lot, and He doesn't seem to mind.

Why we should take it so personally is a problem. Likewise if we wish to have a tea party with the atom, let us: or with the wriggling little unit of energy, or the ether, or the Libido, or the Élan Vital, or any other Cause. Only don't let us have sex for tea. We've all got too much of it under the table; and really, for my part, I prefer to keep mine there, no matter what the Freudians say about me.

But it is tiring to go to any more tea parties with the Origin, or the Cause, or even the Lord. Let us pronounce the mystic Om, from the pit of the stomach, and proceed.

There's not a shadow of doubt about it, the First Cause is just unknowable to us, and we'd be sorry if it wasn't. Whether it's God or the Atom. All I say is Om!

The first business of every faith is to declare its ignorance. I don't know where I come from—nor where I exit to. I don't know the origins of life nor the goal of death. I don't know how the two parent cells which are my biological origin became the me which I am. I don't in the least know what those two parent cells were. The chemical analysis is just a farce, and my father and mother were just vehicles. And yet, I must say, since I've got to know about the two cells, I'm glad I do know.

The Moses of Science and the Aaron of Idealism have got the whole bunch of us here on top of Pisgah. It's a tight squeeze, and we'll be falling very, very foul of one another in five minutes, unless some of us climb down. But before leaving our eminence let us have a look round, and get our bearings.

They say that way lies the New Jerusalem of universal love: and over there the happy valley of indulgent Pragmatism: and there, quite near, is the chirpy land of the Vitalists: and in those dark groves the home of successful Analysis, surnamed Psycho: and over those blue hills the Supermen are prancing about, though you can't see them. And there is Besantheim, and there is Eddyhowe, and there, on that queer little tableland, is Wilsonia, and just round the corner is Rabindranathopolis. . . .

But Lord, I can't see anything. Help me, heaven, to a telescope, for I see blank nothing.

I'm not going to try any more. I'm going to sit down on my posterior and sluther full speed down this Pisgah, even if it cost me my trouser seat. So ho! Away we go.

In the beginning—there never was any beginning, but let it pass. We've got to make a start somehow. In the very beginning of all things, time and space and cosmos and being, in the beginning of all these was a little living creature. But I don't know even if it was little. In the beginning was a living creature, its plasm quivering and its life-pulse throbbing. This little creature died, as little creatures always do. But not before it had had young ones. When the daddy creature died, it fell to pieces. And that was the beginning of the cosmos. Its little body fell down to a speck of dust, which the young ones clung to because they must cling to something. Its little breath flew asunder, the hotness and brightness of the little beast—I beg your pardon, I mean the radiant energy from the corpse flew away to the right hand, and seemed to shine warm in the air, while the clammy energy from the body flew away to the left hand, and seemed dark and cold. And so, the first little master was dead and done for, and instead of his little living body there was a speck of dust in the middle, which became the earth, and on the right hand was a brightness which became the sun, rampaging with all the energy that had come out of the dead little master, and on the left hand a darkness which felt like an unrisen moon. And that was how the Lord created the world. Except that I know nothing about the Lord, so I shouldn't mention it.

But I forgot the soul of the little master. It probably did a bit of flying as well—and then came back to the young ones. It seems most natural that way.

Which is my account of the Creation. And I mean by it, that Life is not and never was anything but living creatures. That's what life is and will be, just living creatures, no matter how large you make the capital L. Out of living creatures the material cosmos was made: out of the death of living creatures, when their little living bodies fell dead and fell asunder into all sorts of matter and forces and energies, sun, moons, stars, and worlds. So you

got the universe. Where you got the living creature from, that
first one, don't ask me. He was just there. But he was a little person with a soul of his own. He wasn't Life with a capital L.

If you don't believe me, then don't. I'll even give you a little
song to sing.

> "If it be not true to me
>   What care I how true it be? . . ."

That's the kind of man I really like, chirping his insouciance. And
I chirp back:

> "Though it be not true to thee
>   It's gay and gospel truth to me. . . ."

The living live, and then die. They pass away, as we know, to
dust and to oxygen and nitrogen and so on. But what we don't
know, and what we might perhaps know a little more, is how
they pass away direct into life itself—that is, direct into the living.
That is, how many dead souls fly over our untidiness like swallows and build under the eaves of the living. How many dead
souls, like swallows, twitter and breed thoughts and instincts under the thatch of my hair and the eaves of my forehead, I don't
know. But I believe a good many. And I hope they have a good
time. And I hope not too many are bats.

I am sorry to say I believe in the souls of the dead. I am almost
ashamed to say, that I believe the souls of the dead in some way
re-enter and pervade the souls of the living: so that life is always
the life of living creatures, and death is always our affair. This
bit, I admit, is bordering on mysticism. I'm sorry, because I don't
like mysticism. It has no trousers and no trousers seat: *n'a pas de
quoi.* And I should feel so uncomfortable if I put my hand behind
me and felt an absolute blank.

Meanwhile a long, thin, brown caterpillar keeps on pretending
to be a dead thin beech-twig, on a little bough at my feet. He had
got his hind feet and his fore feet on the twig, and his body
looped up like an arch in the air between, when a fly walked up
the twig and began to mount the arch of the imitator, not having
the least idea that it was on a gentleman's coat-tails. The caterpil-

lar shook his stern, and the fly made off as if it had seen a ghost. The dead twig and the live twig now remain equally motionless, enjoying their different ways. And when, with this very pencil, I push the head of the caterpillar off from the twig, he remains on his tail, arched forward in air, and oscillating unhappily, like some tiny pendulum ticking. Ticking, ticking in midair, arched away from his planted tail. Till at last, after a long minute and a half, he touches the twig again, and subsides into twigginess. The only thing is, the dead beech-twig can't pretend to be a wagging caterpillar. Yet how the two commune! However—we have our exits and our entrances, and one man in his time plays many parts. More than he dreams of, poor darling. And I am entirely at a loss for a moral!

Well, then, we are born. I suppose that's a safe statement. And we become at once conscious, if we weren't so before. *Nem. con.* And our little baby body is a little functioning organism, a little developing machine or instrument or organ, and our little baby mind begins to stir with all our wonderful psychical beginnings. And so we are in bud.

But it won't do. It is too much of a Pisgah sight. We overlook too much. *Descendez, cher Moïse. Vous voyez trop loin.* You see too far all at once, dear Moses. Too much of a bird's-eye view across the Promised Land to the shore. Come down, and walk across, old fellow. And you won't see all that milk and honey and grapes the size of duck's eggs. All the dear little budding infant with its tender virginal mind and various clouds of glory instead of a napkin. Not at all, my dear chap. No such luck of a promised land.

Climb down, Pisgah, and go to Jericho. *Allons*, there is no road yet, but we are all Aarons with rods of our own.

The Holy Family

We are all very pleased with Mr. Einstein for knocking that eternal axis out of the universe. The universe isn't a spinning wheel. It is a cloud of bees flying and veering round. Thank goodness for that, for we were getting drunk on the spinning wheel.

So that now the universe has escaped from the pin which was pushed through it, like an impaled fly vainly buzzing: now that the multiple universe flies its own complicated course quite free, and hasn't got any hub, we can hope also to escape.

We won't be pinned down, either. We have no one law that governs us. For me there is only one law: *I am I*. And that isn't a law, it's just a remark. One is one, but one is not all alone. There are other stars buzzing in the centre of their own isolation. And there is no straight path between them. There is no straight path between you and me, dear reader, so don't blame me if my words fly like dust into your eyes and grit between your teeth, instead of like music into your ears. I am I, but also you are you, and we are in sad need of a theory of human relativity. We need it much more than the universe does. The stars know how to prowl round one another without much damage done. But you and I, dear reader, in the first conviction that you are me and that I am you, owing to the oneness of mankind, why, we are always falling foul of one another, and chewing each other's fur.

You are *not* me, dear reader, so make no pretentions to it. Don't get alarmed if *I* say things. It isn't your sacred mouth which is opening and shutting. As for the profanation of your sacred ears, just apply a little theory of relativity, and realize that what I say is not what you hear, but something uttered in the midst of my isolation, and arriving strangely changed and travel-worn down the long curve of your own individual circumambient atmosphere. I may say Boh, but heaven alone knows what the goose hears. And you may be sure that a red rag is, to a bull, something far more mysterious and complicated than a socialist's necktie.

So I hope now I have put you in your place, dear reader. Sit you like Watts' Hope on your own little blue globe, and I'll sit on mine, and we won't bump into one another if we can help it. You can twang your old hopeful lyre. It may be music to you, so I don't blame you. It is a terrible wowing in my ears. But that may be something in my individual atmosphere; some strange deflection as your music crosses the space between us. Certainly I never hear the concert of World Regeneration and Hope Revived Again without getting a sort of lock-jaw, my teeth go so keen on edge from the twanging harmony. Still, the world-regenerators may *really* be quite excellent performers on their own jews'-harps. Blame the edginess of my teeth.

Now I am going to launch words into space, so mind your cosmic eye.

As I said in my small but naturally immortal book, *Psychoanalysis and the Unconscious*, there's more in it than meets the eye. There's more in you, dear reader, than meets the eye. What, don't you believe it? Do you think you're as obvious as a poached egg on a piece of toast, like the poor lunatic? Not a bit of it, dear reader. You've got a solar plexus, and a lumbar ganglion not far from your liver, and I'm going to tell everybody. Nothing brings a man home to himself like telling everybody. And I *will* drive you home to yourself, do you hear? You've been poaching in my private atmospheric grounds long enough, identifying yourself with me and me with everybody. A nice row there'd be in heaven if Aldebaran caught Sirius by the tail and said, "Look here, you're not to look so green, you damn dog-star! It's an offense against star regulations."

Which reminds me that the Arabs say the shooting stars, meteorites, are starry stones which the angels fling at the poaching demons whom they catch sight of prowling too near the palisades of heaven. I must say I like Arab angels. My heaven would coruscate like a Catherine wheel, with white-hot star-stones. Away, you dog, you prowling cur. Got him under the left ear-hole, Gabriel—! See him, see him, Michael! That hopeful blue devil! Land him one! Biff on your bottom, you hoper.

But I wish the Arabs wouldn't entice me, or you, dear reader, provoke me to this. I feel with you, dear reader, as I do with a deaf man when he pushes his vulcanite ear, his listening machine, towards my mouth. I want to shout down the telephone ear-hole all kinds of improper things, to see what effect they will have on the stupid dear face at the end of the coil of wire. After all, words must be very different after they've trickled round and round a long wire coil. Whatever becomes of them! And I, who am a bit deaf myself, and may in the end have a deaf-machine to poke at my friends, it ill becomes me to be so unkind, yet that's how I feel. So there we are.

Help me to be serious, dear reader.

In that little book, *Psychoanalysis and the Unconscious*, I tried rather wistfully to convince you, dear reader, that you had a solar plexus and a lumbar ganglion and a few other things. I don't know why I took the trouble. If a fellow doesn't believe he's got a nose, the best way to convince him is gently to waft a little pepper into his nostrils. And there was I painting my own nose purple, and wistfully inviting you to look and believe. No more, though.

You've got first and foremost a solar plexus, dear reader; and the solar plexus is a great nerve center which lies behind your stomach. I can't be accused of impropriety or untruth, because any book of science or medicine which deals with the nerve-system of the human body will show it to you quite plainly. So don't wriggle or try to look spiritual. Because, willy-nilly, you've got a solar plexus, dear reader, among other things. I'm writing a good sound science book, which there's no gainsaying.

Now, your solar plexus, most gentle of readers, is where you are you. It is your first and greatest and deepest centre of consciousness. If you want to know *how* conscious and *when* conscious, I must refer you to that little book, *Psychoanalysis and the Unconscious*.

At your solar plexus you are primarily conscious: there, behind your stomach. There you have the profound and pristine conscious awareness that you are you. Don't say you haven't. I know you have. You might as well try to deny the nose on your face. There is your first and deepest seat of awareness. There you are triumphantly aware of your own individual existence in the universe. Absolutely there is the keep and central stronghold of your triumphantly conscious self. There you *are*, and you know it. So stick out your tummy gaily, my dear, with a *Me voilà*. With a *Here I am!* With an *Ecco mi!* With a *Da bin ich!* There you are, dearie.

But not only a triumphant awareness that *There you are*. An exultant awareness also that outside this quiet gate, this navel, lies a whole universe on which you can lay tribute. Aha—at birth you closed the central gate forever. Too dangerous to leave it open. Too near the quick. But there are other gates. There are eyes and mouths and ears and nostrils, besides the two lower gates of the passionate body, and the closed but not locked gates of the breasts. Many gates. And besides the actual gates, the marvelous wireless communication between the great centre and the surrounding or contiguous world.

Authorized science tells you that this first great plexus, this all-potent nerve-centre of consciousness and dynamic life-activity is a sympathetic centre. From the solar plexus as from your castle-keep you look around and see the fair lands smiling, the corn and fruit and cattle of your increase, the cottages of your dependents and the halls of your beloveds. From the solar plexus you know that all the world is yours, and all is goodly.

This is the great centre, where, in the womb, your life first sparkled in individuality. This is the centre that drew the gestating maternal blood-stream upon you, in the nine-months lurking, drew it on you for your increase. This is the centre whence the navel-string broke, but where the invisible string of dynamic consciousness, like a dark electric current connecting you with the rest of life, will never break until you die and depart from corporate individuality.

They say, by the way, that doctors now perform a little operation on the born baby, so that no more navel shows. No more
belly-buttons, dear reader! Lucky I caught you this generation,
before the doctors had saved your appearances. Yet, *caro mio*,
whether it shows or not, there you once had immediate connection with the maternal blood-stream. And, because the male
nucleus which derived from the father still lies sparkling and potent within the solar plexus, therefore that great nerve-centre of
you still has immediate knowledge of your father, a subtler but
still vital connection. We call it the tie of blood. So be it. It is a
tie of blood. But much more definite than we imagine. For true
it is that the one bright male germ which went to your begetting
was drawn from the blood of the father. And true it is that that
same bright male germ lies unquenched and unquenchable at the
centre of you, within the famous solar plexus. And furthermore
true is it that this unquenched father-spark within you sends forth
vibrations and dark currents of vital activity all the time; connecting direct with your father. You will never be able to get away
from it while you live.

The connection with the mother may be more obvious. Is
there not your ostensible navel, where the rupture between you
and her took place? But because the mother-child relation is more
plausible and flagrant, is that any reason for supposing it deeper,
more vital, more intrinsic? Not a bit. Because if the large parent
mother-germ still lives and acts vividly and mysteriously in the
great fused nucleus of your solar plexus, does the smaller, brilliant
male-spark that derived from your father act any less vividly? By
no means. It is different—it is less ostensible. It may be even in
magnitude smaller. But it may be even more vivid, even more intrinsic. So beware how you deny the father-quick of yourself.
You may be denying the most intrinsic quick of all.

In the same way it follows that, since brothers and sisters have
the same father and mother, therefore in every brother and sister
there is a direct communication such as can never happen between strangers. The parent nuclei do not die within the new
nucleus. They remain there, marvelous naked sparkling dynamic
life-centres, nodes, well-heads of vivid life itself. Therefore in

every individual the parent nuclei live, and give direction connection, blood connection we call it, with the rest of the family. It *is* blood connection. For the fecundating nuclei are the very spark-essence of the blood. And while life lives the parent nuclei maintain their own centrality and dynamic effectiveness within the solar plexus of the child. So that every individual has mother and father both sparkling within himself.

But this is rather a preliminary truth than an intrinsic truth. The intrinsic truth of every individual is the new unit of unique individuality which emanates from the fusion of the parent nuclei. This is the incalculable and intangible Holy Ghost each time —each individual his own Holy Ghost. When, at the moment of conception, the two parent nuclei fuse to form a new unit of life, then takes place the great mystery of creation. A new individual appears—not the result of the fusion merely. Something more. The quality of individuality cannot be derived. The new individual, in his singleness of self, is a perfectly new whole. He is not a permutation and combination of old elements, transferred through the parents. No, he is something underived and utterly unprecedented, unique, a new soul.

This quality of pure individuality is, however, only the one supreme quality. It consummates all other qualities, but does not consume them. All the others are there, all the time. And only at his maximum does an individual surpass all his derivative elements, and become purely himself. And most people never get there. In his own pure individuality a man surpasses his father and mother, and is utterly unknown to them. "Woman, what have I to do with thee?" But this does not alter the fact that within him lives the mother-quick and the father-quick, and that though in his wholeness he is rapt away beyond the old mother-father connections, they are still there within him, consummated but not consumed. Nor does it alter the fact that very few people surpass their parents nowadays, and attain any individuality beyond them. Most men are half-born slaves: the little soul they are born with just atrophies, and merely the organism emanates, the new self, the new soul, the new swells into manhood, like big potatoes.

So there we are. But considering man at his best, he is at the start faced with the great problem. At the very start he has to undertake his tripartite being, the mother within him, the father within him, and the Holy Ghost, the self which he is supposed to consummate, and which mostly he doesn't.

And there it is, a hard physiological fact. At the moment of our conception, the father nucleus fuses with the mother nucleus, and the wonder emanates, the new self, the new soul, the new individual cell. But in the new individual cell the father-germ and the mother-germ do not relinquish their identity. There they remain still, incorporated and never extinguished. And so, the blood-stream of race is one stream, forever. But the moment the mystery of pure individual newness ceased to be enacted and fulfilled, the blood-stream would dry up and be finished. Mankind would die out.

Let us go back then to the solar plexus. There sparkle the included mother-germ and father-germ, giving us direct, immediate blood-bonds, family connection. The connection is as direct and as subtle as between the Marconi stations, two great wireless stations. A family, if you like, is a group of wireless stations, all adjusted to the same, or very much the same vibration. All the time they quiver with the interchange, there is one long endless flow of vitalistic communication between members of one family, a long, strange *rapport*, a sort of life-unison. It is a ripple of life through many bodies as through one body. But all the time there is the jolt, the rupture of individualism, the individual asserting himself beyond all ties or claims. The highest goal for every man is the goal of pure individual being. But it is a goal you cannot reach by the mere rupture of all ties. A child isn't born by being torn from the womb. When it is born by natural process that is rupture enough. But even then the ties are not broken. They are only subtilized.

From the solar plexus first of all pass the great vitalistic communications between child and parents, the first interplay of primal, pre-mental knowledge and sympathy. It is a great subtle interplay, and from this interplay the child is built up, body and psyche. Impelled from the primal conscious centre in the abdomen, the child seeks the mother, seeks the breast, opens a blind mouth, and gropes for the nipple. Not mentally directed and yet certainly directed. Directed from the dark pre-mind centre of the solar plexus. From this centre the child seeks, the mother knows. Hence the true mindlessness of the pristine, healthy mother. She does not need to think, mentally to know. She knows so profoundly and actively at the great abdominal life-centre.

But if the child thus seeks the mother, does it then know the mother alone? To an infant the mother is the whole universe. Yet the child needs more than the mother. It needs as well the presence of men, the vibration from the present body of the man. There may not be any actual, palpable connection. But from the great voluntary centre in the man pass unknowable communications and untellable nourishment of the stream of manly blood, rays which we cannot see, and which so far we have refused to know, but none the less essential quickening dark rays which pass from the great dark abdominal life-centre in the father to the corresponding centre in the child. And these rays, these vibrations, are not like the mother-vibrations. Far, far from it. They do not need the actual contact, the handling and the caressing. On the contrary, the true male instinct is to avoid physical contact with a baby. It may not need even actual presence. But, present or absent, there should be between the baby and the father that strange, intangible communication, that strange pull and circuit such as the magnetic pole exercises upon a needle, a vitalistic pull and flow which lays all the life-plasm of the baby into the line of vital quickening, strength, knowing. And any lack of this vital circuit, this vital interchange between father and child, man and child, means an inevitable impoverishment to the infant.

The child exists in the interplay of two great life-waves, the womanly and the male. In appearance, the mother is everything. In truth, the father has actively very little part. It does not matter much if he hardly sees his child. Yet see it he should, sometimes, and touch it sometimes, and renew with it the connection, the life-circuit, not allow it to lapse, and so vitally starve his child.

But remember, dear reader, please, that there is not the slightest need for you to believe me, or even read me. Remember, it's just your own affair. Don't implicate me.

☙ III ☙

Plexuses, Planes, and So On

The primal consciousness in man is pre-mental, and has nothing to do with cognition. It is the same as in the animals. And this pre-mental consciousness remains as long as we live the powerful root and body of our consciousness. The mind is but the last flower, the cul-de-sac.

The first seat of our primal consciousness is the solar plexus, the great nerve-centre situated behind the stomach. From this centre we are first dynamically conscious. For the primal consciousness is always dynamic, and never, like mental consciousness, static. Thought, let us say what we will about its magic powers, is instrumental only, the soul's finest instrument for the business of living. Thought is just a means to action and living. But life and action take rise actually at the great centres of dynamic consciousness.

The solar plexus, the greatest and most important centre of our dynamic consciousness, is a sympathetic centre. At this main centre of your first-mind we know as we can never mentally know. Primarily we know, each man, each living creature knows, profoundly and satisfactorily and without question, that *I am I*. This root of all knowledge and being is established in the solar plexus; it is dynamic, pre-mental knowledge, such as cannot be transferred into thought. Do not ask me to transfer the pre-mental dynamic knowledge into thought. It cannot be done. The knowledge that *I am I* can never be thought: only known.

This being the very first term of our life-knowledge, a knowledge established physically and psychically the moment the two parent nuclei fused, at the moment of the conception, it remains integral as a piece of knowledge in every subsequent nucleus derived from this one original. But yet the original nucleus, formed from the two parent nuclei at our conception, remains always primal and central, and is always the original fount and home of the first and supreme knowledge that *I am I*. This original nucleus is embodied in the solar plexus.

But the original nucleus divides. The first division, as science knows, is a division of recoil. From the perfect oneing of the two parent nuclei in the egg-cell results a recoil or new assertion. That which was perfect *one* now divides again, and in the recoil becomes again two.

This second nucleus, the nucleus born of recoil, is the nuclear origin of all the great nuclei of the voluntary system, which are the nuclei of assertive individualism. And it remains central in the adult human body as it was in the egg-cell. In the adult human body the first nucleus of independence, first-born from the great original nucleus of our conception, lies always established in the lumbar ganglion. Here we have our positive centre of independence, in a multifarious universe.

At the solar plexus, the dynamic knowledge is this, that *I am I*. The solar plexus is the centre of all the sympathetic system. The great prime knowledge is sympathetic in nature. I am I, in vital centrality. I am I, the vital centre of all things. I am I, the clue to the whole. All is one with me. It is the one identity.

But at the lumbar ganglion, which is the center of separate identity, the knowledge is of a different mode, though the term is the same. At the lumbar ganglion I know that I am I, in distinction from a whole universe, which is not as I am. This is the first tremendous flash of knowledge of singleness and separate identity. I am I, not because I am at one with all the universe, but because I am other than all the universe. It is my distinction from all the rest of things which makes me myself. Because I am set utterly apart and distinguished from all that is the rest of the universe, therefore *I am I*. And this root of our knowledge in separateness lies rooted all the time in the lumbar ganglion. It is the second term of our dynamic psychic existence.

It is from the great sympathetic centre of the solar plexus that the child rejoices in the mother and in its own blissful centrality, its unison with the as yet unknown universe. Look at the pictures of Madonna and Child, and you will even *see* it. It is from this centre that it draws all things unto itself, winningly, drawing love for the soul, and actively drawing in milk. The same centre controls the great intake of love and of milk, of psychic and of physical nourishment.

And it is from the great voluntary centre of the lumbar ganglion that the child asserts its distinction from the mother, the single identity of its own existence, and its power over its surroundings. From this centre issues the violent little pride and lustiness which kicks with glee, or crows with tiny exultance in its own being, or which claws the breast with a savage little rapacity, and an incipient masterfulness of which every mother is aware. This incipient mastery, this sheer joy of a young thing in its own single existence, the marvellous playfulness of early youth, and the roguish mockery of the mother's love, as well as the bursts of temper and rage, all belong to infancy. And all this flashes spontaneously, *must* flash spontaneously from the first great centre of independence, the powerful lumbar ganglion, great dynamic centre of all the voluntary system, of all the spirit of pride and joy in independent existence. And it is from this centre too that the milk is urged away down the infant bowels, urged away towards excretion. The motion is the same, but here it applies to the material, not to the vital relation. It is from the lumbar ganglion that the dynamic vibrations are emitted which thrill from the stomach and bowels, and promote the excremental function of digestion. It is the solar plexus which controls the assimilatory function in digestion.

So, in the first division of the egg-cell is set up the first plane of psychic and physical life, remaining radically the same throughout the whole existence of the individual. The two original nuclei of the egg-cell remain the same two original nuclei within the corpus of the adult individual. Their psychic and their

physical dynamic is the same in the solar plexus and lumbar ganglion as in the two nuclei of the egg-cell. The first great division
in the egg remains always the same, the unchanging great division in the psychic and the physical structure; the unchanging
great division in knowledge and function. It is a division into polarized duality, psychical and physical, of the human being. It is
the great vertical division of the egg-cell, and of the nature of
man.

Then, this division having taken place, there is a new thrill of
conjunction or collision between the divided nuclei, and at once
the second birth takes place. The two nuclei now split horizontally. There is a horizontal division across the whole egg-cell, and
the nuclei are now four, two above, and two below. But those below retain their original nature, those above are new in nature.
And those above correspond again to those below.

In the developed child, the great horizontal division of the egg-
cell, resulting in four nuclei, this remains the same. The horizontal division-wall is the diaphragm. The two upper nuclei are the
two great nerve-centres, the cardiac plexus and the thoracic ganglion. We have again a sympathetic centre primal in activity and
knowledge, and a corresponding voluntary centre. In the centre
of the breast, the cardiac plexus acts as the great sympathetic
mode of new dynamic activity, new dynamic consciousness. And
near the spine, by the wall of the shoulders, the thoracic ganglion
acts as the powerful voluntary centre of separateness and power,
in the same vertical line as the lumbar ganglion, but horizontally
so different.

Now we must change our whole feeling. We must put off the
deep way of understanding which belongs to the lower body of
our nature, and transfer ourselves into the upper plane, where being and functioning are different.

At the cardiac plexus, there in the centre of the breast, we have
now a new great sun of knowledge and being. Here there is no
more of self. Here there is no longer the dark, exultant knowledge that *I am I*. A change has come. Here I know no more of
myself. Here I am not. Here I only know the delightful revelation that you are you. The wonder is no longer within me, my

own dark, centrifugal, exultant self. The wonder is without me. The wonder is outside me. And I can no longer exult and know myself the dark, central sun of the universe. Now I look with wonder, with tenderness, with joyful yearning towards that which is outside me, beyond me, not me. Behold, that which was once negative has now become the only positive. The other being is now the great positive reality, I myself am as nothing. Positivity has changed places.

If we want to see the portrayed look, then we must turn to the North, to the fair, wondering, blue-eyed infants of the Northern masters. They seem so frail, so innocent and wondering, touching outwards to the mystery. They are not the same as the Southern child, nor the opposite. Their whole life mystery is different. Instead of consummating all things within themselves, as the dark little Southern infants do, the Northern Jesus-children reach out delicate little hands of wondering innocence towards delicate, flower-reverential mothers. Compare a Botticelli Madonna, with all her wounded and abnegating sensuality, with a Hans Memling Madonna, whose soul is pure and only reverential. Beyond me is the mystery and the glory, says the Northern mother: let me have no self, let me only seek that which is all-pure, all-wonderful. But the Southern mother says: This is mine, this is mine, this is my child, my wonder, my master, my lord, my scourge, my own.

From the cardiac plexus the child goes forth in bliss. It seeks the revelation of the unknown. It wonderingly seeks the mother. It opens its small hands and spreads its small fingers to touch her. And bliss, bliss, bliss, it meets the wonder in mid-air and in mid-space it finds the loveliness of the mother's face. It opens and shuts its little fingers with bliss, it laughs the wonderful, selfless laugh of pure baby-bliss, in the first ecstasy of finding all its treasure, groping upon it and finding it in the dark. It opens wide, child-wide eyes to see, to see. But it cannot see. It is puzzled, it wrinkles its face. But when the mother puts her face quite near, and laughs and coos, then the baby trembles with an ecstasy of love. The glamour, the wonder, the treasure beyond. The great uplift of rapture. All this surges from that first centre of the breast, the sun of the breast, the cardiac plexus.

And from the same centre acts the great function of the heart and breath. Ah, the aspiration, the aspiration, like a hope, like a yearning constant and unfailing with which we take in breath. When we breathe, when we take in breath, it is not as when we take in food. When we breathe in we aspire, we yearn towards the heaven of air and light. And when the heart dilates to draw in the stream of dark blood, it opens its arms as to a beloved. It dilates with reverent joy, as a host opening his doors to an honored guest, whom he delights to serve: opening his doors to the wonder which comes to him from beyond, and without which he were nothing.

So it is that our heart dilates, our lungs expand. They are bidden by that great and mysterious impulse from the cardiac plexus, which bids them seek the mystery and the fulfillment of the beyond. They seek the beyond, the air of the sky, the hot blood from the dark underworld. And so we live.

And then, they relax, they contract. They are driven by the opposite motion from the powerful voluntary centre of the thoracic ganglion. That which was drawn in, was invited, is now relinquished, allowed to go forth, negatively. Not positively dismissed, but relinquished.

There is a wonderful complementary duality between the voluntary and the sympathetic activity on the same plane. But between the two planes, upper and lower, there is a further dualism, still more startling, perhaps. Between the dark, glowing first term of knowledge at the solar plexus: *I am I, all is one in me;* and the first term of volitional knowledge: *I am myself, and these others are not as I am*—there is a world of difference. But when the world changes again, and on the upper plane we realize the wonder of other things, the difference is almost shattering. The thoracic ganglion is a ganglion of power. When the child in its delicate bliss seeks the mother and finds her and is added on to her, then it fulfills itself in the great upper sympathetic mode. But then it relinquishes her. It ceases to be aware of her. And if she tries to force its love to play upon her again, like light revealing her to herself, then the child turns away. Or it will lie, and look at her with the strange, odd, curious look of knowledge, like a little imp who is spying her out. This is the curious look that many mothers cannot bear. Involuntarily it arouses a sort of hate in them—the look of scrutinizing curiosity, apart, and as it were studying, balancing them up. Yet it is a look which comes into every child's eyes. It is the reaction of the great voluntary plexus between the shoulders. The mother is suddenly set apart, as an object of curiosity, coldly, sometimes dreamily, sometimes puzzled, sometimes mockingly observed.

Again, if a mother neglect her child, it cries, it weeps for her love and attention. Its pitiful lament is one of the forms of compulsion from the upper centre. This insistence on pity, on love, is quite different from the rageous weeping, which is compulsion from the lower centre, below the diaphragm. Again, some children just drop everything they can lay hands on over the edge of their crib, or their table. They drop everything out of sight. And then they look up with a curious look of negative triumph. This is again a form of recoil from the upper centre, the obliteration of the thing which is outside. And here a child is acting quite differently from the child who joyously *smashes*. The desire to smash comes from the lower centres.

We can quite well recognize the will exerted from the lower centre. We call it headstrong temper and masterfulness. But the peculiar will of the upper centre—the sort of nervous, critical objectivity, the deliberate forcing of sympathy, the play upon pity and tenderness, the plaintive bullying of love, or the benevolent bullying of love—these we don't care to recognize. They are the extravagance of spiritual *will*. But in its true harmony the thoracic ganglion is a centre of happier activity: of real, eager curiosity, of the delightful desire to pick things to pieces, and the desire to put them together again, the desire to "find out," and the desire to invent: all this arises on the upper plane, at the volitional centre of the thoracic ganglion.

❦ IV ❦

Trees and Babies and Papas and Mamas

Oh, damn the miserable baby with its complicated ping-pong table of an unconscious. I'm sure, dear reader, you'd rather have to listen to the brat howling in its crib than to me expounding its plexuses. As for "mixing those babies up," I'd mix him up like a shot if I'd anything to mix him with. Unfortunately he's my own anatomical specimen of a pickled rabbit, so there's nothing to be done with the bits.

But he gets on my nerves. I come out solemnly with a pencil and an exercise book, and take my seat in all gravity at the foot of a large fir-tree, and wait for thoughts to come, gnawing like a squirrel on a nut. But the nut's hollow.

I think there are too many trees. They seem to crowd round and stare at me, and I feel as if they nudged one another when I'm not looking. I can *feel* them standing there. And they won't let me get on about the baby this morning. Just their cussedness. I felt they encouraged me like a harem of wonderful silent wives, yesterday.

It is half rainy too—the wood so damp and still and so secret, in the remote morning air. Morning, with rain in the sky, and the forest subtly brooding, and me feeling no bigger than a pea-bug between the roots of my fir. The trees seem so much bigger than me, so much stronger in life, prowling silent around. I seem to feel them moving and thinking and prowling, and they overwhelm me. Ah, well, the only thing is to give way to them.

It is the edge of the Black Forest—sometimes the Rhine far off, on its Rhine plain, like a bit of magnesium ribbon. But not today. Today only trees, and leaves, and vegetable presences. Huge straight fir-trees, and big beech-trees sending rivers of roots into the ground. And cuckoos, like noise falling in drops off the leaves. And me, a fool, sitting by a grassy wood-road with a pencil and a book, hoping to write more about that baby.

Never mind. I listen again for noises, and I smell the damp moss. The looming trees, so straight. And I listen for their silence. Big, tall-bodied trees, with a certain magnificent cruelty about them. Or barbarity. I don't know why I should say cruelty. Their magnificent, strong, round bodies! It almost seems I can hear the slow, powerful sap drumming in their trunks. Great full-blooded trees, with strange tree-blood in them, soundlessly drumming.

Trees that have no hands and faces, no eyes. Yet the powerful sap-scented blood roaring up the great columns. A vast individual life, and an overshadowing will. The will of a tree. Something that frightens you.

Suppose you want to look a tree in the face? You can't. It hasn't got a face. You look at the strong body of a trunk: you look above you into the matted body-hair of twigs and boughs: you see the soft green tips. But there are no eyes to look into, you can't meet its gaze. You keep on looking at it in part and parcel.

It's no good looking at a tree, to know it. The only thing is to sit among the roots and nestle against its strong trunk, and not bother. That's how I write all about these planes and plexuses, between the toes of a tree, forgetting myself against the great ankle of the trunk. And then, as a rule, as a squirrel is stroked into its wickedness by the faceless magic of a tree, so am I usually stroked into forgetfulness, and into scribbling this book. My tree-book, really.

I come so well to understand tree-worship. All the old Aryans worshipped the tree. My ancestors. The tree of life. The tree of knowledge. Well, one is bound to sprout out some time or other, chip of the old Aryan block. I can so well understand tree-worship. And fear the deepest motive.

Naturally. This marvellous vast individual without a face, without lips or eyes or heart. This towering creature that never had a face. Here am I between his toes like a pea-bug, and him noiselessly over-reaching me. And I feel his great blood-jet surging. And he has no eyes. But he turns two ways. He thrusts himself tremendously down to the middle earth, where dead men sink in darkness, in the damp, dense undersoil, and he turns himself about in high air. Whereas we have eyes on one side of our head only, and only grow upwards.

Plunging himself down into the black humus, with a root's gushing zest, where we can only rot dead; and his tips in high air, where we can only look up to. So vast and powerful and exultant in his two directions. And all the time, he has no face, no thought: only a huge, savage, thoughtless soul. Where does he even keep his soul? Where does anybody?

A huge, plunging, tremendous soul. I would like to be a tree for a while. The great lust of roots. Root-lust. And no mind at all. He towers, and I sit and feel safe. I like to feel him towering round me. I used to be afraid. I used to fear their lust, their rushing black lust. But now I like it, I worship it. I always felt them huge primeval enemies. But now they are my only shelter and strength. I lose myself among the trees. I am so glad to be with them in their silent, intent passion, and their great lust. They feed my soul. But I can understand that Jesus was crucified on a tree.

And I can so well understand the Romans, their terror of the bristling Hercynian wood. Yet when you look from a height down upon the rolling of the forest—this Black Forest—it is as suave as a rolling, oily sea. Inside only, it bristles horrific. And it terrified the Romans.

The Romans! They too seem very near. Nearer than Hindenburg or Foch or even Napoleon. When I look across the Rhine plain, it is Rome and the legionaries of the Rhine that my soul notices. It must have been wonderful to come from South Italy to the shores of this sea-like forest: this dark, moist forest, with its enormously powerful intensity of tree life. Now I know, coming myself from rock-dry Sicily, open to the day.

The Romans and the Greeks found everything human. Everything had a face, and a human voice. Men spoke, and their fountains piped an answer.

But when the legions crossed the Rhine they found a vast impenetrable life which had no voice. They met the faceless silence of the Black Forest. This huge, huge wood did not answer when they called. Its silence was too crude and massive. And the soldiers shrank: shrank before the trees that had no faces, and no answer. A vast array of non-human life, darkly self-sufficient, and bristling with indomitable energy. The Hercynian wood, not to be fathomed. The enormous power of these collective trees, stronger in their somber life even than Rome.

No wonder the soldiers were terrified. No wonder they thrilled with horror when, deep in the woods, they found the skulls and trophies of their dead comrades upon the trees. The trees had devoured them: silently, in mouthfuls, and left the white bones. Bones of the mindful Romans—and savage, preconscious trees, indomitable. The true German has something of the sap of trees in his veins even now: and a sort of pristine savageness, like trees, helpless, but most powerful, under all his mentality. He is a tree-soul, and his gods are not human. His instinct still is to nail skulls and trophies to the sacred tree, deep in the forest. The tree of life and death, tree of good and evil, tree of abstraction and of immense, mindless life; tree of everything except the spirit, spirituality.

But after bone-dry Sicily, and after the gibbering of myriad people all rattling their personalities, I am glad to be with the profound indifference of faceless trees. Their rudimentariness cannot know why we care for the things we care for. They have no faces, no minds and bowels: only deep, lustful roots stretching in earth, and vast, lissome life in air, and primeval individuality. You can sacrifice the whole of your spirituality on their altar still. You can nail your skull on their limbs. They have no skulls, no minds nor faces, they can't make eyes of love at you. Their vast life dispenses with all this. But they will live you down.

The normal life of one of these big trees is about a hundred years. So the Herr Baron told me.

One of the few places that my soul will haunt, when I am dead, will be this. Among the trees here near Ebersteinburg, where I have been alone and written this book. I can't leave these trees. They have taken some of my soul.

Excuse my digression, gentle reader. At first I left it out, thinking we might not see wood for trees. But it doesn't much matter what we see. It's nice just to look round, anywhere.

So there are two planes of being and consciousness and two modes of relation and of function. We will call the lower plane the sensual, the upper the spiritual. The terms may be unwise, but we can think of no other.

Please read that again, dear reader; you'll be a bit dazzled, coming out of the wood.

It is obvious that from the time a child is born, or conceived, it has a permanent relation with the outer universe, a relation in the two modes, not one mode only. There are two ways of love, two ways of activity in independence. And there needs some sort of equilibrium between the two modes. In the same way, in physical function there is eating and drinking, and excrementation, on the lower plane; and respiration and heart-beat on the upper plane.

Now the equilibrium to be established is fourfold. There must be a true equilibrium between what we eat and what we reject again by excretion: likewise between the systole and diastole of the heart, the inspiration and expiration of our breathing. Suffice to say the equilibrium is never quite perfect. Most people are either too fat or too thin, too hot or too cold, too slow or too quick. There is no such thing as an *actual* norm, a living norm. A norm is merely an abstraction, not a reality.

The same on the psychical plane. We either love too much, or impose our will too much, are too spiritual or too sensual. There is not and cannot be any actual norm of human conduct. All depends, first, on the unknown inward need within the very nuclear centres of the individual himself, and secondly on his circumstance. Some men *must* be too spiritual, some *must* be too sensual. Some *must* be too sympathetic, and some *must* be too proud. We have no desire to say what men *ought* to be. We only wish to say there are all kinds of ways of being, and there is no such thing as human perfection. No man can be anything more than just himself, in genuine living relation to all his surroundings. But that which *I* am, when I am myself, will certainly be anathema to those who hate individual integrity, and want to swarm. And that which I, being myself, am in myself, may make the hair bristle with rage on a man who is also himself, but very different from me. Then let it bristle. And if mine bristle back again, then let us, if we must, fly at one another like two enraged men. It is how it should be. We've got to learn to live from the centre of our own responsibility only, and let other people do the same.

To return to the child, however, and his development on his two planes of consciousness. There is all the time a direct dynamic connection between child and mother, child and father also, from the start. It is a connection on two planes, the upper and lower. From the lower sympathetic centre the profound intake of love or vibration from the living co-respondent outside. From the upper sympathetic centre the outgoing of devotion and the passionate vibration of *given* love, given attention. The two sympathetic centres are always, or should always be, counterbalanced by their corresponding voluntary centres. From the great voluntary ganglion of the lower plane, the child is self-willed, independent, and masterful.

In the activity of this centre a boy refuses to be kissed and pawed about, maintaining his proud independence like a little wild animal. From this centre he likes to command and to receive obedience. From this centre likewise he may be destructive and defiant and reckless, determined to have his own way at any cost.

From this centre, too, he learns to use his legs. The motion of walking, like the motion of breathing, is twofold. First, a sympathetic cleaving to the earth with the foot: then the voluntary rejection, the spurning, the kicking away, the exultance in power and freedom.

From the upper voluntary centre the child watches persistently, wilfully, for the attention of the mother: to be taken notice of, to be caressed, in short to exist in and through the mother's attention. From this centre, too, he coldly refuses to notice the mother when she insists on too much attention. This cold refusal is different from the active rejection of the lower centre. It is passive, but cold and negative. It is the great force of our day. From the ganglion of the shoulders, also, the child breathes and his heart beats. From the same centre he learns the first use of his arms. In the gesture of sympathy, from the upper plane, he embraces his mother with his arms. In the motion of curiosity, or interest, which derives from the thoracic ganglion, he spreads his fingers, touches, feels, explores. In the motion of rejection he drops an undesired object deliberately out of sight.

And then, when the four centres of what we call the first *field* of consciousness are fully active, then it is that the eyes begin to gather their sight, the mouth to speak, the ears to awake to their intelligent hearings; all as a result of the great fourfold activity of the first dynamic field of consciousness. And then also, as a result, the mind wakens to its impressions and to its incipient control. For at first the control is non-mental, even non-cerebral. The brain acts only as a sort of switchboard.

The business of the father, in all this incipient child-development, is to stand outside as a final authority and make the necessary adjustments. Where there is too much sympathy, then the great voluntary centres of the spine are weak, the child tends to be delicate. Then the father by instinct supplies the roughness, the sternness which stiffens in the child the centres of resistance and independence, right from the very earliest days. Often, for a mere infant, it is the father's fierce or stern presence, the vibration of his voice, which starts the frictional and independent activity of the great voluntary ganglion and gives the first impulse to the independence which later on is life itself.

But on the other hand, the father, from his distance, supports, protects, nourishes his child, and it is ultimately on the remote but powerful father-love that the infant rests, in a rest which is beyond mother-love. For in the male the dominant centres are naturally the volitional centres, centres of responsibility, authority, and care.

It is the father's business, again, to maintain some sort of equilibrium between the two modes of love in his infant. A mother may wish to bring up her child from the lovely upper centres only, from the centres of the breast, in the mode of what we call pure or spiritual love. Then the child will be all gentle, all tender and tender-radiant, always enfolded with gentleness and forbearance, always shielded from grossness or pain or roughness. Now the father's instinct is to be rough and crude, good-naturedly brutal with the child, calling the deeper centres, the sensual centres, into play. "What do you want? My watch? Well, you can't have it, do you see, because it's mine." Not a lot of explanations of the "You see, darling." No such nonsense. Or if a child wails unnecessarily for its mother, the father must be the check. "Stop your noise, you little brat! What ails you, you whiner?" And if children be too sensitive, too sympathetic, then it will do the child no harm if the father occasionally throws the cat out of the window, or kicks the dog, or raises a storm in the house. Storms there must be. And if the child is old enough and robust enough, it can occasionally have its bottom soundly spanked—by the father, if the mother refuses to perform that most necessary duty. For a child's bottom is made occasionally to be spanked. The vibration of the spanking acts direct upon the spinal nerve-system, there is a direct reciprocity and reaction, the spanker transfers his wrath to the great will-centres in the child, and these will-centres react intensely, are vivified and educated.

On the other hand, given a mother who is too generally hard or indifferent, then it rests with the father to provide the delicate sympathy and the refined discipline. Then the father must show the tender sensitiveness of the upper mode. The sad thing today is that so few mothers have any deep bowels of love—or even the breast of love. What they have is the benevolent spiritual will, the will of the upper self. But the will is not love. And benevolence in a parent is a poison. It is bullying. In these circumstances the father must give delicate adjustment, and, above all, some warm, native love from the richer sensual self.

The question of corporal punishment is important. It is no use roughly smacking a shrinking, sensitive child. And yet, if a child is too shrinking, too sensitive, it may do it a world of good cheerfully to spank its posterior. Not brutally, not cruelly, but with real sound, good-natured exasperation. And let the adult take the full responsibility, half humorously, without apology or explanation. Let us avoid self-justification at all costs. Real corporal punishments apply to the sensual plane. The refined punishments of the spiritual mode are usually much more indecent and dangerous than a good smack. The pained but resigned disapprobation of a mother is usually a very bad thing, much worse than the father's shouts of rage. And sendings to bed, and no dessert for a week, and so on, are crueller and meaner than a bang on the head. When a parent gives his boy a beating, there is a living passionate interchange. But in these refined punishments, the parent suffers nothing and the child is deadened. The bullying of the refined, benevolent spiritual will is simply vitriol to the soul. Yet parents administer it with all the righteousness of virtue and good intention, sparing themselves perfectly.

The point is here. If a child makes you so that you really want to spank it soundly, then soundly spank the brat. But know all the time *what* you are doing, and always be responsible for your anger. Never be ashamed of it, and never surpass it. The flashing interchange of anger between parent and child is part of the responsible relationship necessary to growth. Again, if a child offends you deeply, so that you really can't communicate with it any more, then, while the hurt is deep, switch off your connection from the child, cut off your correspondence, your vital communion, and be alone. But never persist in such a state beyond the time when your deep hurt dies down. The only rule is, do what you *really*, impulsively, wish to do. But always act on your own responsibility sincerely. And have the courage of your own strong emotion. They enrich the child's soul.

For a child's primary education depends almost entirely on its relation to its parents, brothers, and sisters. Between mother and child, father and child, the law is this: I, the mother, am myself alone: the child is itself alone. But there exists between us a vital dynamic relation, for which I, being the conscious one, am basically responsible. So, as far as possible, there must be in me no departure from myself, lest I injure the preconscious dynamic relation. I must absolutely act according to my own true spon-

taneous feeling. But, moreover, I must also have wisdom for myself and for my child. Always, always the deep wisdom of responsibility. And always a brave responsibility for the soul's own
spontaneity. Love—what is love? We'd better get a new idea.
Love is, in all, generous impulse—even a good spanking. But wisdom is something else, a deep collectedness in the soul, a deep
abiding by my own integral being, which makes me responsible,
not for the child, but for my certain duties towards the child, and
for maintaining the dynamic flow between the child and myself
as genuine as possible: that is to say, not perverted by ideals or by
my *will*.

Most fatal, most hateful of all things is bullying. But what is
bullying? It is a desire to superimpose my own will upon another
person. Sensual bullying of course is fairly easily detected. What
is more dangerous is ideal bullying. Bullying people into what is
ideally good for them. I embrace for example an ideal, and I seek
to enact this ideal in the person of another. This is ideal bullying.
A mother says that life should be all love, all delicacy and forbearance and gentleness. And she proceeds to spin a hateful sticky
web of permanent forbearance, a gentleness, hushedness around
her naturally passionate and hasty child. This so foils the child as
to make him half imbecile or criminal. I may have ideals if I like
—even of love and forbearance and meekness. But I have no right
to ask another to have these ideals. And to impose *any ideals* upon
a child as it grows is almost criminal. It results in impoverishment
and distortion and subsequent deficiency. In our day, most dangerous is the love and benevolence ideal. It results in neurasthenia,
which is largely a dislocation or collapse of the great voluntary
centres, a derangement of the will. It is in us an insistence upon
the one life-mode only, the spiritual mode. It is a suppression of
the great lower centres, and a living a sort of half-life, almost entirely from the upper centres. Thence, since we live terribly and
exhaustively from the upper centres, there is a tendency now
towards pthisis and neurasthenia of the heart. The great sympathetic centre of the breast becomes exhausted, the lungs, burnt
by the over-insistence of one way of life, become diseased, the
heart, strained in one mode of dilation, retaliates. The powerful

lower centres are no longer fully active, particularly the great lumbar ganglion, which is the clue to our sensual passionate pride and independence, this ganglion is atrophied by suppression. And it is this ganglion which holds the spine erect. So, weak-chested, round-shouldered, we stoop hollowly forward on ourselves. It is the result of the all-famous love and charity ideal, an ideal now quite dead in its sympathetic activity, but still fixed and determined in its voluntary action.

Let us beware and beware, and beware of having a high ideal for ourselves. But particularly let us beware of having an ideal for our children. So doing, we damn them. All we can have is wisdom. And wisdom is not a theory, it is a state of soul. It is the state wherein we know our wholeness and the complicate, manifold nature of our being. It is the state wherein we know the great relations which exist between us and our near ones. And it is the state which accepts full responsibility, first for our own souls, and then for the living dynamic relations wherein we have our being. It is no use expecting the other person to know. Each must know for himself. But nowadays men have even a stunt of pretending that children and idiots alone know best. This is a pretty piece of sophistry, and criminal cowardice, trying to dodge the life-responsibility which no man or woman can dodge without disaster.

The only thing is to be direct. If a child has to swallow castor oil, then say: "Child, you've got to swallow this castor oil. It is necessary for your inside. I say so because it is true. So open your mouth." Why try coaxing and logic and tricks with children? Children are more sagacious than we are. They twig soon enough if there is a flaw in our own intention and our own true spontaneity. And they play up to our bit of falsity till there is hell to pay.

"You love mother, don't you, dear?" Just a piece of indecent trickery of the spiritual will. The great emotions like love are unspoken. Speaking them is a sign of an indecent bullying will.

"Poor pussy! You must love poor pussy!"

What cant! What sickening cant! An appeal to love based on false pity. That's the way to inculcate a filthy pharisaic conceit into a child. If the child ill-treats the cat, say:

"Stop mauling that cat. It's got its own life to live, so let it live it." Then, if the brat persists, give tit for tat.

"What, you pull the cat's tail! Then I'll pull your nose, to see how you like it." And give his nose a proper hard pinch.

Children *must* pull the cat's tail a little. Children *must* steal the sugar sometimes. They *must* occasionally spoil just the things one doesn't want them to spoil. And they *must* occasionally tell stories—tell a lie. Circumstances and life are such that we must all sometimes tell a lie: just as we wear trousers because we don't choose that everybody shall see our nakedness. Morality is a delicate act of adjustment on the soul's part, not a rule or a prescription. Beyond a certain point the child *shall* not pull the cat's tail, *or* steal the sugar, *or* spoil the furniture, *or* tell lies. But I'm afraid you can't fix this certain soul's humour. And so it must. If at a sudden point you fly into a temper and thoroughly beat the boy for hardly touching the cat—well, that's life. All you've got to say to him is: "There, that'll serve you for all the times you *have* pulled her tail and hurt her." And he will feel outraged, and so will you. But what does it matter? Children have an infinite understanding of the soul's passionate variabilities, and forgive even a real injustice, if it was *spontaneous* and not intentional. They know we aren't perfect. What they don't forgive us is if we pretend we are: or if we *bully*.

V

The Five Senses

Science is wretched in its treatment of the human body as a sort of complex mechanism made up of numerous little machines working automatically in a rather unsatisfactory relation to one another. The body is the total machine; the various organs are the included machines; and the whole thing, given a start at birth, or at conception, trundles on by itself. The only god in the machine, the human will or intelligence, is absolutely at the mercy of the machine.

Such is the orthodox view. Soul, when it is allowed an existence at all, sits somewhat vaguely within the machine, never defined. If anything goes wrong with the machine, why, the soul is forgotten instantly. We summon the arch-mechanic of our day, the medicine-man. And a marvellous earnest fraud he is, doing his best. He is really wonderful as a mechanic of the human system. But the life within us fails more and more, while we marvellously tinker at the engines. Doctors are not to blame.

It is obvious that, even considering the human body as a very delicate and complex machine, you cannot keep such a machine running for one day without most exact central control. Still more is it impossible to consider the automatic evolution of such a machine. When did any machine, even a single spinning-wheel, automatically evolve itself? There was a god in the machine before the machine existed.

So there we are with the human body. There must have been, and must be a central god in the machine of each animate corpus.

The little soul of the beetle makes the beetle toddle. The little soul of the Homo sapiens sets him on his two feet. Don't ask me to define the soul. You might as well ask a bicycle to define the young damsel who so whimsically and so god-like pedals her way along the highroad. A young lady skeltering off on her bicycle to meet her young man—why, what could the bicycle make of such a mystery, if you explained it till doomsday? Yet the bicycle wouldn't be spinning from Streatham to Croydon by itself.

So we may as well settle down to the little god in the machine. We may as well call it the individual soul, and leave it there. It's as far as the bicycle would ever get, if it had to define Mademoiselle. But be sure the bicycle would not deny the existence of the young Miss who seats herself in the saddle. Not like us, who try to pretend there is no one in the saddle. Why even the sun would no more spin without a rider than would a cycle-pedal. But, since we have innumerable planets to reckon with, in the spinning we must not begin to define the rider in terms of our own exclusive planet. Nevertheless, rider there is: even a rider of the many-wheeled universe.

But let us leave the universe alone. It is too big a bauble for me. *Revenons.* At the start of me there is me. There is a mysterious little entity which is my individual self, the god who builds the machine and then makes his gay excursion of seventy years within it. Now we are talking at the moment about the machine. For the moment we are the bicycle, and not the feather-brained cyclist. So that all we can do is to define the cyclist in terms of ourself. A bicycle could say: Here, upon my leather saddle, rests a strange and animated force, which I call the force of gravity, as being the one great force which controls my universe. And yet, on second thoughts, I must modify myself. This great force of gravity is not *always* in the saddle. Sometimes it just is not there— and I lean strangely against a wall. I have been even known to turn upside down, with my wheels in the air; spun by the same mysterious Miss. So that I must introduce a theory of Relativity. However, mostly, when I am awake and alive, she is in the saddle; or *it* is in the saddle, the mysterious force. And when it is in the saddle, then two subsidiary forces plunge and claw upon my two pedals, plunge and claw with inestimable power. And at the same time, a kind and mysterious force sways my head-stock, sways most incalculably, and governs my whole motion. This force is not a driving force, but a subtle directing force, beneath whose grip my bright steel body is flexible as a dipping highroad. Then let me not forget the sudden clutch of arrest upon my hurrying wheels. Oh, this is pain to me! While I am rushing forward, surpassing myself in an *élan vital*, suddenly the awful check grips my back wheel, or my front wheel, or both. Suddenly there is a fearful arrest. My soul rushes on before my body, I feel myself strained, torn back. My fibres groan. Then perhaps the tension relaxes.

So the bicycle will continue to babble about itself. And it will inevitably wind up with a philosophy. "Oh, if only the great and divine force rested forever upon my saddle, and if only the mysterious will which sways my steering gear remained in place forever: then my pedals would revolve of themselves, and never cease, and no hideous brake should tear the perpetuity of my motions. Then, oh, then I should be immortal. I should leap through the world forever, and spin to infinity, till I was identified with the dizzy and timeless cycle-race of the stars and the great sun. . . ."

Poor old bicycle. The very thought is enough to start a philanthropic society for the prevention of cruelty to bicycles.

Well, then, our human body is the bicycle. And our individual and incomprehensible self is the rider thereof. And seeing that the universe is another bicycle riding full tilt, we are bound to suppose a rider for that also. But we needn't say what sort of rider. When I see a cockroach scuttling across the floor and turning up its tail I stand affronted, and think: A rum sort of rider *you* must have. You've no business to have such a rider, do you hear? And when I hear the monotonous and plaintive cuckoo in the June woods, I think: Who the devil made *that* clock? And when I see a politician making a fiery speech on a platform, and the crowd gawping, I think: Lord, save me—they've all got riders. But Holy Moses! you could never guess what was coming. And so I shouldn't like, myself, to start guessing about the rider of the universe. I am all too flummoxed by the masquerade in the tourney round about me.

We ourselves then: wisdom, like charity, begins at home. We've each of us got a rider in the saddle: an individual soul. Mostly it can't ride, and can't steer, so mankind is like squadrons of bicycles running amok. We should every one fall off if we didn't ride so thick that we hold each other up. Horrid nightmare!

As for myself, I have a horror of riding *en bloc*. So I grind away uphill, and sweat my guts out, as they say.

Well, well—my body is my bicycle: the whole middle of me is the saddle where sits the rider of my soul. And my front wheel is the cardiac plane, and my back wheel is the solar plexus. And the brakes are the voluntary ganglia. And the steering gear is my head. And the right and left pedals are the right and left dynamics of the body, in some way corresponding to the sympathetic and voluntary division.

So that now I know more or less how my rider rides me, and from what centres controls me. That is, I know the points of vital contact between my rider and my machine: between my invisible and my visible self. I don't attempt to say what is my rider. A bicycle might as well try to define its young Miss by wriggling its handle-bars and ringing its bell.

However, having more or less determined the four primary motions, we can see the further unfolding. In a child, the solar plexus and the cardiac plexus, with corresponding voluntary ganglia, are awake and active. From these centres develop the great functions of the body.

As we have seen, it is the solar plexus, with the lumbar ganglion, which controls the great dynamic system, the functioning of the liver and the kidneys. Any excess in the sympathetic dynamism tends to accelerate the action of the liver, to cause fever and constipation. Any collapse of the sympathetic dynamism causes anaemia. The sudden stimulating of the voluntary center may cause diarrhoea, and so on. But all this depends so completely on the polarized flow between the individual and the correspondent, between the child and mother, child and father, child and sisters or brothers or teacher, or circumambient universe, that it is impossible to lay down laws, unless we state particulars. Nevertheless, the whole of the great organs of the lower body are controlled from the two lower centres, and these organs work well or ill according as there is a true dynamic *psychic* activity at the two primary centres of consciousness. By a *true* dynamic psychic activity we mean an activity which is true to the individual himself, to his own peculiar soul-nature. And a dynamic psychic activity means a dynamic polarity between the individual himself and other individuals concerned in his living; or between him and his immediate surroundings, human, physical, geographical.

On the upper plane, the lungs and heart are controlled from the cardiac plane and the thoracic ganglion. Any excess in the sympathetic mode from the upper centres tends to burn the lungs with oxygen, weaken them with stress, and cause consumption. So it is just criminal to make a child too loving. No child should be induced to love too much. It means derangement and death at last.

But beyond the primary physiological function—and it is the business of doctors to discover the relation between the functioning of the primary organs and the dynamic psychic activity at the four primary consciousness-centres—beyond these physical functions, there are the activities which are half-psychic, half-functional. Such as the five senses.

Of the five senses, four have their functioning in the face-region. The fifth, the sense of touch, is distributed all over the body. But all have their roots in the four great primary centres of consciousness. From the constellation of your nerve-nodes, from the great field of your poles, the nerves run out in every direction, ending on the surface of the body. Inwardly this is an inextricable ramification and communication.

And yet the body is planned out in areas, there is a definite area-control from the four centres. On the back the sense of touch is not acute. There the voluntary centres act in resistance. But in the front of the body, the breast is one great field of sympathetic touch, the belly is another. On these two fields the stimu-

lus of touch is quite different, has a quite different psychic quality and psychic result. The breast-touch is the fine alertness of
quivering curiosity, the belly-touch is a deep thrill of delight and
avidity. Correspondingly, the hands and arms are instruments of
superb delicate curiosity, and deliberate execution. Through the
elbows and the wrists flows the dynamic psychic current, and a
dislocation in the current between two individuals will cause a
feeling of dislocation at the wrists and elbows. On the lower
plane, the legs and feet are instruments of unfathomable gratifi-
cations and repudiations. The thighs, the knees, the feet are intensely alive with love-desire, darkly and superbly drinking in
the love-contact, blindly. Or they are the great centres of resistance, kicking, repudiating. Sudden flushing of great general sympathetic desire will make a man feel weak at the knees. Hatred
will harden the tension of the knees like steel, and grip the feet
like talons. Thus the fields of touch are four, two sympathetic
fields in front of the body from the throat to the feet, two resistant fields behind from the neck to the heels.

There are two fields of touch, however, where the distribution
is not so simple: the face and the buttocks. Neither in the face
nor in the buttocks is there one single mode of sense communication.

The face is of course the great window of the self, the great
opening of the self upon the world, the great gateway. The
lower body has its own gates of exit. But the bulk of our communication with all the outer universe goes on through the face.

And every one of the windows or gates of the face has its direct communication with each of the four great centres of the
first field of consciousness. Take the mouth, with the sense of
taste. The mouth is primarily the gate of the two chief sensual
centres. It is the gateway to the belly and the loins. Through the
mouth we eat and we drink. In the mouth we have the sense of
taste. At the lips, too, we kiss. And the kiss of the mouth is the
first sensual connection.

In the mouth also are the teeth. And the teeth are the instruments of our sensual will. The growth of the teeth is controlled
entirely from the two great sensual centres below the diaphragm.

But almost entirely from the one centre, the voluntary centre. The growth and the life of the teeth depend almost entirely on the lumbar ganglion. During the growth of the teeth the sympathetic mode is held in abeyance. There is a sort of arrest. There is pain, there is diarrhoea, there is misery for the baby.

And we, in our age, have no rest with our teeth. Our mouths are too small. For many ages we have been suppressing the avid, negroid, sensual will. We have been converting ourselves into ideal creatures, all spiritually conscious, and active dynamically only on one plane, the upper, spiritual plane. Our mouth has contracted, our teeth have become soft and unquickened. Where in us are the sharp and vivid teeth of the wolf, keen to defend and devour? If we had them more, we should be happier. Where are the white negroid teeth? Where? In our little pinched mouths they have no room. We are sympathy-rotten, and spirit-rotten, and idea-rotten. We have forfeited our flashing sensual power. And we have false teeth in our mouths. In the same way the lips of our sensual desire go thinner and more meaningless, in the compression of our upper will and our idea-driven impulse. Let us break the conscious, self-conscious love-ideal, and we shall grow strong, resistant teeth once more, and the teething of our young will not be the hell it is.

Teething is strictly the period when the voluntary centre of the lower plane first comes into full activity, and takes for a time the precedence.

So, the mouth is the great sensual gate to the lower body. But let us not forget it is also a gate by which we breathe, the gate through which we speak and go impalpably forth to our object, the gate at which we can kiss the pinched, delicate, spiritual kiss. Therefore, although the main sensual gate of entrance to the lower body, it has its reference also to the upper body.

Taste, the sense of taste, is an intake of a pure communication between us and a body from the outside world. It contains the element of touch, and in this it refers to the cardiac plexus. But taste, *qua* taste, refers purely to the solar plexus.

And then smell. The nostrils are the great gate from the wide atmosphere of heaven to the lungs. The extreme sigh of yearning we catch through the mouth. But the delicate nose advances always into the air, our palpable communicator with the infinite air. Thus it has its first delicate root in the cardiac plexus, the root of its intake. And the root of the delicate-proud exhalation, rejection, is in the thoracic ganglion. But the nostrils have their other function of smell. Here the delicate nerve-ends run direct from the lower centres, from the solar plexus and the lumbar ganglion, or even deeper. There is the refined sensual intake when a scent is sweet. There is the sensual repudiation when a scent is unsavoury. And just as the fullness of the lips and the shape of the mouth depend on the development from the lower or the upper centres, the sensual or the spiritual, so does the shape of the nose depend on the direct control of the deepest centres of consciousness. A perfect nose is perhaps the result of a balance in the four modes. But what is a perfect nose! We only know that a short snub nose goes with an over-sympathetic nature, not proud enough; while a long nose derives from the centre of the upper will, the thoracic ganglion, our great centre of curiosity, and benevolent or objective control. A thick, squat nose is the sensual-sympathetic nose, and the high, arched nose the sensual voluntary nose, having the curve of repudiation, as when we turn up our nose from a bad smell, but also the proud curve of haughtiness and subjective authority. The nose is one of the greatest indicators of character. That is to say, it almost inevitably indicates the mode of predominant dynamic consciousness in the individual, the predominant primary centre from which he lives. When savages rub noses instead of kissing, they are exchanging a more sensitive and a deeper sensual salute than our lip-touch.

The eyes are the third great gateway of the psyche. Here the soul goes in and out of the body, as a bird flying forth and coming home. But the root of conscious vision is almost entirely in the breast. When I go forth from my own eyes, in delight to dwell upon the world which is beyond me, outside me, then I go forth from wide open windows, through which shows the full and living lambent darkness of my present inward self. I go forth, and I leave the lovely open darkness of my sensient self revealed; when I go forth in the wonder of vision to dwell upon the beloved, or upon the wonder of the world, I go from the centre of the glad breast, through the eyes, and who will may look into the full soft darkness of me, rich with my undiscovered presence. But if I am displeased, then hard and cold my self stands in my eyes, and refuses any communication, any sympathy, but merely stares outwards. It is the motion of cold objectivity from the thoracic ganglion. Or, from the same center of will, cold but intense my eyes may watch with curiosity, as a cat watches a fly. It may be into my curiosity will creep an element of warm gladness in the wonder which I am beholding outside myself. Or it may be that my curiosity will be purely and simply the cold, almost cruel curiosity of the upper will, directed from the ganglion of the shoulders: such as is the acute attention of an experimental scientist.

The eyes have, however, their sensual root as well. But this is hard to transfer into language, as all *our* vision, our modern Northern vision, is in the upper mode of actual seeing.

There is a sensual way of beholding. There is the dark, desirous look of a savage who apprehends only that which has direct reference to himself, that which stirs a certain dark yearning within his lower self. Then his eye is fathomless blackness. But there is the dark eye which glances with a certain fire, and has no depth. There is a keen quick vision which watches, which beholds, but which never yields to the object outside: as a cat watching its prey. The dark glancing look which knows the *strangeness*, the danger of its object, the need to overcome the object. The eye which is not wide open to study, to *learn*, but which powerfully, proudly, or cautiously glances, and knows the terror or the pure desirability of *strangeness* in the object it beholds. The savage is all in all in himself. That which he sees outside he hardly notices, or, he sees as something odd, something automatically desirable, something lustfully desirable, or something dangerous. What we call vision, that he has not.

We must compare the look in a horse's eye with the look in a cow's. The eye of the cow is soft, velvety, receptive. She stands and gazes with the strangest intent curiosity. She goes forth from herself in wonder. The root of her vision is in her yearning breast. The same one hears when she moos. The same massive weight of passion is in a bull's breast; the passion to go forth from himself. His strength is in his breast, his weapons are on his head. The wonder is always outside him.

But the horse's eye is bright and glancing. His curiosity is cautious, full of terror, or else aggressive and frightening for the object. The root of his vision is in his belly, in the solar plexus. And he fights with his teeth, and his heels, the sensual weapons.

Both these animals, however, are established in the sympathetic mode. The life-mode in both is sensitively sympathetic, or preponderantly sympathetic. Those animals which like cats, wolves, tigers, hawks, chiefly live from the great voluntary centres, these animals are, in our sense of the word, almost visionless. Sight in them is sharpened or narrowed down to a point: the object of prey. It is exclusive. They see no more than this. And thus they see unthinkably far, unthinkably keenly.

Most animals, however, smell what they see: vision is not very highly developed. They know better by the more direct contact of scent.

And vision in us becomes faulty because we proceed too much in one mode. We see too much, we attend too much. The dark, glancing sightlessness of the intent savage, the narrowed vision of the cat, the single point of vision of the hawk—these we do not know any more. We live far too much from the sympathetic centres, without the balance from the voluntary mode. And we live far, far too much from the *upper* sympathetic centre and voluntary centre, in an endless objective curiosity. Sight is the least sensual of all the senses. And we strain ourselves to see, see, see —everything, everything through the eye, in one mode of objective curiosity. There is nothing inside us, we stare endlessly at the outside. So our eyes begin to fail; to retaliate on us. We go short-sighted, almost in self-protection.

Hearing is the last, and perhaps the deepest of the senses. And here there is no choice. In every other faculty we have the power of rejection. We have a choice of vision. We can, if we choose, see in the terms of the wonderful beyond, the world of light into which we go forth in joy to lose ourselves in it. Or we can see, as the Egyptians saw, in the terms of their own dark souls: seeing the strangeness of the creature outside, the gulf between it and them, but finally its existence in terms of themselves. They saw according to their own unchangeable idea, subjectively, they did not go forth from themselves to seek the wonder outside.

Those are the two chief ways of sympathetic vision. We call our way the objective, the Egyptian the subjective. But objective and subjective are words that depend absolutely on your starting point. Spiritual and sensual are much more descriptive terms.

But there are, of course, also the two ways of volitional vision. We can see with the endless modern critical sight, analytic, and at last deliberately ugly. Or we can see as the hawk sees the one concentrated spot where beats the life-heart of our prey.

In the four modes of sight we have some choice. We have some choice to refuse tastes or smells or touch. In hearing we have the minimum of choice. Sound acts direct upon the great affective centres. We may voluntarily quicken our hearing, or make it dull. But we have really no choice of what we hear. Our will is eliminated. Sound acts direct, almost automatically, upon the affective centres. And we have no power of going forth from the ear. We are always and only recipient.

Nevertheless, sound acts upon us in various ways, according to the four primary poles of consciousness. The singing of birds acts almost entirely upon the centres of the breast. Birds, which live by flight, impelled from the strong conscious-activity of the breast and shoulders, have become for us symbols of the spirit, the upper mode of consciousness. Their legs have become idle, almost insentient twigs. Only the tail flirts from the centre of the sensual will.

But their singing acts direct upon the upper, or spiritual, centres in us. So does almost all our music, which is all Christian in tendency. But modern music is analytical, critical, and it has discovered the power of ugliness. Like our martial music, it is of the upper plane, like our martial songs, our fifes and our brass-bands. These act direct upon the thoracic ganglion. Time was, however, when music acted upon the sensual centres direct. We hear it still in savage music, and in the roll of drums, and in the roaring of lions, and in the howling of cats. And in some voices still we hear the deeper resonance of the sensual mode of consciousness. But the tendency is for everything to be brought on to the upper plane, whilst the lower plane is just worked automatically from the upper.

❦ VI ❦

First Glimmerings of Mind

We can now see what is the true goal of education for a child. It is the full and harmonious development of the four primary modes of consciousness, always with regard to the individual nature of the child.

The goal is *not* ideal. The aim is *not* mental consciousness. We want *effectual* human beings, not conscious ones. The final aim is not *to know*, but *to be*. There never was a more risky motto than that: *Know thyself.* You've got to know yourself as far as possible. But not just for the sake of knowing. You've got to know yourself so that you can at last *be* yourself. "Be yourself" is the last motto.

The whole field of dynamic and effectual consciousness is *always* pre-mental, non-mental. Not even the most knowing man that ever lived would know how he would be feeling next week; whether some new and utterly shattering impulse would have arisen in him and laid his nicely conceived self in ruins. It is the impulse we have to live by, not the ideals or the idea. But we have to know ourselves pretty thoroughly before we can break the automatism of ideals and conventions. The savage in a state of nature is one of the most conventional of creatures. So is a child. Only through fine delicate knowledge can we recognize and release our impulses. Now our whole aim has been to force each individual to a maximum of mental control, and mental consciousness. Our poor little plans of children are put into horrible forcing-beds, called schools, and the young idea is there forced to shoot. It shoots, poor thing, like a potato in a warm cellar. One mass of pallid sickly ideas and ideals. And no root, no life. The ideas shoot, hard enough, in our sad offspring, but they shoot at the expense of life itself. Never was such a mistake. Mental consciousness is a purely individual affair. Some men are born to be highly and delicately conscious. But for the vast majority, much mental consciousness is simply a catastrophe, a blight. It just stops their living.

Our business, at the present, is to prevent at all cost the young idea from shooting. The ideal mind, the brain, has become the vampire of modern life, sucking up the blood and the life. There is hardly an original thought or original utterance possible to us. All is sickly repetition of stale, stale ideas.

Let all schools be closed at once. Keep only a few technical training establishments, nothing more. Let humanity lie fallow, for two generations at least. Let no child learn to read, unless it learns by itself, out of its own individual persistent desire.

That is my serious admonition, gentle reader. But I am not so flighty as to imagine you will pay any heed. But if I thought you would, I should feel my hope surge up. And if you *don't* pay any heed, calamity will at length shut your schools for you, sure enough.

The process of transfer from the primary consciousness to recognized mental consciousness is a mystery like every other transfer. Yet it follows its own laws. And here we begin to approach the confines of orthodox psychology, upon which we have no desire to trespass. But this we *can* say. The degree of transfer from primary to mental consciousness varies with every individual. But in most individuals the natural degree is very low.

The process of transfer from primary consciousness is called sublimation, the sublimating of the potential body of knowledge with the definite reality of the idea. And with this process we have identified all education. The very derivation of the Latin word *education* shows us. Of course it should mean the leading forth of each nature to its fullness. But with us, fools that we are, it is the leading forth of the primary consciousness, the potential or dynamic consciousness, into mental consciousness, which is

finite and static. Now before we set out so gaily to lead our children *en bloc* out of the dynamic into the static way of consciousness, let us consider a moment what we are doing.

A child in the womb can have no *idea* of the mother. I think
orthodox psychology will allow us so much. And yet the child
in the womb must be dynamically conscious of the mother.
Otherwise how could it maintain a definite and progressively
developing relation to her?

This consciousness, however, is utterly non-ideal, non-mental,
purely dynamic, a matter of dynamic polarized intercourse of
vital vibrations, as an exchange of wireless messages which are
never translated from the pulse-rhythm into speech, because
they have no need to be. It is a dynamic polarized intercourse between the great primary nuclei in the foetus and the corresponding nuclei in the dynamic maternal psyche.

This form of consciousness is established at conception, and
continues long after birth. Nay, it continues all life long. But the
particular interchange of dynamic consciousness between mother
and child suffers no interruption at birth. It continues almost the
same. The child has no conception whatsoever of the mother. It
cannot see her, for its eye has no focus. It can hear her, because
hearing needs no transmission into concept, but it has no oral notion of sounds. It knows her, but only by a form of vital dynamic correspondence, a sort of magnetic interchange. The idea
does not intervene at all.

Gradually, however, the dark shadow of our object begins to
loom in the formless mind of the infant. The idea of the mother
is, as it were, gradually photographed on the cerebral plasm. It
begins with the faintest shadow—but the figure is gradually developed through years of experience. It is never quite completed.

How does the figure of the mother gradually develop as a *conception* in the child mind? It develops as the result of the positive
and negative reaction from the primary centres of consciousness.
From the first great centre of sympathy the child is drawn to a
lovely oneing with the mother. From the first great centre of
will comes the independent self-assertion which locates the
mother as something outside, something objective. And as a re-

sult of this twofold notion, a twofold increase in the child. First, the dynamic establishment of the individual consciousness in the infant: and then the first shadow of a mental conception of the mother, in the infant brain. The development of the *original* mind in every child and every man always and only follows from the dual fulfilment in the dynamic consciousness.

But mark further. Each time, after the fourfold interchange between two dynamic polarized lives, there results a development in the individuality and a sublimation into consciousness, both simultaneously in each party: *and this dual development causes at once a diminution in the dynamic polarity between the two parties.* That is, as its individuality and its mental concept of the mother develop in the child, there is a corresponding *waning* of the dynamic relation between the child and the mother. And this is the natural progression of all love. As we have said before, the accomplishment of individuality never finally exhausts the dynamic flow between parents and child. In the same way, a child can never have a finite conception of either of its parents. It can have a very much more finite, finished conception of its aunts or its friends. The portrait of the parent can never be quite completed in the mind of the son or daughter. As long as time lasts it must be left unfinished.

Nevertheless, the inevitable photography of time upon the mental plasm does print at last a very substantial portrait of the parent, a very well-filled concept in the child mind. And the nearer a conception comes towards finality, the nearer does the dynamic relation, out of which this concept has arisen, draw to a close. To know is to lose. When I have a finished mental concept of a beloved, or a friend, then the love and the friendship is dead. It falls to the level of an acquaintance. As soon as I have a finished mental conception, a full idea even of myself, then dynamically I am dead. To know is to die.

But knowledge and death are part of our natural development. Only, of course, most things can never be known by us in full. Which means we do never absolutely die, even to our parents. So that Jesus' question to His mother, "Woman, what have I to do with thee!" while expressing a major truth, still has an exaggerated sound, which comes from its denial of the minor truth.

This progression from dynamic relationship towards a finished individuality and a finished mental concept is carried on from the four great primary centres through the correspondence medium of all the senses and sensibilities. First of all, the child knows the mother only through touch—perfect and immediate contact. And yet, from the moment of conception, the egg-cell repudiated complete adhesion and even communication, and asserted its individual integrity. The child in the womb, perfect a contact though it may have with the mother, is all the time also dynamically polarized against this contact. From the first moment, this relation in touch has a dual polarity, and, no doubt, a dual mode. It is a fourfold interchange of consciousness, the moment the egg-cell has made its two spontaneous divisions.

As soon as the child is born, there is a real severance. The contact of touch is interrupted, it now becomes occasional only. True, the dynamic flow between mother and child is not severed when simple physical contact is missing. Though mother and child may not touch, still the dynamic flow continues between them. The mother knows her child, feels her bowels and her breast drawn to it, even if it be a hundred miles away. But if the severance continue long, the dynamic flow begins to die, both in mother and child. It wanes fairly quickly—and perhaps can never be fully revived. The dynamic relation between parent and child may fairly easily fall into quiescence, a static condition.

For a full dynamic relationship it is necessary that there be actual contact. The nerves run from the four primary dynamos, and end with live ends all over the body. And it is necessary to bring the live ends of the nerves of the child into contact with the live ends of corresponding nerves in the mother, so that a pure circuit is established. Wherever a pure circuit is established, there occurs a pure development in the individual creation, and this is inevitably accompanied by sensation; and sensation is the first term of mental knowledge.

So, from the field of the breast and arms, the upper circuit, and from the field of the knees and feet and belly, the lower circuit.

And then, the moment a child is born, the face is alive. And the face communicates direct with both planes of primary consciousness. The moment a child is born, it begins to grope for the breast. And suddenly a new great circuit is established, the four poles all working at once, as the child sucks. There is the profound desirousness of the lower centre of sympathy, and the superior avidity of the centre of will, and at the same time, the cleaving yearning to the nipple, and the tiny curiosity of lips and gums. The nipple of the mother's breast is one of the great gates of the body, hence of the living psyche. In the nipple terminate vivid nerves which flash their very powerful vibrations through the mouth of the child and deep into its four great poles of being and knowing. Even the nipples of the man are gateways to the great dynamic flow: still gateways.

Touch, taste, and smell are now active in the baby. And these senses, so-called, are strictly sensations. They are the first term of the child's mental knowledge. And on these three *cerebral* reactions the foundation of the future mind is laid.

The moment there is a perfect polarized circuit between the first four poles of dynamic consciousness, at that moment does the mind, the terminal station, flash into cognition. The first cognition is merely sensation: sensation and the remembrance of sensation being the first element in all knowing and in all conception.

The circuit of touch, taste, and smell must be well established before the eyes begin actually to see. All mental knowledge is built up of sensation and of memory. It is the continually recurring sensation of the touch of the mother which forms the basis of the first conception of the mother. After that, the gradually discriminated taste of the mother, and scent of the mother. Till gradually sight and hearing develop and largely usurp the first three senses, as medium of correspondence and of knowledge.

And while, of course, the sensational *knowledge* is being secreted in the brain, in some much more mysterious way the living individuality of the child is being developed in the four first

nuclei, the four great nerve-centres of the primary field of consciousness and being.

As time goes on, the child learns to see the mother. At first he
sees her face as a blur, and, though he knows her, knows her by a
direct glow of communication, as if her face were a warm glowing life-lamp which rejoiced him. But gradually, as the circuit
of touch, taste, and smell become powerfully established; gradually, as the individual develops in the child, and so retreats towards isolation; gradually, as the child stands more immune from
the mother, the circuit of correspondence extends, and the eyes
now communicate across space, the ears begin to discriminate
sounds. Last of all develops discriminate hearing.

Now gradually the picture of the mother is transferred to the
child's mind, and the sound of the first baby-words is imprinted.
And as the child learns to discriminate visually, objectively, between the mother and the nurse, he learns to choose, and becomes
individually free. And still, the dynamic correspondence is not
finished. It only changes its circuit.

While the brain is registering sensations, the four dynamic
centres are coming into perfect relation. Or rather, as we see,
the reverse is the case. As the dynamic centres come into perfect
relation, the mind registers and remembers sensations, and begins
consciously to know. But the great field of activity is still and
always the dynamic field. When a child learns to walk, it learns
almost entirely from the solar plexus and the lumbar ganglion,
the cardiac plexus and the thoracic ganglion balancing the upper
body.

There is a perfected circuit of polarity. The two lower centres
are the positive, the two upper the negative poles. And so the
child strikes out with his feet for the earth, presses, and strikes
away again from the earth, the two upper centres meanwhile
corresponding implicitly in the balance of the upper body. It is
a chain of spontaneous activity in the four primary centres, establishing a circuit through the whole body. But the positive poles
are the lower centres. And the brain has probably nothing at all
to do with it. Even the *desire* to walk is not born in the brain, but
in the primary nuclei.

The same with the use of the hands and arms. It means the establishment of a pure circuit between the four centres, the two upper poles now being the positive, the lower the negative poles, and the hands the live end of the wire. Again the brain is not concerned. Probably, even in the first deliberate grasping of an object, the brain is not concerned. Not until there is an element of recognition and sensation-memory.

All our primal activity originates and circulates purely in the four great nerve-centres. All our active desire, our genuine impulse, our love, our hope, our yearning, everything originates mysteriously at these four great centres or well-heads of our existence: everything vital and dynamic. The mind can only register that which results from the emanation of the dynamic impulse and the collision or communion of this impulse with its object.

So now we see that we can never know ourselves. Knowledge is to consciousness what the signpost is to the traveller: just an indication of the way which has been travelled before. Knowledge is not even in direct proportion to being. There may be great knowledge of chemistry in a man who is a rather poor *being:* and those who *know*, even in wisdom like Solomon, are often at the end of the matter of living, not at the beginning. As a matter of fact, David did the living, the dynamic achievement. To Solomon was left the consummation and the finish, and the dying down.

Yet we *must* know, if only in order to learn not to know. The supreme lesson of human consciousness is to learn how *not to know*. That is, how not to *interfere*. That is, how to live dynamically, from the great Source, and not statically, like machines driven by ideas and principles from the head, or automatically, from one fixed desire. At last, knowledge must be put into its true place in the living activity of man. And we must know deeply, in order even to do that.

So a new conception of the meaning of education.

Education means leading out the individual nature in each man and woman to its true fullness. You can't do that by stimulating the mind. To pump education into the mind is fatal. That which sublimates from the dynamic consciousness into the mental consciousness has alone any value. This, in most individuals, is very little indeed. So that most individuals, under a wise government, would be most carefully protected from all vicious attempts to inject extraneous ideas into them. Every extraneous idea, which has no inherent root in the dynamic consciousness, is as dangerous as a nail driven into a young tree. For the mass of people, knowledge *must* be symbolical, mythical, dynamic. This means you must have a higher, responsible, conscious class: and then in varying degrees the lower classes, varying in their degree of consciousness. Symbols must be true from top to bottom. But the interpretation of the symbols must rest, degree after degree, in the higher, responsible, conscious classes. To *those who cannot divest* themselves again of mental consciousness and definite ideas, mentality and ideas are death, nails through their hands and feet.

✆ VII ✆

First Steps in Education

The first process of education is obviously not a mental process. When a mother talks to a baby, she is not encouraging its little mind to think. When she is coaxing her child to walk, she is not making a theoretic exposition of the science of equilibration. She crouches before the child, at a little distance, and spreads her hands. "Come, baby—come to mother. Come! Baby, walk! Yes, walk! Walk to mother! Come along. A little walk to its mother. Come! Come then! Why yes, a pretty baby! Oh, he can toddle! Yes—yes— No, don't be frightened, a dear. No— Come to mother—" and she catches his little pinafore by the tip—and the infant lurches forward. "There! There! A beautiful walk! A beautiful walker, yes! Walked all the way to mother, baby did. Yes, he did—"

Now who will tell me that this talk has any rhyme or reason? Not a spark of reason. Yet a real rhyme: or rhythm, much more important. The song and the urge of the mother's voice plays direct on the affective centers of the child, a wonderful stimulus and tuition. The words hardly matter. True, this constant repetition in the end forms a mental association. At the moment they have no mental significance at all for the baby. But they ring with a strange palpitating music in his fluttering soul, and lift him into motion.

And this is the way to educate children: the instinctive way of mothers. There should be no effort made to teach children to think, to have ideas. Only to lift them and urge them into dynamic activity. The voice of dynamic sound, not the words of understanding. Damn understanding. Gestures, and touch, and expression of the face, not theory. Never have ideas about children—and never have ideas *for* them.

If we are going to teach children we must teach them first to move. And not by rule or mental dictation. Horror! But by playing and teasing and anger, and amusement. A child must learn to move blithe and free and proud. It must learn the fullness of spontaneous motion. And this it can only learn by continuous reaction from all the centres, through all the emotions. A child must learn to contain itself. It must learn to sit still if need be. Part of the first phase of education is the learning to stay still and be physically self-contained. Then a child must learn to be alone, and to adventure alone, and to play alone. Any peevish clinging should be quite roughly rebuffed. From the very first day, throw a child back on its own resources—even a little cruelly sometimes. But don't neglect it, don't have a negative attitude to it. Play with it, tease it and roll it over as a dog her puppy, mock it when it is too timorous, laugh at it, scold it when it really bothers you—for a child must learn not to bother another person—and when it makes you genuinely angry, spank it soundly. But always remember that it is a single little soul by itself; and that the responsibility for the wise, warm relationship is yours, the adult's.

Then always watch its deportment. Above all things encourage a straight backbone and proud shoulders. Above all things despise a slovenly movement, an ugly bearing and unpleasing manner. And make a mock of petulance and of too much timidity.

We are imbeciles to start bothering about love and so forth in a child. Forget utterly that there is such a thing as emotional reciprocity. But never forget your own honour as an adult individual towards a small individual. It is a question of honour, not of love.

A tree grows straight when it has deep roots and is not too stifled. Love is a spontaneous thing, coming out of the spontaneous effectual soul. As a deliberate principle it is an unmitigated evil. Also morality which is based on ideas, or on an ideal, is an unmitigated evil. A child which is proud and free in its movements, in all its deportment, will be quite as moral as need be. Honour is an instinct, a superb instinct which should be kept keenly alive. Immorality, vice, crime, these come from a suppression or a collapse at one or other of the great primary centres. If one of these centres fails to maintain its true polarity, then there is a physical or psychic derangement, or both. And viciousness or crime are the result of a derangement in the primary system. Pure morality is only an instinctive adjustment which the soul makes in every circumstance, adjusting one thing to another livingly, delicately, sensitively. There can be no law. Therefore, at every cost and charge keep the first four centres alive and alert, active, and vivid in reaction. And then you need fear no perversion. What we have done, in our era, is, first, we have tried as far as possible to suppress or subordinate the two sensual centres. We have so unduly insisted on and exaggerated the upper spiritual or selfless mode—the living in the other person and through the other person—that we have caused already a dangerous overbalance in the natural psyche.

To correct this we go one worse, and try to rule ourselves more and more by the old ideas of sympathy and benevolence. We think that love and benevolence will cure anything. Whereas love and benevolence are our poison, poison to the giver, and still more poison to the receiver. Poison only because there is practically *no* spontaneous love left in the world. It is all *will*, the fatal love-will and insatiable morbid curiosity. The pure sympathetic mode of love long ago broke down. There is now only deadly, exaggerated volition.

This is also why general education should be suppressed as soon as possible. We have fallen into a state of fixed, deadly will. Everything we do and say to our children in school tends simply to fix in them the same deadly will, under the pretence of pure love. Our idealism is the clue to our fixed will. Love, beauty, benevolence, progress, these are the words we use. But the principle we evoke is a principle of barren, sanctified compulsion of all life. We want to put all life under compulsion. "How to outwit the nerves," for example. And therefore, to save the children as far as possible, elementary education should be stopped at once.

No child should be sent to any sort of public institution before the age of ten years. If I could but advise, I would advise that this notice should be sent through the length and breadth of the land.

Parents, the State can no longer be responsible for the mind and character of your children. From the first day of the coming year, all schools will be closed for an indefinite period. Fathers, see that your boys are trained to be men. Mothers, see that your daughters are trained to be women.

All schools will shortly be converted either into public workshops or into gymnasia. No child will be admitted into the workshops under ten years of age. Active training in primitive modes of fighting and gymnastics will be compulsory for all boys over ten years of age.

All girls over ten years of age must attend at one domestic workshop. All girls over ten years of age may, in addition, attend at one workshop of skilled labour, or of technical industry, or of art. Admission for three months' probation.

All boys over ten years of age must attend at one workshop of domestic crafts, and at one workshop of skilled labour, or of technical industry, or of art. A boy may choose, with his parents' consent, his school of labour, or technical industry or art, but the directors reserve the right to transfer him to a more suitable department, if necessary, after a three months' probation.

It is the intention of this State to form a body of active, energetic citizens. The danger of a helpless, presumptuous, newspaper-reading population is universally recognized.

All elementary education is left in the hands of the
parents, save such as is necessary to the different
branches of industry.

Schools of mental culture are free to all individuals
over fourteen years of age.

Universities are free to all who obtain the first
culture degree.

The fact is, our process of universal education is today so uncouth, so psychologically barbaric, that it is the most terrible
menace to the existence of our race. We seize hold of our children, and by parrot-compulsion we force into them a set of
mental tricks. By unnatural and unhealthy compulsion we force
them into a certain amount of cerebral activity. And then, after
a few years, with a certain number of windmills in their
heads, we turn them loose, like so many inferior Don Quixotes,
to make a mess of life. All that they have learnt in their heads
has no reference at all to their dynamic souls. The windmills spin
and spin in a wind of words, Dulcinea del Toboso beckons round
every corner, and our nation of inferior Quixotes jumps on and
off tramcars, trains, bicycles, motor-cars, buses, in one mad chase
of the divine Dulcinea, who is all the time chewing chocolates
and feeling very, very bored. It is no use telling the poor devils
to stop. They read in the newspapers about more Dulcineas and
more chivalry due to them and more horrid persons who injure
the fair fame of these bored females. And round they skelter,
after their own tails. That is, when they are not forced to grind
out their lives for a wage. Though work is the only thing that
prevents our masses from going quite mad.

To tell the truth, ideas are the most dangerous germs mankind
has ever been injected with. They are introduced into the brain
by injection, in schools and by means of newspapers, and then
we are done for.

An idea which is merely introduced into the brain, and started
spinning there like some outrageous insect, is the cause of all our
misery today. Instead of living from the spontaneous centres, we

live from the head. We chew, chew, chew at some theory, some idea. We grind, grind, grind in our mental consciousness, till we are beside ourselves. Our primary affective centres, our centres of spontaneous being, are so utterly ground round and automatized that they squeak in all stages of disharmony and incipient collapse. We are a people—and not we alone—of idiots, imbeciles, and epileptics, and we don't even know we are raving.

And all is due, directly and solely, to that hateful germ we call the Ideal. The Ideal is *always* evil, no matter what ideal it be. No idea should ever be raised to a governing throne.

This does not mean that man should immediately cut off his head and try to develop a pair of eyes in his breasts. But it does mean this: that an idea is just the final concrete or registered result of living dynamic interchange and reactions: that no idea is ever perfectly expressed until its dynamic cause is finished; and that to continue to put into dynamic effect an already perfected idea means the nullification of all living activity, the substitution of mechanism, and all the resultant horrors of *ennui*, ecstasy, neurasthenia, and a collapsing psyche.

The whole tree of our idea of life and living is dead. Then let us leave off hanging ourselves and our children from its branches like medlars.

The idea, the actual idea, must rise ever fresh, ever displaced, like the leaves of a tree, from out of the quickness of the sap, and according to the forever incalculable effluence of the great dynamic centres of life. The tree of life is a gay kind of tree that is forever dropping its leaves and budding out afresh quite different ones. If the last lot were thistle leaves, the next lot may be vine. You never can tell with the tree of life.

So we come back to that precious child who costs us such a lot of ink. By what right, I ask you, are we going to inject into him our own disease-germs of ideas and infallible motives? By the right of the diseased, who want to infect everybody.

There are *few, few people* in whom the living impulse and reaction develops and sublimates into mental consciousness. There are all kinds of trees in the forest. But few of them indeed bear the apples of knowledge. The modern world insists, however, that every individual shall bear the apples of knowledge. So we go through the forest of mankind, cut back every tree, and try to graft it into an apple-tree. A nice wood of monsters we make by so doing.

It is not the *nature* of most men to know and to understand and to reason very far. Therefore, why should they make a pretence of it? It is the nature of some few men to reason, then let them reason. Those whose nature it is to be rational will instinctively ask why and wherefore, and wrestle with themselves for an answer. But why every Tom, Dick, and Harry should have the why and wherefore of the universe rammed into him, and should be allowed to draw the conclusion hence that he is the ideal person and responsible for the universe, I don't know. It is a lie anyway—for neither the whys nor the wherefores are his own, and he is but a parrot with his nut of a universe.

Why should we cram the mind of a child with facts that have nothing to do with his own experiences, and have no relation to his own dynamic activity? Let us realize that every extraneous idea effectually introduced into a man's mind is a direct obstruction of his dynamic activity. Every idea which is introduced from outside into a man's mind, and which does not correspond to his own dynamic nature, is a fatal stumbling-block for that man: is a cause of arrest for his true individual activity, and a derangement to his psychic being.

For instance, if I teach a man the idea that all men are equal. Now this idea has no foundation in experience, but is logically deduced from certain ethical or philosophic principles. But there is a disease of idealism in the world, and we all are born with it. Particularly teachers are born with it. So they seize on the idea of equality, and proceed to instil it. With what result? Your man is no longer a man, living his own life from his own spontaneous centres. He is a theoretic imbecile trying to frustrate and dislocate all life.

It is the death of all life to force a pure *idea* into practice. Life must be lived from the deep, self-responsible spontaneous centres of every individual, in a vital, *non-ideal* circuit of dynamic relation between individuals. The passions or desires which are thought-born are deadly. Any particular mode of passion or desire which receives an exclusive ideal sanction at once becomes poisonous.

If this is true for men, it is much more true for women. Teach a woman to act from an idea, and you destroy her womanhood forever. Make a woman self-conscious, and her soul is barren as a sandbag. Why were we driven out of Paradise? Why did we fall into this gnawing disease of unappeasable dissatisfaction? Not because we sinned. Ah, no. All the animals in Paradise enjoyed the sensual passion of coition. Not because we sinned. But because we got our sex into our head.

When Eve ate that particular apple, she became aware of her own womanhood, mentally. And mentally she began to experiment with it. She has been experimenting ever since. So has man. To the rage and horror of both of them.

These sexual experiments are really anathema. But once a woman is sexually self-conscious, what is she to do? There it is, she is born with the disease of her own self-consciousness, as was her mother before her. She is bound to experiment and try one idea after another, in the long run always to her own misery. She is bound to have fixed one, and then another idea of herself, herself as woman. First she is the noble spouse of a not-quite-so-noble male: then a *Mater Dolorosa:* then a ministering Angel: then a competent social unit, a Member of Parliament or a Lady Doctor or a platform speaker: and all the while, as a sideshow, she is the Isolde of some Tristan, or the Guinevere of some Lancelot, or the Fata Morgana of all men—in her own idea. She can't stop having an idea of herself. She can't get herself out of her own head. And there she is, functioning away from her own head and her own consciousness of herself and her own automatic self-will, till the whole man-and-woman game has become just a hell, and men with any backbone would rather kill themselves than go on with it—or kill somebody else.

Yet we are going to inculcate more and more self-conscious-

ness, teach every little Mary to be more and more a nice little
Mary out of her own head, and every little Joseph to theorize
himself up to the scratch.

And the point lies here. There will *have* to come an end.
Every race which has become self-conscious and idea-bound in
the past has perished. And then it has all started afresh, in a different way, with another race. And man has never learnt any better. We are really far, far more life-stupid than the dead Greeks
or the lost Etruscans. Our day is pretty short, and closing fast.
We can pass, and another race can follow later.

But there is another alternative. We still have in us the power
to discriminate between our own idealism, our own self-conscious will, and that other reality, our own true spontaneous self.
Certainly we are so overloaded and diseased with ideas that we
can't get well in a minute. But we can set our faces stubbornly
against the disease, once we recognize it. The disease of love, the
disease of "spirit," the disease of niceness and benevolence and
feeling good on our own behalf and good on somebody else's
behalf. Pah, it is all a gangrene. We can retreat upon the proud,
isolate self, and remain there alone, like lepers, till we are cured
of this ghastly white disease of self-conscious idealism.

And we really can make a move on our children's behalf. We
really can refrain from thrusting our children any more into
those hot-beds of the self-conscious disease, schools. We really
can prevent their eating much more of the tissues of leprosy,
newspapers and books. For a time, there should be no compulsory teaching to read and write at all. *The great mass of humanity should never learn to read and write—never.*

And instead of this gnawing, gnawing disease of mental
consciousness and awful, unhealthy craving for stimulus and for
action, we must substitute genuine action. The war was really
not a bad beginning. But we went out under the banners of
idealism, and now the men are home again, the virus is more
active than ever, rotting their very souls.

The mass of the people will never *mentally understand.* But
they will soon instinctively fall into line.

Let us substitute action, all kinds of action, for the mass of people, in place of mental activity. Even twelve hours' work a day is better than a newspaper at four in the afternoon and a grievance for the rest of the evening. But particularly let us take care of the children. At all cost, try to prevent a girl's mind from dwelling on herself. Make her act, work, play: assume a rule over her girlhood. Let her learn the domestic arts in their perfection. Let us even artificially set her to spin and weave. Anything to keep her busy, to prevent her reading and becoming self-conscious. Let us awake as soon as possible to the repulsive machine quality of machine-made things. They smell of death. And let us insist that the home is sacred, the hearth, and the very things of the home. Then keep the girls apart from any familiarity or being "pals" with the boys. The nice clean intimacy which we now so admire between the sexes is sterilizing. It makes neuters. Later on, no deep, magical sex-life is possible.

The same with the boys. First and foremost establish a rule over them, a proud, harsh, manly rule. Make them *know* that at every moment they are in the shadow of a proud, strong, adult authority. Let them be soldiers, but as individuals, not machine units. There are wars in the future, great wars, which not machines will finally decide, but the free, indomitable life spirit. No more wars under the banners of the ideal, and in the spirit of sacrifice. But wars in the strength of individual men. And then, pure individualistic training to fight, and preparation for a whole new way of life, a new society. Put money into its place, and science and industry. The leaders must stand for life, and they must not ask the simple followers to point out the direction. When the leaders assume responsibility they relieve the followers forever of the burden of finding a way. Relieved of this hateful incubus of responsibility for general affairs, the populace can again become free and happy and spontaneous, leaving matters to their superiors. No newspapers—the mass of the people never learning to read. The evolving once more of the great spontaneous gestures of life.

We can't go on as we are. Poor, nerve-worn creatures, fretting our lives away and hating to die because we have never lived. The secret is to commit into the hands of the sacred few the responsibility which now lies like torture on the mass. Let the few, the leaders, be increasingly responsible for the whole. And let the mass be free: free, save for the choice of leaders.

Leaders—this is what mankind is craving for.

But men must be prepared to obey, body and soul, once they have chosen the leader. And let them choose the leader for life's sake only.

Begin then—there is a beginning.

✑ VIII ✑

Education and Sex in Man, Woman, and Child

The one thing we have to avoid, then, even while we carry on our own old process of education, is this development of the powers of so-called self-expression in a child. Let us beware of artificially stimulating his self-consciousness and his so-called imagination. All that we do is to pervert the child into a ghastly state of self-consciousness, making him affectedly try to show off as we wish him to show off. The moment the least little trace of self-consciousness enters in a child, good-bye to everything except falsity.

Much better just pound away at the A B C and simple arithmetic and so on. The modern methods do make children sharp, give them a sort of slick finesse, but it is the beginning of the mischief. It ends in the great "unrest" of a nervous, hysterical proletariat. Begin to teach a child of five to "understand." To understand the sun and moon and daisy and the secrets of procreation, bless your soul. Understanding all the way. And when the child is twenty he'll have a hysterical understanding of his own invented grievance, and there's an end of him. Understanding is the devil.

A child mustn't understand things. He must have them his own way. His vision isn't ours. When a boy of eight sees a horse, he doesn't see the correct biological object we intend him to see. He sees a big living presence of no particular shape with hair dangling from its neck and four legs. If he puts two eyes in the profile, he is quite right. Because he does *not* see with optical, photographic vision. The image on his retina is *not* the image of his consciousness. The image on his retina just does not go into him. His unconsciousness is filled with a strong, dark, vague prescience of a powerful presence, a two-eyed, four-legged, long-maned presence looming imminent.

And to *force* the boy to see a correct one-eyed horse-profile is just like pasting a placard in front of his vision. It simply kills his inward seeing. We don't *want* him to see a proper horse. The child is *not* a little camera. He is a small vital organism which has direct dynamic *rapport* with the objects of the outer universe. He perceives from his breast and his abdomen, with deep-sunken realism, the elemental nature of the creature. So that to this day a Noah's Ark tree is more real than a Corot tree or a Constable tree: and a flat Noah's Ark cow has a deeper vital reality than even a Cuyp cow.

The mode of vision is not one and final. The mode of vision is manifold. And the optical image is a mere vibrating blur to a child—and, indeed, to a passionate adult. In this vibrating blur the soul sees its own true correspondent. It sees, in a cow, horns and squareness, and a long tail. It sees, for a horse, a mane, and a long face, round nose, and four legs. And in each case a darkly vital presence. Now horns and squareness and a long thin ox-tail, these are the fearful and wonderful elements of the cow-form, which the dynamic soul perfectly perceives. The ideal-image is just outside nature, for a child—something false. In a picture, a child wants elemental recognition, and not correctness or expression, or least of all what we call understanding. The child distorts inevitably and dynamically. But the dynamic abstraction is more than mental. If a huge eye sits in the middle of the cheek, in a child's drawing, this shows that the deep dynamic consciousness of the eye, its relative exaggeration, is the life-truth, even if it is a scientific falsehood.

On the other hand, what on earth is the good of saying to a child, "The world is a flattened sphere, like an orange." It is simply pernicious. You had much better say the world is a poached egg in a frying pan. *That* might have some dynamic meaning. The only thing about the flattened orange is that the child just sees this orange disporting itself in blue air, and never bothers to associate it with the earth he treads on. And yet it would be so much better for the mass of mankind if they never heard of the flattened sphere. They should never be told that the earth is round. It only makes everything unreal to them. They are balked in their impression of the flat good earth, they can't get over this sphere business, they live in a fog of abstraction, and nothing is anything. Save for purposes of abstraction, the earth is a great plain, with hills and valleys. Why force abstractions and kill the reality, when there's no need?

As for children, will we never realize that their abstractions are never based on observations, but on subjective exaggerations? If there is an eye in the face, the face is all eye. It is the child-soul which cannot get over the mystery of the eye. If there is a tree in a landscape, the landscape is all tree. Always this partial focus. The attempt to make a child focus for a whole view—which is really a generalization and an adult abstraction—is simply wicked. Yet the first thing we do is to set a child making relief-maps in clay, for example: of his own district. Imbecility! He has not even the faintest impression of the total hill on which his home stands. A steepness going up to a door—and front garden railings—and perhaps windows. That's the lot.

The top and bottom of it is that it is a crime to teach a child anything at all, school-wise. It is just evil to collect children together and teach them through the head. It causes absolute starvation in the dynamic centres, and sterile substitute of brain knowledge is all the gain. The children of the middle classes are so vitally impoverished that the miracle is they continue to exist at all. The children of the lower classes do better, because they escape into the streets. But even the children of the proletariat are now infected.

And, of course, as my critics point out, under all the school-smarm and newspaper-cant man is today as savage as a cannibal, and more dangerous. The living dynamic self is denaturalized instead of being educated.

We talk about education—leading forth the natural intelligence of a child. But ours is just the opposite of leading forth. It is a ramming in of brain facts through the head, and a consequent distortion, suffocation, and starvation of the primary centres of consciousness. A nice day of reckoning we've got in front of us.

Let us lead forth, by all means. But let us not have mental knowledge before us as the goal of the leading. Much less let us make of it a vicious circle in which we lead the unhappy child-mind, like a cow in a ring at a fair. We don't want to educate children so that they may understand. Understanding is a fallacy and a vice in most people. I don't even want my child to know, much less to understand. *I* don't want my child to know that five fives are twenty-five, any more than I want my child to wear my hat or my boots. I *don't* want my child to *know*. If he wants five fives let him count them on his fingers. As for his little mind, give it a rest, and let his dynamic self be alert. He will ask "why" often enough. But he more often asks why the sun shines, or why men have moustaches, or why grass is green, than anything sensible. Most of a child's questions are, and should be, unanswerable. They are not questions at all. They are exclamations of wonder, they are *remarks* half-sceptically addressed. When a child says, "Why is grass green?" he half implies, "Is it really green, or is it just taking me in?" And we solemnly begin to prate about chlorophyll. Oh, imbeciles, idiots, inexcusable owls!

The whole of a child's development goes on from the great dynamic centres, and is basically non-mental. To introduce mental activity is to arrest the dynamic activity, and stultify true dynamic development. By the age of twenty-one our young people are helpless, hopeless, selfless, floundering mental entities, with nothing in front of them, because they have been starved from the roots, systematically, for twenty-one years, and fed through the head. They have had all their mental excitements, sex and everything, all through the head, and when it comes to the actual thing, why, there's nothing in it. *Blasé*. The affective centres have been exhausted from the head.

Before the age of fourteen, children should be taught only to move, to act, to *do*. And they should be taught as little as possible even of this. Adults simply cannot and do not know any more what the mode of childish intelligence is. Adults *always* interfere. They *always* force the adult mental mode. Therefore children must be preserved from adult instructions.

Make a child work—yes. Make it do little jobs. Keep a fine and delicate and fierce discipline, so that the little jobs are performed as perfectly as is consistent with the child's nature. Make the child alert, proud, and becoming in its movements. Make it know very definitely that it shall not and must not trespass on other people's privacy or patience. Teach it songs, tell it tales. But *never* instruct it school-wise. And mostly, leave it alone, send it away to be with other children and to get in and out of mischief, and in and out of danger. Forget your child altogether as much as possible.

All this is the active and strenuous business of parents, and must not be shelved off on to strangers. It is the business of parents *mentally* to forget but dynamically never to forsake their children.

It is no use expecting parents to know *why* schools are closed, and *why* they, the parents, must be quite responsible for their own children during the first ten years. If it is quite useless to expect parents to understand a theory of relativity, much less will they understand the development of the dynamic consciousness. But why should they understand? It is the business of very few to understand and for the mass, it is their business to believe and not to bother, but to be honourable and humanly to fulfill their human responsibilities. To give active obedience to their leaders, and to possess their own souls in natural pride.

Some must understand why a child is not to be mentally educated. Some must have a faint inkling of the processes of consciousness during the first fourteen years. Some must know what a child beholds when it looks at a horse, and what it means when it says, "Why is grass green?" The answer to this question, by the way, is "Because it is."

The interplay of the four dynamic centres follows no one conceivable law. Mental activity continues according to a law of co-relation. But there is no logical or rational co-relation in the dynamic consciousness. It pulses on inconsequential, and it would be impossible to determine any sequence. Out of the very lack of sequence in dynamic consciousness does the individual himself develop. The dynamic abstraction of a child's precepts follows no mental law, and even no law which can ever be mentally propounded. And this is why it is utterly pernicious to set a child making a clay relief-map of its own district, or to ask a child to draw conclusions from given observations. Dynamically, a child draws no conclusions. All things still remain dynamically possible. A conclusion drawn is a nail in the coffin of a child's developing being. Let a child make a clay landscape, if it likes. But entirely according to its own fancy, and without conclusions drawn. Only, let the landscape be vividly made—always the discipline of the soul's full attention. "Oh, but where are the factory chimneys?"—or else—"Why have you left out the gas-works?" or "Do you call that sloppy thing a church?" The particular focus should be vivid, and the record in some way true. The soul must give earnest attention, that is all.

And so actively disciplined, the child develops for the first ten years. We need not be afraid of letting children see the passions and reactions of adult life. Only we must not strain the *sympathies* of a child, in *any* direction, particularly the direction of love and pity. Nor must we introduce the fallacy of right and wrong. Spontaneous distaste should take the place of right and wrong. And least of all must there be a cry: "You see, dear, you don't understand. When you are older—" A child's sagacity is better than an adult understanding, anyhow.

Of course it is ten times criminal to tell young children facts about sex, or to implicate them in adult relationships. A child has a strong evanescent sex-consciousness. It instinctively writes impossible words on back walls. But this is not a fully conscious mental act. It is a kind of dream act—quite natural. The child's curious, shadowy, indecent sex-knowledge is quite in the course of nature. And does nobody any harm at all. Adults had far better not notice it. But if a child sees a cockerel tread a hen, or two dogs coupling, well and good. It *should* see these things. Only, without comment. Let nothing be exaggeratedly hidden. By instinct, let us preserve the decent privacies. But if a child occasionally sees its parent nude, taking a bath, all the better. Or even sitting in the w.c. Exaggerated secrecy is bad. But indecent exposure is also very bad. But worst of all is dragging in the *mental* consciousness of these shadowy dynamic realities.

In the same way, to talk to a child about an adult is vile. Let adults keep their adult feelings and communications for people of their own age. But if a child sees its parents violently quarrel, all the better. There must be storms. And a child's dynamic understanding is far deeper and more penetrating than our sophisticated interpretation. But *never* make a child a party to adult affairs. Never drag the child in. Refuse its sympathy on such occasions. Always treat it as if it had *no* business to hear, even if it is present and *must* hear. Truly, it has no business mentally to hear. And the dynamic soul will always weigh things up and dispose of them properly, if there be no interference of adult comment or adult desire for sympathy. It is despicable for any one parent to accept a child's sympathy against the other parent. And the one who *received* the sympathy is always more contemptible than the one who is hated.

Of course so many children are born today unnaturally mentally awake and alive to adult affairs, that there is nothing left but to tell them everything, crudely: or else, much better, to say: "Ah, get out, you know too much, you make me sick."

To return to the question of sex. A child is born sexed. A child is either male or female, in the whole of its psyche and physique is either male or female. Every single living cell is either male or female, and will remain either male or female as long as life lasts. And every single cell in every male child is male, and every cell in every female child is female. The talk about a third sex, or about the indeterminate sex, is just to pervert the issue.

Biologically, it is true, the rudimentary formation of both sexes is found in every individual. That doesn't mean that every individual is a bit of both, or either, *ad lib*. After a sufficient period of idealism, men become hopelessly self-conscious. That is, the great affective centres no longer act spontaneously, but always wait for control from the head. This always breeds a great fluster in the psyche, and the poor self-conscious individual cannot help posing and posturing. Our ideal has taught us to be gentle and wistful: rather girlish and yielding, and *very* yielding in our sympathies. In fact, many young men feel so very like what they imagine a girl must feel, that hence they draw the conclusion that they must have a large share of female sex inside them. False conclusion.

These girlish men have often, today, the finest maleness, once it is put to the test. How is it then that they feel, and look, so girlish? It is largely a question of the direction of the polarized flow. Our ideal has taught us to be *so* loving and *so* submissive and *so* yielding in our sympathy, that the mode has become automatic in many men. Now in what we will call the "natural" mode, man has his positivity in the volitional centres, and women in the sympathetic. In fulfilling the Christian love ideal, however, men have reversed this. Man has assumed the gentle, all-sympathetic role, and woman has become the energetic party, with the authority in her hands. The male is the sensitive, sympathetic nature, the woman the active, effective, authoritative. So that the male acts as the passive, or recipient pole of attraction, the female as the active, positive, exertive pole, in human relations. Which is a reversal of the old flow. The woman is now the initiator, man the responder. They seem to play each other's parts. But man is purely male, playing woman's part, and woman is purely female, however manly. The gulf between Heliogabalus, or the most womanly man on earth, and the most manly woman, is just the same as ever: just the same old gulf between the sexes. The man is male, the woman is female. Only they are playing one another's parts, as they must at certain periods. The dynamic polarity has swung around.

If we look a little closer, we can define this positive and negative business better. As a matter of fact, positive and negative, passive and active cuts both ways. If the man, as thinker and doer, is active, or positive, and the woman negative, then, on the other hand, as the initiator of emotion, of feeling, and of sympathetic understanding the woman is positive, the man negative. The man may be the initiator in action, but the woman is initiator in emotion. The man has the initiative as far as voluntary activity goes, and the woman the initiative as far as sympathetic activity goes. In love, it is the woman naturally who loves, the man who is loved. In love, woman is the positive, man the negative. It is woman who asks, in love, and man who answers. In life, the reverse is the case. In knowing and in doing, man is positive and woman negative: man initiates, and woman lives up to it.

Naturally this nicely arranged order of things may be reversed. Action and utterance, which are male, are polarized against feeling, emotion, which are female. And which is positive, which negative? Was man, the eternal protagonist, born of woman, from her womb of fathomless emotion? Or was woman, with her deep womb of emotion, born from the rib of active man, the first created? Man, the doer, the knower, the original in *being*, is he lord of life? Or is woman, the great Mother, who bore us from the womb of love, is she the supreme Goddess?

This is the question of all time. And as long as man and woman endure, so will the answer be given, first one way, then the other. Man, as the utterer, usually claims that Eve was created out of his spare rib: from the field of the creative, upper dynamic consciousness, that is. But woman, as soon as she gets a word in, points to the fact that man inevitably, poor darling, is the issue of his mother's womb. So the battle rages.

But some men always agree with the woman. Some men always yield to woman the creative positivity. And in certain periods, such as the present, the majority of men concur in regarding woman as the source of life, the first term in creation: woman, the mother, the prime being.

And then, the whole polarity shifts over. Man still remains the doer and thinker. But he is so only in the service of emotional and procreative woman. His highest moment is now the emotional moment when he gives himself up to the woman, when he forms the perfect answer for her great emotional and procreative asking. All his thinking, all his activity in the world only contributes to this great moment, when he is fulfilled in the emotional passion of the woman, the birth of rebirth, as Whitman calls it. In his consummation in the emotional passion of a woman, man is reborn, which is quite true.

And there is the point at which we all now stick. Life, thought, and activity, all are devoted truly to the great end of Woman, wife and mother.

Man has now entered on to his negative mode. Now, his consummation is in feeling, not in action. Now, his activity is all of the domestic order and all his thought goes to proving that nothing matters except that birth shall continue and woman shall rock in the nest of this globe like a bird who covers her eggs in some tall tree. Man is the fetcher, the carrier, the sacrifice, the crucified, and the reborn of woman.

This being so, the whole tendency of his nature changes. Instead of being assertive and rather insentient, he becomes wavering and sensitive. He begins to have as many feelings—nay, more than a woman. His heroism is all in altruistic endurance. He worships pity and tenderness and weakness, even in himself. In short, he takes on very largely the original role of woman. Woman meanwhile becomes the fearless, inwardly relentless, determined positive party. She grips the responsibility. The hand that rocks the cradle rules the world. Nay, she makes man discover that cradles should not be rocked, in order that her hands may be left free. She is now a queen of the earth, and inwardly a fearsome tyrant. She keeps pity and tenderness emblazoned on her banners. But God help the man whom she pities. Ultimately she tears him to bits.

Therefore we see the reversal of the old poles. Man becomes the emotional party, woman the positive and active. Man begins to show strong signs of the peculiarly strong passive sex desire, the desire to be taken, which is considered characteristic of woman. Man begins to have all the feelings of woman—or all the feelings which he attributed to woman. He becomes more feminine than woman ever was, and worships his own femininity, calling it the highest. In short, he begins to exhibit all signs of sexual complexity. He begins to imagine he really is half female. And certainly woman seems very male. So the hermaphrodite fallacy revives again.

But it is all a fallacy. Man, in the midst of all his effeminacy, is still male and nothing but male. And woman, though she harangue in Parliament or patrol the streets with a helmet on her head, is still completely female. They are only playing each other's roles, because the poles have swung into reversion. The compass is reversed. But that doesn't mean that the north pole has become the south pole, or that each is a bit of both.

Of course a woman should stick to her own natural emotional positivity. But then man must stick to his own positivity of *being*, of action, *disinterested, non-domestic, male* action, which is not devoted to the increase of the female. Once man vacates his camp of sincere, passionate positivity in disinterested being, his supreme responsibility to fulfil his own profoundest impulses, with reference to none but God or his own soul, not taking woman into count at all, in this primary responsibility to his own deepest soul; once man vacates this strong citadel of his own genuine, not spurious, divinity; then in comes woman, picks up the sceptre, and begins to conduct a rag-time band.

Man remains man, however he may put on wistfulness and tenderness like petticoats, and sensibilities like pearl ornaments. Your sensitive little big-eyed boy, so much more gentle and loving than his harder sister, is male for all that, believe me. Perhaps evilly male, so mothers may learn to their cost: and wives still more.

Of course there should be a great balance between the sexes. Man, in the daytime, must follow his own soul's greatest impulse, and give himself to life-work and risk himself to death. It is not woman who claims the highest in man. It is a man's own religious soul that drives him on beyond woman, to his supreme activity. For his highest, man is responsible to God alone. He may not pause to remember that he has a life to lose, or a wife and children to leave. He must carry forward the banner of life, though seven worlds perish, with all the wives and mothers and children in them. Hence Jesus, "Woman, what have I to do with thee?" Every man that lives has to say it again to his wife or mother, once he has any work or mission in hand, that comes from his soul.

But again, no man is a blooming marvel for twenty-four hours a day. Jesus or Napoleon or any other of them ought to have been man enough to be able to come home at tea-time and put his slippers on and sit under the spell of his wife. For there you are, the woman has her world, her positivity: the world of love, of emotion, of sympathy. And it behooves every man in his hour to take off his shoes and relax and give himself up to his woman and her world. Not to give up his purpose. But to give up himself for a time to her who is his mate. And so it is one detests the clockwork Kant, and the petit-bourgeois Napoleon divorcing his Josephine for a Hapsburg—or even Jesus, with his "Woman, what have I to do with thee?" He might have added "just now." They were all failures.

IX

The Birth of Sex

The last chapter was a chapter of semi-digression. We now return to the straight course. Is the straightness none too evident? Ah well, it's a matter of relativity. A child is born with one sex only, and remains always single in his sex. There is no intermingling, only a great change of roles is possible. But man in the female role is still male.

Sex—that is to say, maleness and femaleness—is present from the moment of birth, and in every act or deed of every child. But sex in the real sense of dynamic sexual relationship, this does not exist in a child, and cannot exist until puberty and after. True, children have a sort of sex-consciousness. Little boys and little girls may even commit indecencies together. And still it is nothing vital. It is a sort of shadow activity, a sort of dream-activity. It has no very profound effect.

But still, boys and girls should be kept apart as much as possible, that they may have some sort of respect and fear for the gulf that lies between them in nature, and for the great strangeness which each has to offer the other, finally. We are all wrong when we say there is no vital difference between the sexes. There is every difference. Every bit, every cell in a boy is male, every cell is female in a woman, and must remain so. Women can never feel or know as men do. And in the reverse men can never feel and know, dynamically, as women do. Man, acting in the passive or feminine polarity, is still man, and he doesn't have one single unmanly feeling. And women, when they speak and write, utter not one single word that men have not taught them. Men learn their feelings from women, women learn their mental consciousness from men. And so it will ever be. Meanwhile, women live forever by feeling, and men live forever from an inherent sense of *purpose*. Feeling is an end in itself. This is unspeakable truth to a woman, and never true for one minute to a man. When man, in the Epicurean spirit, embraces feeling, he makes himself a martyr to it— like Maupassant or Oscar Wilde. Woman will *never* understand the depth of the spirit of purpose in man, his deeper spirit. And man will never understand the sacredness of feeling to woman. Each will play at the other's game, but they will remain apart.

The whole mode, the whole everything is really different in man and woman. Therefore we should keep boys and girls apart, that they are pure and virgin in themselves. On mixing with one another, in becoming familiar, in being "pals," they lose their own male and female integrity. And they lose the treasure of the future, the vital sex polarity, the dynamic magic of life. For the magic and the dynamism rests on *otherness*.

For actual sex is a vital polarity. And a polarity which rouses into action, as we know, at puberty.

And how? As we know, a child lives from the great field of dynamic consciousness established between the four poles of the dynamic psyche, two great poles of sympathy, two great poles of will. The solar plexus and the lumbar ganglion, great nerve-centres below the diaphragm, act as the dynamic origin of all consciousness in man, and are immediately polarized by the other two nerve-centres, the cardiac plexus and the thoracic ganglion above the diaphragm. At these four poles the whole flow, both within the individual and from without him, of dynamic consciousness and dynamic creative relationship is centred. These four first poles constitute the first field of dynamic consciousness for the first twelve or fourteen years of the life of every child.

And then a change takes place. It takes place slowly, gradually and inevitably, utterly beyond our provision or control. The living soul is unfolding itself in another great metamorphosis.

What happens, in the biological psyche, is that deeper centres of consciousness and function come awake. Deep in the lower body the great sympathetic centre, the hypogastric plexus has been acting all the time in a kind of dream-automatism, balanced by its corresponding voluntary centre, the sacral ganglion. At the age of twelve these two centres begin slowly to rumble awake, with a deep reverberant force that changes the whole constitution of the life of the individual.

And as these two centres, the sympathetic centre of the deeper abdomen, and the voluntary centre of the loins, gradually sparkle into wakeful, *conscious* activity, their corresponding poles are roused in the upper body. In the region of the throat and neck, the so-called cervical plexuses and the cervical ganglia dawn into activity.

We have now another field of dawning dynamic consciousness, that will extend far beyond the first. And now various things happen to us. First of all actual sex establishes its strange and troublesome presence within us. This is the massive wakening of the lower body. And then, in the upper body, the breasts of a woman begin to develop, her throat changes its form. And in the man, the voice breaks, the beard begins to grow round the lips and on to the throat. There are the obvious physiological changes resulting from the gradual bursting into free activity of the hypogastric plexus and the sacral ganglion, in the lower body, and of the cervical plexuses and ganglia of the neck, in the upper body.

Why the growth of hair should start at the lower and upper sympathetic regions we cannot say. Perhaps for protection. Perhaps to preserve these powerful yet supersensitive nodes from the inclemency of changes in temperature, which might cause a derangement. Perhaps for the sake of protective warning, as hair warns when it is touched. Perhaps for a screen against various dynamic vibrations, and as a receiver of other suited dynamic vibrations. It may be that even the hair of the head acts as a sensitive vibration-medium for conveying currents of physical and vitalistic activity to and from the brain. And perhaps from the centers of intense vital surcharge hair springs as a sort of annunciation or declaration, like a crest of life-assertion. Perhaps all these things, and perhaps others.

But with the bursting awake of the four new poles of dynamic consciousness and being, change takes place in everything, the features now begin to take individual form, the limbs develop out of the soft round matrix of child-form, the body resolves itself into distinctions. A strange creative change in being has taken place. The child before puberty is quite another thing from the child after puberty. Strange indeed is this new birth, this rising from the sea of childhood into a new being. It is a resurrection which we fear.

And now, a new world, a new heaven and a new earth. Now new relationships are formed, the old ones retire from their prominence. Now mother and father inevitably give way before masters and mistresses, brothers and sisters yield to friends. This is the period of *Schwärmerei*, of young adoration and of real initial friendships. A child before puberty has playmates. After puberty he has friends and enemies.

A whole new field of passional relationship. And the old bonds relaxing, the old love retreating. The father and mother bonds now relax, though they never break. The family love wanes, though it never dies.

It is the hour of the stranger. Let the stranger now enter the soul.

And it is the first hour of true individuality, the first hour of genuine, responsible solitariness. A child knows the abyss of forlornness. But an adolescent alone knows the strange pain of growing into his own isolation of individuality.

All this change is an agony and a bliss. It is a cataclysm and a new world. It is our most serious hour, perhaps. And yet we cannot be responsible for it.

Now sex comes into active being. Until puberty, sex is submerged, nascent, incipient only. After puberty, it is a tremendous factor.

What is sex, really? We can never say, satisfactorily. But we know so much: we know that it is a dynamic polarity between human beings, and a circuit of force *always* flowing. The psychoanalyst is right so far. There can be no vivid relation between two adult individuals which does not consist in a dynamic polarized flow of vitalistic force or magnetism or electricity, call it what you will, between these two people. Yet is this dynamic flow inevitably sexual in nature?

This is the moot point for psychoanalysis. But let us look at sex, in its obvious manifestation. The *sexual* relation between man and woman consummates in the act of coition. Now what is the act of coition? We know its functional purpose of procreation. But, after all our experience and all our poetry and novels we know that the procreative purpose of sex is, to the individual man and woman, just a sideshow. To the individual, the act of coition is a great psychic experience, a vital experience of tremendous importance. On this vital individual experience the life and very being of the individual largely depends.

But what is the experience? Untellable. Only, we know something. We know that in the act of coition the *blood* of the individual man, acutely surcharged with intense vital electricity—we know no word, so say "electricity," by analogy—rises to a culmination, in a tremendous magnetic urge towards the magnetic blood of the female. The whole of the living blood in the two individuals forms a field of intense, polarized magnetic attraction. So, the two poles must be brought into contact. In the act of coition, the two seas of blood in the two individuals, rocking and surging towards contact, as near as possible, clash into a oneness. A great flash of interchange occurs, like an electric spark when two currents meet or like lightning out of the densely surcharged clouds. There is a lightning flash which passes through the blood of both individuals, there is a thunder of sensation which rolls in diminishing crashes down the nerves of each—and then the tension passes.

The two individuals are separate again. But are they as they were before? Is the air the same after a thunder-storm as before? No. The air is as it were new, fresh, tingling with newness. So is the blood of man and woman after successful coition. After a false coition, like prostitution, there is not newness but a certain disintegration.

But after coition, the actual chemical constitution of the blood is so changed, that usually sleep intervenes, to allow the time for chemical, biological readjustment through the whole system.

So, the blood is changed and renewed, refreshed, almost recreated, like the atmosphere after thunder. Out of the newness of the living blood pass the new strange waves which beat upon the great dynamic centres of the nerves: primarily upon the hypogastric plexus and the sacral ganglion. From these centres rise new impulses, new vision, new being, rising like Aphrodite from the foam of the new tide of blood. And so individual life goes on.

Perhaps, then, we will allow ourselves to say what, in psychic individual reality, is the act of coition. It is the bringing together of the surcharged electric blood of the male with the polarized electric blood of the female, with the result of a tremendous flashing interchange, which alters the constitution of the blood, and the very quality of *being*, in both.

And this, surely, is sex. But is this the whole of sex? That is the question.

After coition, we say the blood is renewed. We say that from the new, finely sparkling blood new thrills pass into the great affective centres of the lower body, new thrills of feeling, of impulse, of energy. And what about these new thrills?

Now, a new story. The new thrills are passed on to the great upper centres of the dynamic body. The individual polarity now changes, within the individual system. The upper centres, cardiac plexus and cervical plexuses, thoracic ganglion and cervical ganglia, now assume positivity. These, the upper polarized centers, have now the positive role to play, the solar and the hypogastric plexuses, the lumbar and the sacral ganglia, these have the submissive, negative role for the time being.

And what then? What now, that the upper centers are finely active in positivity? Now it is a different story. Now there is new vision in the eyes, new hearing in the ears, new voice in the throat and speech on the lips. Now the new song rises, the brain tingles to new thought, the heart craves for new activity.

The heart craves for new activity. For new *collective* activity. That is, for a new polarized connection with other beings, other men.

Is this new craving for polarized communion with others, this craving for a new unison, is it sexual, like the original craving for the woman? Not at all. The whole polarity is different. Now, the positive poles are the poles of the breast and shoulders and throat, the poles of activity and full consciousness. Men, being themselves made new after the act of coition, wish to make the world new. A new, passionate polarity springs up between men who are bent on the same activity, the polarity between man and woman sinks to passivity. It is now daytime, and time to forget sex, time to be busy making a new world.

Is this new polarity, this new circuit of passion between comrades and co-workers, is this also sexual? It is a vivid circuit of polarized passion. Is it hence sex?

It is not. Because what are the poles of positive connection? The upper, busy poles. What is the dynamic contact? A unison in spirit, in understanding, and a pure commingling in one great *work*. A mingling of the individual passion into one great *purpose*. Now this is also a grand consummation for men, this mingling of many with one great impassioned purpose. But is this sex? Knowing what sex is, can we call this other also sex? We cannot.

This meeting of many in one great passionate purpose is not sex, and should never be confused with sex. It is a great motion in the opposite direction. And I am sure that the ultimate, greatest desire in men is this desire for great *purposive* activity. When man loses his deep sense of purposive, creative activity, he feels lost, and is lost. When he makes the sexual consummation the supreme consummation, even in his *secret* soul, he falls into the beginnings of despair. When he makes woman, or the woman and child the great centre of life and of life-significance, he falls into the beginnings of despair.

Man must bravely stand by his own soul, his own responsibility as the creative vanguard of life. And he must also have the courage to go home to his woman and become a perfect answer to her deep sexual call. But he must never confuse his two issues. Primarily and supremely man is *always* the pioneer of life, adventuring onward into the unknown, alone with his own temerarious, dauntless soul. Woman for him exists only in the twilight, by the camp fire, when day has departed. Evening and the night are hers.

The psychoanalysts, driving us back to the sexual consummation always, do us infinite damage.

We have to break away, back to the great unison of manhood in some passionate *purpose*. Now this is not like sex. Sex is always individual. A man has his own sex: nobody else's. And sexually he goes as a single individual; he can mingle only singly. So that to make sex a general affair is just a perversion and a lie. You can't get people and talk to them about their sex, as if it were a common interest.

We have got to get back to the great purpose of manhood, a passionate unison in actively making a world. This is a real commingling of many. And in such a commingling we forfeit the individual. In the commingling of sex we are alone with *one* partner. It is an individual affair, there is no superior or inferior. But in the commingling of a passionate purpose, each individual sacredly abandons his individual. In the living faith of his soul, he surrenders his individuality to the great urge which is upon him. He may have to surrender his name, his fame, his fortune, his life, everything. But once a man, in the integrity of his own individual soul, *believes*, he surrenders his own individuality to his belief, and becomes one of a united body. He knows what he does. He makes the surrender honourably, in agreement with his own soul's deepest desire. But he surrenders, and remains responsible for the purity of his surrender.

But what if he believes that his sexual consummation is his supreme consummation? Then he serves the great purpose to which he pledges himself only as long as it pleases him. After which he turns it down, and goes back to sex. With sex as the one accepted prime motive, the world drifts into despair and anarchy.

Of all countries, America has most to fear from anarchy, even from one single moment's lapse into anarchy. The old nations are *organically* fixed into classes, but America not. You can shake Europe to atoms. And yet peasants fall back to peasantry, artisans to industrial labor, upper classes to their control—inevitably. But can you say the same of America?

America must not lapse for one single moment into anarchy.

It would be the end of her. She must drift no nearer to anarchy. She is near enough.

Well, then, Americans must make a choice. It is a choice between belief in man's creative, spontaneous soul, and man's automatic power of production and reproduction. It is a choice between serving *man*, or woman. It is a choice between yielding the soul to a leader, leaders, or yielding only to the woman, wife, mistress, or mother.

The great collective passion of belief which brings men together, comrades and co-workers, passionately obeying their soul-chosen leader or leaders, this is not a sex passion. Not in any sense. Sex holds any *two* people together, but it tends to disintegrate society, unless it is subordinated to the great dominating male passion of collective *purpose*.

But when the sex passion submits to the great purposive passion, then you have fullness. And no great purposive passion can endure long unless it is established upon the fulfilment in the vast majority of individuals of the true sexual passion. No great motive or ideal or social principle can endure for any length of time unless based upon the sexual fulfilment of the vast majority of individuals concerned.

It cuts both ways. Assert sex as the predominant fulfilment, and you get the collapse of living purpose in man. You get anarchy. Assert *purposiveness* as the one supreme and pure activity of life, and you drift into barren sterility, like our business life of today, and our political life. You become sterile, you make anarchy inevitable. And so there you are. You have got to base your great purposive activity upon the intense sexual fulfilment of all your individuals. That was how Egypt endured. But you have got to keep your sexual fulfilment even then subordinate, just subordinate to the great passion of purpose: subordinate by a hair's breadth only: but still, by that hair's breadth, subordinate.

Perhaps we can see now a little better—to go back to the child —where Freud is wrong in attributing a sexual motive to all human activity. It is obvious there is no real sexual motive in a child, for example. The great sexual centres are not even awake. True, even in a child of three, rudimentary sex throws strange shadows on the wall, in its approach from the distance. But these are only an uneasy intrusion from the as-yet-uncreated, unready biological centres. The great sexual centres of the hypogastric plexus, and the immensely powerful sacral ganglion are slowly prepared, developed in a kind of prenatal gestation during childhood before puberty. But even an unborn child kicks in the womb. So do the great sex-centres give occasional blind kicks in a child. It is part of the phenomenon of childhood. But we must be most careful not to charge these rather unpleasant apparitions or phenomena against the individual boy or girl. We must be *very* careful not to drag the matter into mental consciousness. Shoo it away. Reprimand it with a pah! and a faugh! and a bit of contempt. But do not get into any heat or any fear. Do not startle a passional attention. Drive the whole thing away like the shadow it is, and be *very* careful not to drive it into the consciousness. Be very careful to plant no seed of burning shame or horror. Throw over it merely the cold water of contemptuous indifference, dismissal.

After puberty, a child may as well be told the simple and necessary facts of sex. As things stand, the parent may as well do it. But briefly, coldly, and with as cold a dismissal as possible. "Look here, you're not a child any more; you know it, don't you? You're going to be a man. And you know what that means. It means you're going to marry a woman later on, and get children. You know it, and I know it. But in the meantime, leave yourself alone. I know you'll have a lot of bother with yourself, and your feelings. I know what is happening to you. And I know you get excited about it. But you needn't. Other men have all gone through it. So don't you go creeping off by yourself and doing things on the sly. It won't do you any good. I know what you'll do, because we've all been through it. I know the thing will keep coming on you at night. But remember that I know. Remember. And remember that I want you to leave yourself alone. I know what it is, I tell you. I've been through it all myself. You've got to go through these years, before you find a woman you want to marry, and whom you can marry. I went through them myself, and got myself worked up a good deal more than was good for me. Try to contain yourself. Always try to contain yourself, and be a man. That's the only thing. Always try and be manly, and quiet in yourself. Remember I know what it is. I've been the same, in the same state that you are in. And probably I've behaved more foolishly and perniciously than ever you will. So come to me if anything *really* bothers you. And don't feel sly and secret. I do know just what you've got and what you haven't. I've been as bad and perhaps worse than you. And the only thing I want of you is to be manly. Try and be manly, and quiet in yourself."

That is about as much as a father can say to a boy, at puberty. You have to be *very* careful what you do: especially if you are a parent. To translate sex into mental ideas is vile, to make a scientific fact of it is death.

As a matter of fact there should be some sort of initiation into true adult consciousness. Boys should be taken away from their mothers and sisters as much as possible at adolescence. They should be given into some real manly charge. And there should be some actual initiation into sex life. Perhaps like the savages, who make the boy die again, symbolically, and pull him forth through some narrow aperture, to be born again, and make him suffer and endure terrible hardships, to make a great dynamic effect on the consciousness, a terrible dynamic sense of change in the very being. In short, a long, violent initiation, from which the lad emerges emaciated, but cut off forever from childhood, entered into the serious, responsible pale of manhood. And with his whole consciousness convulsed by a great change, as his dynamic psyche actually is convulsed. And something in the same way, to initiate girls into womanhood.

There should be the intense dynamic reaction: the physical suffering and the physical realization sinking deep into the soul, changing the soul forever. Sex should come upon us as a terrible thing of suffering and privilege and mystery: a mysterious metamorphosis come upon us, and a new terrible power given us, and a new responsibility. Telling? What's the good of telling? The mystery, the terror, and the tremendous power of sex should never be explained away. The mass of mankind should *never* be acquainted with the scientific biological facts of sex: *never*. The mystery must remain in its dark secrecy, and its dark, powerful dynamism. The reality of sex lies in the great dynamic convulsions in the soul. And as such it should be realized, a great creative-convulsive seizure upon the soul. To make it a matter of test-tube mixtures, chemical demonstrations, and trashy lock-and-key symbols is just blasting. Even more sickening is the line: "You see, dear, one day you'll love a man as I love Daddy, more than anything else in the *whole* world. And then, dear, I hope you'll marry him. Because if you do you'll be happy, and I want you to be happy, my love. And so I hope you'll marry the man you really love [kisses the child]. And then, darling, there will come a lot of things you know nothing about now. You'll want to have a dear little baby, won't you, darling? Your own dear little baby. And your husband's as well. Because it'll be his, too. You know that, don't you, dear? It will be born from both of you. And you don't know how, do you? Well, it will come from right inside you, dear, out of your own inside. You came out of mother's inside," etc., etc.

But I suppose there's really nothing else to be done, given the world and society as we've got them now. The mother is doing her best.

But it is all wrong. It is wrong to make sex appear as if it were part of the dear-darling-love smarm: the spiritual love. It is even worse to take the scientific test-tube line. It all kills the great effective dynamism of life, and substitutes the mere ash of mental ideas and tricks.

The scientific fact of sex is no more sex than a skeleton is a man. Yet you'd think twice before you stock a skeleton in front of a lad and said, "You see, my boy, this is what you are when you come to know yourself." And the ideal, lovey-dovey "explanation" of sex as something wonderful and extra lovey-dovey, a bill-and-coo process of obtaining a sweet little baby—or else "God made us so that we must do this, to bring another dear little baby to life"—well, it just makes one sick. It is disastrous to the deep sexual life. But perhaps that is what we want.

When humanity comes to its senses it will realize what a fearful Sodom apple our understanding is. What terrible mouths and stomachs full of bitter ash we've all got. And then we shall take away "knowledge" and "understanding," and lock them up along with the rest of poisons, to be administered in small doses only by competent people.

We have almost poisoned the mass of humanity to death with *understanding*. The period of actual death and race-extermination is not far off. We could have produced the same barrenness and frenzy of nothingness in people, perhaps, by dinning it into them that every man is just a charnel-house skeleton of unclean bones. Our "understanding," our science and idealism have produced in people the same strange frenzy of self-repulsion as if they saw their own skulls each time they looked in the mirror. A man is a thing of scientific cause-and-effect and biological process, draped in an ideal, is he? No wonder he sees the skeleton grinning through the flesh.

Our leaders have not loved men: they have loved ideas, and have been willing to sacrifice passionate men on the altars of the blood-drinking, ever-ash-thirsty ideal. Has President Wilson, or Karl Marx, or Bernard Shaw ever felt one hot blood-pulse of love for the working man, the half-conscious, deluded working man? Never. Each of these leaders has wanted to abstract him away from his own blood and being, into some foul Methuselah or abstraction of a man.

And me? There is no danger of the working man ever reading my books, so I shan't hurt him that way. But oh, I would like to save him alive, in his living, spontaneous, original being. I can't help it. It is my passionate instinct.

I would like him to give me back the responsibility for general affairs, a responsibility which he can't acquit, and which saps his life. I would like him to give me back the responsibility for the future. I would like him to give me back the responsibility for thought, for direction. I wish we could take hope and belief together. I would undertake my share of the responsibility, if he gave me his belief.

I would like him to give me back books and newspapers and theories. And I would like to give him back, in return, his old insouciance, and rich, original spontaneity and fullness of life.

✑ X ✑

Parent Love

In the serious hour of puberty, the individual passes into his second phase of accomplishment. But there cannot be a perfect transition unless all the activity is in full play in all the first four poles of the psyche. Childhood is a chrysalis from which each must extricate himself. And the struggling youth or maid cannot emerge unless by the energy of all powers; he can never emerge if the whole mass of the world and the tradition of love hold him back.

Now we come to the greater peril of our particular form of idealism. It is the idealism of love and of the spirit: the idealism of yearning, outgoing love, of pure sympathetic communion and "understanding." And this idealism recognizes as the highest earthly love, the love of mother and child.

And what does this mean? It means, for every delicately brought up child, indeed for all the children who matter, a steady and persistent pressure upon the upper sympathetic centres, and a steady and persistent starving of the lower centres, particularly the great voluntary centre of the lower body. The centre of sensual, manly independence, of exultation in the sturdy, defiant self, wilfulness and masterfulness and pride, this centre is steadily suppressed. The warm, swift, sensual self is steadily and persistently denied, damped, weakened, throughout all the period of childhood. And by sensual we do not mean greedy or ugly, we mean the deeper, more impulsive reckless nature. Life must be always refined and superior. Love and happiness must be the watchword.

The wilful, critical element of the spiritual mode is never absent, the silent, if forbearing disapproval and distaste is always ready. Vile bullying forbearance.

With what result? The centre of upper sympathy is abnormally, inflamedly excited; and the centres of will are so deranged that they operate in jerks and spasms. The true polarity of the sympathetic-voluntary system within the child is so disturbed as to be almost deranged. Then we have an exaggerated sensitiveness alternating with a sort of helpless fury: and we have delicate frail children with nerves or with strange whims. And we have the strange, cold obstinacy of the spiritual will, cold as hell, fixed in a child.

Then one parent, usually the mother, is the object of blind devotion, whilst the other parent, usually the father, is an object of resistance. The child is taught, however, that both parents should be loved, and only loved: and that love, gentleness, pity, charity, and all "higher" emotions, these alone are genuine feelings, all the rest are false, to be rejected.

With what result? The upper centres are developed to a degree of unnatural acuteness and reaction—or again they fall numbed and barren. And then between parents and children a painfully false relation grows up: a relation as of two adults, either of two pure lovers, or of two love-appearing people who are really trying to bully one another. Instead of leaving the child with its own limited but deep and incomprehensible feelings, the parent, hopelessly involved in the sympathetic mode of selfless love, and spiritual love-will, stimulates the child into a consciousness which does not belong to it, on the one plane, and robs it of its own spontaneous consciousness and freedom on the other plane.

And this is the fatality. Long before puberty, by an exaggeration and an intensity of spiritual love from the parents, the second centres of sympathy are artificially aroused into response. And there is an irreparable disaster. Instead of seeing as a child should see, through a glass, darkly, the child now opens premature eyes of sympathetic cognition. Instead of knowing in part, as it should know, it begins, at a fearfully small age, to know in full. The cervical plexuses and the cervical ganglia, which should only begin to awake after adolescence, these centres of the higher dynamic sympathy and cognition, are both artificially stimulated, by the adult personal love-emotion and love-will into response, in a quite young child, sometimes even in an infant. This is a holy obscenity.

Our particular mode of idealism causes us to suppress as far as possible the sensual centres, to make them negative. The whole of the activity is concentrated, as far as possible, in the upper or spiritual centres, the centres of the breast and throat, which we will call the centres of dynamic cognition, in contrast to the centres of sensual comprehension below the diaphragm.

And then a child arrives at puberty, with its upper nature already roused into precocious action. The child nowadays is almost invariably precocious in "understanding." In the north, spiritually precocious, so that by the time it arrives at adolescence it already has experienced the extended sympathetic reactions which should have lain utterly dark. And it has experienced these extended reactions with whom? With the parent or parents.

Which is man devouring his own offspring. For to the parents belongs, once and for all, the dynamic reaction on the first plane of consciousness only, the reaction and relationship at the first four poles of dynamic consciousness. When the second, the farther plane of consciousness rouses into action, the relationship is with strangers. All human instinct and all ethnology will prove this to us. What sex-instinct there is in a child is always *adverse* to the parents.

But also, the parents are all too quick. They all proceed to swallow their children before the children can get out of their clutches. And even if parents do send away their children at the age of puberty—to school or elsewhere—it is not much good. The mischief has been done before. For the first twelve years the parents and the whole community forcibly insist on the child's living from the upper centres only, and particularly the upper sympathetic centres, without the balance of the warm, deep sensual self. Parents and community alike insist on rousing an adult sympathetic response, and a mental answer in the child-schools, Sunday-schools, books, home-influence—all works in this **one** pernicious way. But it is the home, the parents, that work most effectively and intensely. There is the most intimate mesh of love, love-bullying, and "understanding" in which a child is entangled.

So that a child arrives at the age of puberty already stripped of its childhood's darkness, bound, and delivered over. Instead of waking now to a whole new field of consciousness, a whole vast and wonderful new dynamic impulse towards new connections, it finds itself fatally bound. Puberty accomplishes itself. The hour of sex strikes. But there is your child, bound, helpless. You have already aroused in it the dynamic response to your own insatiable love-will. You have already established between your child and yourself the dynamic relation in the further plane of consciousness. You have got your child as sure as if you had woven its flesh again with your own. You have done what it is vicious for any parent to do: you have established between your child and yourself the bond of adult love: the love of man for man, woman for woman, or man for woman. All your tenderness, your cherishing will not excuse you. It only deepens your guilt. You have established between your child and yourself the bond of further sympathy. I do not speak of sex. I speak of pure sympathy, sacred love. The parents establish between themselves and their child the bond of the higher love, the further spiritual love, the sympathy of the adult soul.

And this is fatal. It is a sort of incest. It is a dynamic *spiritual* incest, more dangerous than sensual incest, because it is more intangible and less instinctively repugnant. But let psychoanalysis fall into what discredit it may, it has done us this great service of proving to us that the intense upper sympathy, indeed the dynamic relation either of love-will or love-sympathy, between parent and child, upon the upper plane, inevitably involves us in a conclusion of incest.

For although it is our aim to establish a purely spiritual dynamic relation on the upper plane only, yet, because of the inevitable polarity of the human psychic system, we shall arouse at the same time a dynamic sensual activity on the lower plane, the deeper sensual plane. We may be as pure as angels, and yet, being human, this will and must inevitably happen. When Mrs. Ruskin said that

John Ruskin should have married his mother she spoke the truth. He *was* married to his mother. For in spite of all our intention, all our creed, all our purity, all our desire, and all our will, once we arouse the dynamic relation in the upper, higher plane of love, we inevitably evoke a dynamic consciousness on the lower, deeper plane of sensual love. And then what?

Of course, parents can reply that their love, however intense, is pure, and has absolutely no sensual element. Maybe—and maybe not. But admit that it is so. It does not help. The intense excitement of the upper centres of sympathy willy-nilly arouses the lower centres. It arouses them to activity, even if it denies them any expression or any polarized connection. Our psyche is so framed that activity aroused on one plane provokes activity on the corresponding plane, automatically. So the intense *pure* love-relation between parent and child inevitably arouses the lower centres in the child, the centres of sex. Now the deeper sensual centres, once aroused, should find response from the sensual body of some other, some friend or lover. The response is impossible between parent and child. Myself, I believe that biologically there is radical sex-aversion between parent and child, at the deeper sensual centres. The sensual circuit *cannot* adjust itself spontaneously between the two.

So what have you? Child and parent intensely linked in adult love-sympathy and love-will, on the upper plane, and in the child, the deeper sensual centres aroused, but finding no correspondent, no objective, no polarized connection with another person. There they are, the powerful centres of sex, acting spasmodically, without balance. They must be polarized somehow. So they are polarized to the active upper centres within the child, and you get an introvert.

This is how introversion begins. The lower sexual centres are aroused. They find no sympathy, no connection, no response from outside, no expression. They are dynamically polarized by the upper centres within the individual. That is, the whole of the sexual or deeper sensual flow goes on upwards in the individual, to his own upper, from his own lower centres. The upper centres hold the lower in positive polarity. The flow goes on upwards.

There *must* be some reaction. And so you get, first and foremost, self-consciousness, an intense consciousness in the upper self of the lower self. This is the first disaster. Then you get the upper body exploiting the lower body. You get the hands exploiting the sensual body, in feeling, fingering, and in masturbation. You get a pornographic longing with regard to the self. You get the obscene postcards which most youths possess. You get the absolute lust for dirty stories, which so many men have. And you get various mild sex perversions, such as masturbation, and so on.

What does all this mean? It means that the activity of the lower psyche and lower body is polarized by the upper body. Eyes and ears want to gather sexual activity and knowledge. The mind becomes full of sex: and always, in an introvert, of his *own* sex. If we examine the apparent extroverts, like the flaunting Italian, we shall see the same thing. It is his own sex which obsesses him.

And today what have we but this? Almost inevitably we find in a child now an intense, precocious, secret sexual preoccupation. The upper self is rabidly engaged in exploiting the lower self. A child and its own roused, inflamed sex, its own shame and masturbation, its own cruel, secret sexual excitement and sex *curiosity*, this is the greatest tragedy of our day. The child does not so much want to *act* as to *know*. The thought of actual sex connection is usually repulsive. There is an aversion from the normal coition act. But the craving to feel, to see, to taste, to *know*, mentally in the head, this is insatiable. Anything, so that the sensation and experience shall come through the *upper* channels. This is the secret of our introversion and our perversion today. Anything rather than spontaneous, direct action from the sensual self. Anything rather than the merely normal passion. Introduce any trick, any idea, any mental element you can into sex, but make it an affair of the upper consciousness, the mind and eyes and mouth and fingers. This is our vice, our dirt, our disease.

And the adult, and the ideal are to blame. But the tragedy of our children, in their inflamed, solitary sexual excitement, distresses us beyond any blame.

It is time to drop the word love, and more than time to drop the ideal of love. Every frenzied individual is told to find fulfilment in love. So he tries. Whereas, there is no fulfilment in love. Half of our fulfilment comes *through* love, through strong, sensual love. But the central fulfilment, for a man, is that he possess his own soul in strength within him, deep and alone. The deep, rich aloneness, reached and perfected through love. And the passing beyond any further *quest* of love.

This central fullness of self-possession is our goal, if goal there be any. But there are two great *ways* of fulfilment. The first, the way of fulfilment through complete love, complete, passionate, deep love. And the second, the greater, the fulfilment through the accomplishment of religious purpose, the soul's earnest purpose. We work the love way falsely, from the upper self, and work it to death. The second way, of active unison in strong purpose, and in faith, this we only sneer at.

But to return to the child and the parent. The coming to the fulfilment of single aloneness, through love, is made impossible for us by the ideal, the monomania of more love. At the very *âge dangereuse*, when a woman should be accomplishing her own fulfilment into maturity and rich quiescence, she turns rabidly to seek a new lover. At the very crucial time when she should be coming to a state of pure equilibrium and rest with her husband, she turns rabidly against rest or peace or equilibrium or husband in any shape or form, and demands more love, more love, a new sort of lover, one who will "understand" her. And as often as not she turns to her son.

It is true, a woman reaches her goal of fulfilment through feeling. But through being "understood" she reaches nowhere, unless the lover understands what a vice it is for a woman to get herself and her sex into her head. A woman reaches her fulfilment through love, deep sensual love, and exquisite sensitive communion. But once she reaches the point of fulfilment, she should not break off to ask for more excitements. She should take the beauty of maturity and peace and quiet faithfulness upon her.

This she won't do, however, unless the man, her husband, goes on beyond her. When a man approaches the beginning of maturity and the fulfilment of his individual self, about the age of thirty-five, then is not his time to come to rest. On the contrary.

Deeply fulfilled through marriage, and at one with his own soul, he must now undertake the responsibility for the next step into the future. He must now give himself perfectly to some further purpose, some passionate purposive activity. Till a man makes the great resolution of aloneness and singleness of being, till he takes upon himself the silence and central appeasedness of maturity; and *then, after this*, assumes a sacred responsibility for the next purposive step into the future, there is no rest. The great resolution of aloneness and appeasedness, and the further deep assumption of responsibility in purpose—this is necessary to every parent, every father, every husband, at a certain point. If the resolution is never made, the responsibility never embraced, then the love-craving will run on into frenzy, and lay waste to the family. In the woman particularly the love-craving will run on to frenzy and disaster.

Seeking, seeking the fulfilment in the deep passional self; diseased with self-consciousness and sex in the head, foiled by the very loving weakness of the husband who has not the courage to withdraw into his own stillness and singleness, and put the wife under the spell of his fulfilled decision; the unhappy woman beats about for her insatiable satisfaction, seeking whom she may devour. And usually, she turns to her child. Here she provokes what she wants. Here, in her own son who belongs to her, she seems to find the last perfect response for which she is craving. He is a medium to her, she provokes from him her own answer. So she throws herself into a last great love for her son, a final and fatal devotion, that which would have been the richness and strength of her husband and is poison to her boy. The husband, irresolute, never accepting his own higher responsibility, bows and accepts. And the fatal round of introversion and "complex" starts once more. If man will never accept his own ultimate being, his final aloneness, and his last responsibility for life, then he must expect woman to dash from disaster to disaster, rootless and uncontrolled.

"*On revient toujours à son premier amour.*" It sounds like a cynicism today. As if we really meant: "*On ne revient jamais à son premier amour.*" But as a matter of fact, a man never leaves his first love, once the love is established. He may leave his first attempt at love. Once a man establishes a full dynamic communication, at the deeper and the higher centres, with a woman, this can never be broken. But sex in the head breaks down, and half circuits break down. Once the full circuit is established, however, this can never break down.

Nowadays, alas, we start off self-conscious, with sex in the head. We find a woman who is the same. We marry because we are "pals." The sex is a rather nasty fiasco. We keep up a pretense of "pals"—and nice love. Sex spins wilder in the head than ever. There is either a family of children whom the dissatisfied parents can devote themselves to, thereby perverting the miserable little creatures: or else there is a divorce. And at the great dynamic centres nothing has happened at all. Blank nothing. There has been no vital interchange at all in the whole of this beautiful marriage affair.

Establish between yourself and another individual a dynamic connection at only *two* of the four further poles, and you will have the devil of a job to break the connection. Especially if it be the first connection you have made. Especially if the other individual be the first in the field.

This is the case of the parents. Parents are first in the field of the child's further consciousness. They are criminal trespassers in that field. But that makes no matter. They are first in the field. They establish a dynamic connection between the two upper centres, the centres of the throat, the centres of the higher dynamic sympathy and cognition. They establish this circuit. And break it if you can. Very often not even death can break it.

And as we see, the establishment of the upper love-and-cognition circuit inevitably provokes the lower sex-sensual centres into action, even though there be no correspondence on the sensual plane between the two individuals concerned. Then see what happens. If you want to see the real desirable wife-spirit, look at a mother with her boy of eighteen. How she serves him, how she stimulates him, how her true female self is his, is wife-submissive to him as never, never it could be to a husband. This is the quiescent, flowering love of a mature woman. It is the very flower of a woman's love: sexually asking nothing, asking nothing of the be-loved, save that he shall be himself, and that for his living he shall accept the gift of her love. This is the perfect flower of married love, which a husband should put in his cap as he goes forward into the future in his supreme activity. For the husband, it is a great pledge, and a blossom. For the son also it seems wonderful. The woman now feels for the first time as a true wife might feel. And her feeling is towards her son.

Or, instead of mother and son, read father and daughter.

And then what? The son gets on swimmingly for a time, till he is faced with the actual fact of sex necessity. He gleefully inherits his adolescence and the world at large, without an obstacle in his way, mother-supported, mother-loved. Everything comes to him in glamour, he feels he sees wondrous much, understands a whole heaven, mother-stimulated. Think of the power which a mature woman thus infuses into her boy. He flares up like a flame in oxygen. No wonder they say geniuses mostly have great mothers. They mostly have sad fates.

And then? And then, with this glamorous youth? What is he actually to do with his sensual, sexual self? Bury it? Or make an effort with a stranger? For he is taught, even by his mother, that his manhood must not forego sex. Yet he is linked up in ideal love already, the best he will ever know.

No woman will give to a stranger that which she gives to her son, her father, or her brother: that beautiful and glamorous sub-mission which is truly the wife-submission. To a stranger, a hus-band, a woman insists on being queen, goddess, mistress, the posi-tive, the adored, the first and foremost and the one and only. This she will not ask from her near blood-kin. Of her blood-kin, there is always one she will love devotedly.

And so, the charming young girl who adores her father, or one of her brothers, is sought in marriage by the attractive young man who loves his mother devotedly. And a pretty business the mar-riage is. We can't think of it. Of course they may be good pals. It's the only thing left.

And there we are. The game is spoilt before it is begun. Within the circle of the family, owing to our creed of insatiable love, intense adult sympathies are provoked in quite young children. In Italy, the Italian stimulates adult sex-consciousness and sex-sympathy in his child, almost deliberately. But with us, it is usually spiritual sympathy and spiritual criticism. The adult experiences are provoked, the adult devotional sympathies are linked up, prematurely, as far as the child is concerned. We have the heart-wringing spectacle of intense parent-child love, a love intense as the love of man and woman, but not sexual; or else the great brother-sister devotion. And thus, the great love-experience which should lie in the future is forestalled. Within the family, the love-bond forms quickly, without the shocks and ruptures inevitable between strangers. And so, it is easiest, intensest—and seems the best. It seems the highest. You will not easily get a man to believe that his carnal love for the woman he has made his wife is as high a love as that he felt for his mother or sister.

The cream is licked off from life before the boy or the girl is twenty. Afterwards—repetition, disillusion, and barrenness.

And the cause? Always the same. That parents will not make the great resolution to come to rest within themselves, to possess their own souls in quiet and fullness. The man has not the courage to withdraw at last into his own soul's stillness and aloneness, and *then*, passionately and faithfully, to strive for the living future. The woman has not the courage to give up her hopeless insistence on love and her endless demand for love, demand of being loved. She has not the greatness of soul to relinquish her own self-assertion, and believe in the man who believes in himself and in his own soul's efforts: if there *are* any such men nowadays, which is very doubtful.

Alas, alas, the future! Your son, who has tasted the real beauty of wife-response in his mother or sister. Your daughter, who adores her brother, and who marries some woman's son. They are so charming to look at, such a lovely couple. And at first it is all such a good game, such good sport. Then each one begins to fret for the beauty of the lost, non-sexual, partial relationship. The sexual part of marriage has proved so—so empty. While that other loveliest thing—the poignant touch of devotion felt for mother or father or brother—why, this is missing altogether. The best is missing. The rest isn't worth much. Ah well, such is life. Settle down to it, and bring up the children carefully to more of the same. The future! You've had all your good days by the time you're twenty.

And, I ask you, what good will psychoanalysis do you in this state of affairs? Introduce an extra sex-motive to excite you for a bit and make you feel how thrillingly immoral things really are. And then—it all goes flat again. Father complex, mother complex, incest dreams: pah, when we've had the little excitement out of them we shall forget them as we have forgotten so many other catch-words. And we shall be just where we were before: unless we are worse, with *more* sex in the head, and more introversion, only more brazen.

⑤ XI ⑤

The Vicious Circle

Here is a very vicious circle. And how to get out of it? In the first place, we have to break the love-ideal, once and for all. Love, as we see, is not the only dynamic. Taking love in its greatest sense, and making it embrace every form of sympathy, every flow from the great sympathetic centres of the human body, still it is not the whole of the dynamic flow, it is only the one-half. There is always the other voluntary flow to reckon with, the intense motion of independence and singleness of self, the pride of isolation, and the profound fulfilment through power.

The very first thing of all to be recognized is the danger of idealism. It is the one besetting sin of the human race. It means the fall into automatism, mechanism, and nullity.

We know that life issues spontaneously at the great nodes of the psyche, the great nerve-centres. At first these are four only: then, after puberty, they become eight: later there may still be an extension of the dynamic consciousness, a further polarization. But eight is enough at the moment.

First at four, and then at eight dynamic centres of the human body, the human nervous system, life starts spontaneously into being. The soul bursts day by day into fresh impulses, fresh desire, fresh purpose, at these our polar centres. And from these dynamic generative centres issue the vital currents which put us into connection with our object. We have really no will and no choice, in the first place. It is our soul which acts within us, day by day unfolding us according to our own nature.

From the objective circuits and from the subjective circuits which establish and fulfil themselves at the first four centres of consciousness we derive our first being, our child-being, and also our first mind, our child-mind. By the objective circuits we mean those circuits which are established between the self and some external object: mother, father, sister, cat, dog, bird, or even tree or plant, or even further still, some particular place, some particular inanimate object, a knife or a chair or a cap or a doll or a wooden horse. For we must insist that every object which really enters effectively into our lives does so by direct connection. If I love my mother, it is because there is established between me and her a direct, powerful circuit of vital magnetism, call it what you will, but a direct flow of dynamic *vital* interchange and intercourse. I will not call this vital flow a *force*, because it depends on the incomprehensible initiative and control of the individual soul or self. Force is that which is directed only from some universal will or law. Life is *always* individual, and therefore never controlled by one law, one God. And therefore, since the living really sway the universe, even if unknowingly; therefore there is no one universal law, even for the physical forces. Because we insist that even the sun depends, for its heart-beat, its respiration, its pivotal motion, on the beating hearts of men and beast, on the dynamic of the soul-impulse in individual creatures. It is from the aggregate heart-beat of living individuals, of we know not how many or what sort of worlds, that the sun rests stable.

Which may be dismissed as metaphysics, although it is quite as valid or even as demonstrable as Newton's Law of Gravitation, which law still remains a law, even if not quite so absolute as heretofore.

But this is a digression. The argument is that between an individual and any external object with which he has an affective connection there exists a definite vital flow, as definite and concrete as the electric current whose polarized circuit sets our tramcars running and our lamps shining, or our Marconi wires vibrating. Whether this object be human, or animal, or plant, or quite inanimate, there is still a circuit. My dog, my canary has a polarized connection with me. Nay, the very cells in the ash-tree I loved as a child had a dynamic vibratory connection with the nuclei in my own centres of primary consciousness. And further still, the boots I have worn are so saturated with my own magnetism, my own vital activity, that if anyone else wear them I feel it is a trespass, almost as if another man used my hand to knock away a fly. I doubt very much if a blood-hound, when it takes a scent, *smells*, in our sense of the word. It receives at the infinitely sensitive telegraphic center of the dog's nostrils the vital vibration which remains in the inanimate object from the individual with whom the object was associated. I should like to know if a dog would trace a pair of quite new shoes which had merely been dragged at the end of a string. That is, does he follow the smell of the leather itself, or the vibration track of the individual whose vitality is communicated to the leather?

So, there is a definite vibratory rapport between a man and his surroundings, once he definitely gets into contact with these surroundings. Any particular locality, any house which has been lived in has a vibration, a transferred vitality of its own. This is either sympathetic or antipathetic to the succeeding individual in varying degree. But certain it is that the inhabitants who live at the foot of Etna will always have a certain pitch of life-vibration, antagonistic to the pitch of vibration even of a Palermitan, in some measure. And old houses are saturated with human presence, at last to a degree of indecency, unbearable. And tradition, in its most elemental sense, means the continuing of the same peculiar pitch of vital vibration.

Such is the objective dynamic flow between the psychic poles of the individual and the substance of the external object, animate or inanimate. The subjective dynamic flow is established between the four primary poles within the individual. Every dynamic connection begins from one or the other of the sympathetic centres: is, or should be, almost immediately polarized from the corresponding voluntary centre. Then a complete flow is set up, in one plane. But this always rouses the activity on the other, corresponding plane, more or less intense. There is a whole field of consciousness established, with positive polarity of the first plane, negative polarity of the second. Which being so, a whole fourfold field of dynamic consciousness now working within the individual, direct cognition takes place. The mind begins to know, and to strive to know.

The business of the mind is first and foremost the pure joy of knowing and comprehending the pure joy of consciousness. The second business is to act as medium, as interpreter, as agent between the individual and his object. The mind should *not* act as a director or controller of the spontaneous centres. These the soul alone must control: the soul being that forever unknowable reality which causes us to rise into being. There is continual conflict between the soul, which is forever sending forth incalculable impulses, and the psyche, which is conservative, and wishes to persist in its old motions, and the mind, which wishes to have "freedom," that is spasmodic, idea-driven control. Mind, and conservative psyche, and the incalculable soul, these three are a trinity of powers in every human being. But there is something even beyond these. It is the individual in his pure singleness, in his totality of consciousness, in his oneness of being: the Holy Ghost which is with us after our Pentecost, and which we may not deny. When I say to myself, "I am wrong," knowing with sudden insight that I *am* wrong, then this is the whole self speaking, the Holy Ghost. It is no piece of mental inference. It is not just the soul sending forth a flash. It is my whole being speaking in one voice, soul and mind and psyche transfigured into oneness. This voice of my being I may *never* deny. When at last, in all my storms, my whole self speaks, then there is a pause. The soul collects itself into pure silence and isolation—perhaps after much pain. The mind suspends its knowledge, and waits. The psyche becomes strangely still. And then, after the pause, there is fresh beginning, a new life adjustment. Conscience is the being's consciousness, when the individual is conscious *in toto*, when he knows in full. It is something which includes and which far surpasses mental consciousness. Every man must live as far as he can by his own soul's conscience. But not according to any ideal. To submit the conscience to a creed, or an idea, or a tradition, or even an impulse, is our ruin.

To make the mind the absolute ruler is as good as making a

Cook's tourist-interpreter a king and a god because he can speak several languages and make an Arab understand that an Englishman wants fish for supper. And to make an ideal a ruling principle is about as stupid as if a bunch of travellers should never cease giving each other and their dragoman sixpence because the dragoman's main idea of virtue is the virtue of sixpence-giving. In the same way, we *know* we cannot live purely by impulse. Neither can we live solely by tradition. We must live by all three, ideal, impulse, and tradition, each in its hour. But the real guide is the pure conscience, the voice of the self in its wholeness, the Holy Ghost.

We have fallen now into the mistake of idealism. Man always falls into one of the three mistakes. In China, it is tradition. And in the South Seas, it seems to have been impulse. Ours is idealism. Each of the three modes is a true life-mode. But any one, alone or dominant, brings us to destruction. We must depend on the wholeness of our being, ultimately only on that, which is our Holy Ghost within us. Whereas, in an ideal of love and benevolence, we have tried to automatize ourselves into little love-engines always stoked with the sorrows or beauties of other people, so that we can get up steam of charity or righteous wrath. A great trick is to pour on the fire the oil of our indignation at somebody else's wickedness, and then, when we've got up steam like hell, back the engine and run bish! smash! against the belly of the offender. Because he said he didn't want to love any more, we hate him for evermore, and try to run over him, every bit of him, with our love-tanks. And all the time we yell at him: "Will you deny love, you villain? Will you?" And by the time he faintly squeaks, "I want to be loved! I want to be loved!" we have got so used to running over him with our love-tanks that we don't feel in a hurry to leave off.

> *"Sois mon frère, ou je te tue."*
> *"Sois mon frère, ou je me tue."*

There are the two parrot-threats of love, on which our loving centuries have run as on a pair of railway-lines. Excuse me if I want to get out of the train. Excuse me if I can't get up any love-steam any more. My boilers are burst.

We have made a mistake, laying down love like the permanent way of a great emotional transport system. There we are, however, running on wheels on the lines of our love. And of course we have only two directions, forwards and backwards. "Onward, Christian soldiers, towards the great terminus where bottles of sterilized milk for the babies are delivered at the bedroom windows by noiseless airplanes each morn, where the science of dentistry is so perfect that teeth are planted in a man's mouth without his knowing it, where twilight sleep is so delicious that every woman longs for her next confinement, and where nobody ever has to do anything except turn a handle now and then in a spirit of universal love—" That is the forward direction of the English-speaking race. The Germans unwisely backed their engine. "We have a city of light. But instead of lying ahead it lies direct behind us. So reverse engines. Reverse engines, and away, away to our city, where the sterilized milk is delivered by noiseless airplanes, *at the very precise minute when our great doctors of the Fatherland have diagnosed that it is good for you:* where the teeth are not only so painlessly planted that they grow like living rock, but where their composition is such that the friction of eating stimulates the cells of the jaw-bone and develops the *superman strength of will which makes us gods:* and where not only is twilight sleep serene, but into the sleeper are inculcated the most useful and instructive dreams, calculated to perfect the character of the young citizen at this crucial period, and to enlighten permanently the mind of the happy mother, with regard to her new duties towards her child and towards our great Fatherland—"

Here you see we are, on the railway, with New Jerusalem ahead, and New Jerusalem away behind us. But of course it was very wrong of the Germans to reverse their engines, and cause one long collision all along the line. Why should we go *their* way to the New Jerusalem, when of course they might so easily have kept on going our way. And now there's wreckage all along the line! But clear the way is our motto—or make the Germans clear it. Because get on we will.

Meanwhile we sit rather in the cold, waiting for the train to get a start. People keep on signalling with green lights and red lights. And it's all very bewildering.

As for me, I'm off. I'm damned if I'll be shunted along any more. And I'm thrice damned if I'll go another yard towards that sterilized New Jerusalem, either forwards or backwards. New Jerusalem may rot, if it waits for me. I'm not going.

So good-bye! There we leave humanity, encamped in an appalling mess beside the railway-smash of love, sitting down, however, and having not a bad time, some of 'em, feeding themselves fat on the plunder: others, farther down the line, with mouths green from eating grass. But all grossly, stupidly, automatically gabbling about getting the love-service running again, the trains booked for the New Jerusalem well on the way once more. And occasionally a good engine gives a screech of love, and something seems to be about to happen. And sometimes there is enough steam to set the indignation-whistles whistling. But never any more will there be enough love-steam to get the system properly running. It is done.

Good-bye, then! You may have laid your line from one end to the other of the infinite. But still there's plenty of hinterland. I'll go. Good-bye. Ach, it will be so nice to be alone: not to hear you, not to see you, not to smell you, humanity. I wish you no ill, but wisdom. Good-bye!

To be alone with one's own soul. Not to be alone without my own soul, mind you. But to be alone with one's own soul! This, and the joy of it, is the real goal of love. My own soul, and myself. Not my ego, my conceit of myself. But my very soul. To be at one in my own self. Not to be questing any more. Not to be yearning, seeking, hoping, desiring, aspiring. But to pause, and be alone.

And to have one's own "gentle spouse" by one's side, of course, to dig one in the ribs occasionally. Because really, being alone in peace means being two people together. Two people who can be silent together, and not conscious of one another outwardly. Me in my silence, she in hers, and the balance, the equilibrium, the pure circuit between us. With occasional lapses of course: digs in the ribs if one gets too vague or self-sufficient.

They say it is better to travel than to arrive. It's not been my experience, at least. The journey of love has been rather a lacerating, if well-worth-it, journey. But to come at last to a nice place under the trees, with your "amiable spouse" who has at last learned to hold her tongue and not to bother about rights and wrongs: her own particularly. And then to pitch a camp, and cook your rabbit, and eat him: and to possess your own soul in silence, and to feel all the clamour lapse. That is the best I know.

I think it is terrible to be young. The ecstasies and agonies of love, the agonies and ecstasies of fear and doubt and drop-by-drop fulfilment, realization. The awful process of human relationships, love and marital relationships especially. Because we all make a very, very bad start today, with our idea of love in our head, and our sex in our head as well. All the fight till one is bled of one's self-consciousness and sex-in-the-head. All the bitterness of the conflict with this devil of an amiable spouse, who has got herself so stuck in her own head. It is terrible to be young. But one fights one's way through it, till one is cleaned: the self-consciousness and sex-idea burned out of one, cauterized out bit by bit, and the self whole again, and at last free.

The best thing I have known is the stillness of accomplished marriage, when one possesses one's own soul in silence, side by side with the amiable spouse, and has left off craving and raving and being only half one's self. But I must say, I know a great deal more about the craving and raving and sore ribs than about the accomplishment. And I must confess that I feel this self-same "accomplishment" of the fulfilled being is only a preparation for new responsibilities ahead, new unison in effort and conflict, the effort to make, with other men, a little new way into the future, and to break through the hedge of the many.

But—to your tents, my Israel. And to that precious baby you've left slumbering there. What I meant to say was, in each phase of life you have a great circuit of human relationship to establish and fulfil. In childhood, it is the circuit of family love, established at the first four consciousness centres, and gradually fulfilling itself, completing itself. At adolescence, the first circuit of family love should be completed, dynamically finished. And then, it falls into quiescence. After puberty, family love should fall quiescent in a child. The love never breaks. It continues static and basic, the basis of the emotional psyche, the foundation of the self. It is like the moon when the moon at last subsides into her eternal orbit, round the earth. She travels in her orbit so inevitably that she forgets, and becomes unaware. She only knits her brows over the earth's greater aberrations in space.

The circuit of parental love, once fulfilled, is not done away with, but only established into silence. The child is then free to establish the new connections, in which he surpasses his parents. And let us repeat, parents should never try to establish adult relations, of sympathy or interest or anything else, between themselves and their children. The attempt to do so only deranges the deep primary circuit which is the dynamic basis of our living. It is a clambering upwards only by means of a broken foundation. Parents should remain parents, children children, forever, and the great gulf preserved between the two. Honour thy father and thy mother should always be a leading commandment. But this can only take place when father and mother keep their true parental distances, dignity, reserve, and limitation. As soon as father and mother try to become the *friends* and *companions* of their children, they break the root of life, they rupture the deepest dynamic circuit of living, they derange the whole flow of life for themselves and their children.

For let us reiterate and reiterate: you cannot mingle and confuse the various modes of dynamic love. If you try, you produce horrors. You cannot plant the heart below the diaphragm or put an ocular eye in the navel. No more can you transfer parent love into friend love or adult love. Parent love is established at the great primary centres, where man is father and child, playmate and brother, but where he *cannot* be comrade or lover. Comrade and lover, this is the dynamic activity of the further centres, the second four centres. And these second four centres must be active in the parent, their intense circuit established even if not fulfilled, long before the child is born. The circuit of friendship, of personal companionship, of sexual love must needs be established before the child is begotten, or at least before it attains to adolescence. These circuits of the extended field are already fully established in the parent before the centres of correspondence in the child are even formed. When therefore the four great centres of the extended consciousness arouse in a child, at adolescence, they must needs seek a strange complement, a foreign conjunction.

Not only is this the case, but the actual dynamic impulse of the new life which rouses at puberty is *alien* to the original dynamic flow. The new wave-length by no means corresponds. The new vibration by no means harmonizes. Force the two together, and you cause a terrible frictional excitement and jarring. It is this instinctive recognition of the different dynamic vibrations from different centres, in different modes, and in different directions of positive and negative, which lies at the base of savage taboo. After puberty, members of one family should be taboo to one another. There should be the most definite limits to the degree of contact. And mothers-in-law should be taboo to their daughters' husbands, and fathers-in-law to their sons' wives. We must again begin to learn the great laws of the first dynamic life-circuits. These laws we now make havoc of, and consequently we make havoc of our own soul, psyche, mind, and health.

This book is written primarily concerning the child's consciousness. It is not intended to enter the field of the post-puberty consciousness. But yet, the dynamic relation of the child is established so directly with the physical and psychical soul of the parent, that to get any inkling of dynamic child-consciousness we must understand something of parent-consciousness.

We assert that the parent-child love-mode excludes the possibility of the man-and-woman or friend-and-friend love mode. We assert that the polarity of the first four poles is inconsistent with the polarity of the second four poles. Nay, between the two great fields is a certain dynamic opposition, resistance, even antipathy. So that in the natural course of life there is no possibility of confusing parent love and adult love.

But we are mental creatures, and with the explosive and mechanistic aid of ideas we can pervert the whole psyche. Only, however, in a destructive degree, not in a positive or constructive.

Let us return then. In the ordinary course of development, by the time that the child is born and grown to puberty the whole dynamic soul of the mother is engaged: first, with the children, and second, on the further, higher plane, with the husband, and with her own friends. So that when the child reaches adolescence it must inevitably cast abroad for connection.

But now let us remember the actual state of affairs today, when the poles are reversed between the sexes. The woman is now the responsible party, the law-giver, the culture-bearer. She is the conscious guide and director of the man. She bears his soul between her two hands. And her sex is just a function or an instrument of power. This being so, the man is really the servant and the fount of emotion, love and otherwise.

Which is all very well, while the fun lasts. But like all perverted processes, it is exhaustive, and like the fun wears out. Leaving an exhaustion, and an irritation. Each looks on the other as a perverter of life. Almost invariably a married woman, as she passes the age of thirty, conceives a dislike or a contempt of her husband, or a pity which is too near contempt. Particularly if he be a good husband, a true modern. And he, for his part, though just as jarred inside himself, resents only the fact that he is not loved as he ought to be.

Then starts a new game. The woman, even the most virtuous, looks abroad for new sympathy. She will have a new man-friend, if nothing more. But as a rule she has got something more. She has got her children.

A relation between mother and child today is practically *never* parental. It is personal—which means, it is critical and deliberate, and adult in provocation. The mother, in her new role of idealist and life-manager never, practically for one single moment, gives her child the unthinking response from the deep dynamic centres. No, she gives it what is good for it. She shoves milk in its mouth as the clock strikes, she shoves it to sleep when the milk is swallowed, and she shoves it ideally through baths and massage, promenades and practice, till the little organism develops like a mushroom to stand on its own feet. Then she continues her ideal shoving of it through all the stages of an ideal up-bringing, she loves it as a chemist loves his test-tubes in which he analyses his salts. The poor little object is his mother's ideal. But of her head she dictates his providential days, and by the force of her deliberate mentally-directed love-will she pushes him up into boyhood. The poor little devil never knows one moment when he is not encompassed by the beautiful, benevolent, idealistic, Botticelli-pure, and finally obscene love-will of the mother. Never, never one mouthful does he drink of the milk of human kindness: always the sterilized milk of human benevolence. There is no mother's milk today, save in tigers' udders, and in the udders of sea-whales. Our children drink a decoction of ideal love, at the breast.

Never for one moment, poor baby, the deep warm stream of love from the mother's bowels to his bowels. Never for one moment the dark proud recoil into rest, the soul's separation into deep, rich independence. Never this lovely rich forgetfulness, as a cat trots off and utterly forgets her kittens, utterly, richly forgets them, till suddenly, click, the dynamic circuit reverses itself in her, and she remembers, and rages round in a frenzy, shouting for her young.

Our miserable infants never know this joy and richness and pang of real maternal warmth. Our wonderful mothers never let us out of their minds for one single moment. Not for a second do they allow us to escape from their ideal benevolence. Not one single breath does a baby draw, free from the imposition of the pure, unselfish, Botticelli-holy, detestable *love-will* of the mother. Always the *will*, the will, the love-will, the ideal will, directed from the ideal mind. Always this stone, this scorpion of maternal nourishment. Always this infernal self-conscious Madonna starving our living guts and bullying us to death with her love.

We have made the idea supplant both impulse and tradition.

We have no spark of wholeness. And we live by an evil love-will. Alas, the great spontaneous mode is abrogated. There is no lovely great flux of vital sympathy, no rich rejoicing of pride into isolation and independence. There is no reverence for great traditions of parenthood. No, there is substitute for everything—life-substitute—just as we have butter-substitute, and meat-substitute, and sugar-substitute, and leather-substitute, and silk-substitute, so we have life-substitute. We have beastly benevolence, and foul good-will, and stinking charity, and poisonous ideals.

The poor modern brat, shoved horribly into life by an effort of will, and shoved up towards manhood by every appliance that can be applied to it, especially the appliance of the maternal will, it is really too pathetic to contemplate. The only thing that prevents us wringing our hands is the remembrance that the little devil will grow up and beget other similar little devils of his own, to invent more airplanes and hospitals and germ-killers and food-substitutes and poison-gases. The problem of the future is a question of the strongest poison-gas. Which is certainly a very sure way out of our vicious circle.

There is no way out of a vicious circle, of course, except breaking the circle. And since the mother-child relationship is today the viciousest of circles, what are we to do? Just wait for the results of the poison-gas competition, presumably.

Oh, ideal humanity, how detestable and despicable you are! And how you deserve your own poison-gases! How you deserve to perish in your own stink.

It is no use contemplating the development of the modern child, born out of the mental-conscious love-will, born to be another unit of self-conscious love-will: an ideal-born beastly little entity with a devil's own will of its own, benevolent, of course, and a Satan's own seraphic self-consciousness, like a beastly Botticelli brat.

Once we really consider this modern process of life and the love-will, we could throw the pen away, and spit, and say three cheers for the inventors of poison-gas. Is there not an American who is supposed to have invented a breath of heaven whereby, drop one popcornful in Hampstead, one in Brixton, one in East Ham, and one in Islington, and London is a Pompeii in five minutes! Or was the American only bragging? Because anyhow, whom has he experimented on? I read it in the newspaper, though. London a Pompeii in five minutes. Makes the gods look silly!

XII

Litany of Exhortations

I thought I'd better turn over a new leaf, and start a new chapter. The intention of the last chapter was to find a way out of the vicious circle. And it ended in poison-gas.

Yes, dear reader, so it did. But you've not silenced me yet, for all that.

We're in a nasty mess. We're in a vicious circle. And we're making a careful study of poison-gases. The secret of Greek fire was lost long ago, when the world left off being wonderful and ideal. Now it is wonderful and ideal again, much wonderfuller and *much* more ideal. So we ought to do something rare in the way of poison-gas. London a Pompeii in five minutes! How to outdo Vesuvius!—title of a new book by American authors.

There is only one single other thing to do. And it's more difficult than poison-gas. It is to leave off loving. It is to leave off benevolenting and having a good will. It is to cease utterly. Just leave off. Oh, parents, see that your children get their dinners and clean sheets, but don't love them. Don't love them one single grain, and don't let anybody else love them. Give them their dinners and leave them alone. You've already loved them to perdition. Now leave them alone, to find their own way out.

Wives, don't love your husbands any more: even if they cry for it, the great babies! Sing: "I've had enough of that old sauce." And leave off loving them or caring for them one single bit. Don't even hate them or dislike them. Don't have any stew with them at all. Just boil the eggs and fill the salt-cellars and be quite nice, and in your own soul be alone and be still. Be alone, and be still, preserving all the human decencies, and abandoning the indecency of desires and benevolencies and devotions, those beastly poison-gas apples of the Sodom vine of the love-will.

Wives, don't love your husbands nor your children nor anybody. Sit still, and say Hush! And while you shake the duster out of the drawing-room window, say to yourself—"In the sweetness of solitude." And when your husband comes in and says he's afraid he's got a cold and is going to have double pneumonia, say quietly: "Surely not." And if he wants the ammoniated quinine, give it him if he can't get it for himself. But don't let him drive you out of your solitude, your singleness within yourself. And if your little boy falls down the steps and makes his mouth bleed, nurse and comfort him, but say to yourself, even while you tremble with the shock: "Alone. Alone. Be alone, my soul." And if the servant smashes three electric-light-bulbs in three minutes, say to her: "How very inconsiderate and careless of you!" But say to yourself: "Don't hear it, my soul. Don't take fright at the pop of a light-bulb."

Husbands, don't love your wives any more. If they flirt with men younger or older than yourselves, let your blood not stir. If you can go away, go away. But if you must stay and see her, then say to her, "I would rather you didn't flirt in my presence, Eleanora." Then, when she goes red and loosens torrents of indignation, don't answer any more. And when she floods into tears, say quietly in your own self, "My soul is my own"; and go away, be alone as much as possible. And when she works herself up, and says she must have love or she will die, then say: "Not my love, however." And to all her threats, her tears, her entreaties, her reproaches, her cajolements, her winsomenesses, answer nothing, but say to yourself: "Shall I be implicated in this display of the love-will? Shall I be blasted by this false lightning?" And though you tremble in every fibre, and feel sick, vomit-sick with the scene, still contain yourself, and say: "My soul is my own. It shall not be violated." And learn, learn, learn the one and only lesson worth learning at last. Learn to walk in the sweetness of the possession of your own soul. And whether your wife weeps as she takes off her amber beads at night, or whether your neighbor in the train sits in your coat bottoms, or whether your superior in the office makes supercilious remarks, or your inferior is familiar and impudent; or whether you read in the newspaper that Lloyd George is performing another iniquity, or the Germans plotting another plot, say to yourself: "My soul is my own. My soul is with myself, and beyond implication." And wait, quietly, in possession of your own soul, till you meet another man who has made the choice, and kept it. Then you will know him by the look on his face: half a dangerous look, a look of Cain, and half a look of gathered beauty. Then you two will make the nucleus of a new society—Ooray! Bis! Bis!!

But if you should never meet such a man: and if your wife should torture you every day with her love-will: and even if she should force herself into a consumption, like Catherine Linton in *Wuthering Heights*, owing to her obstinate and determined love-will (which is quite another matter than love): and if you see the world inventing poison-gas and falling into its poisoned grave: never give in, but be alone, and utterly alone with your own soul, in the stillness and sweet possession of your own soul. And don't even be angry. And *never* be sad. Why should you? It's not your affair.

But if your wife should accomplish for herself the sweetness of her own soul's possession, then gently, delicately let the new mode assert itself, the new mode of relation between you, with something of spontaneous paradise in it, the apple of knowledge at last digested. But, my word, what belly-aches meanwhile. That apple is harder to digest than a lead gun-cartridge.

XIII

Cosmological

Well, dear reader, Chapter XII was short, and I hope you found it sweet.

But remember, this is an essay on Child Consciousness, not a tract on Salvation. It isn't my fault that I am led at moments into exhortation.

Well, then, what about it? One fact now seems very clear—at any rate to me. We've got to pause. We haven't got to gird our loins with a new frenzy and our larynxes with a new Glory Song. Not a bit of it. Before you dash off to put salt on the tail of a new religion or of a new Leader of Men, dear reader, sit down quietly and pull yourself together. Say to yourself: "Come now, what is it all about?" And you'll realize, dear reader, that you're all in a fluster, inwardly. Then say to yourself: "Why am I in such a fluster?" And you'll see you've no reason at all to be so: except that it's rather exciting to be in a fluster, and it may seem rather stale eggs to be in no fluster at all about anything. And yet, dear little reader, once you consider it quietly, it's *so* much nicer *not* to be in a fluster. It's so much nicer not to feel one's deeper innards storming like the Bay of Biscay. It is so much better to get up and say to the waters of one's own troubled spirit: Peace, be still . . . ! And they will be still . . . perhaps.

And then one realizes that all the wild storms of anxiety and frenzy were only so much breaking of eggs. It isn't our business to live anybody's life, or to die anybody's death, except our own. Nor to save anybody's soul, nor to put anybody in the right; nor yet in the wrong, which is more the point today. But to be still, and to ignore the false fine frenzy of the seething world. To turn away, now, each one into the stillness and solitude of his own soul. And there to remain in the quiet with the Holy Ghost which is to each man his own true soul.

This is the way out of the vicious circle. Not to rush round on the periphery, like a rabbit in a ring, trying to break through. But to retreat to the very centre, and there to be filled with a new strange stability, polarized in unfathomable richness with the center of centres. We are so silly, trying to invent devices and machines for flying off from the surface of the earth. Instead of realizing that for us the deep satisfaction lies not in escaping, but in getting into the perfect circuit of the earth's terrestrial magnetism. Not in breaking away. What is the good of trying to break away from one's own? What is the good of a tree desiring to fly like a bird in the sky, when a bird is rooted in the earth as surely as a tree is? Nay, the bird is only the topmost leaf of the tree, fluttering in the high air, but attached as close to the tree as any other leaf. Mr. Einstein's Theory of Relativity does not supersede the Newtonian Law of Gravitation or of Inertia. It only says, "Beware! The Law of Inertia is not the simple ideal proposition you would like to make of it. It is a vast complexity. Gravitation is not one elemental uncouth force. It is a strange, infinitely complex, subtle aggregate of forces." And yet, however much it may waggle, a stone does fall to earth if you drop it.

We should like, vulgarly, to rejoice and say that the new Theory of Relativity releases us from the old obligation of centrality. It does no such thing. It only makes the old centrality much more strange, subtle, complex, and vital. It only robs us of the nice old ideal simplicity. Which ideal simplicity and logicalness has become such a fish-bone stuck in our throats.

The universe is once more in the mental melting-pot. And you can melt it down as long as you like, and mutter all the jargon and abracadabra, *aldeboronti fosco fornio* of science that mental monkey-tricks can teach you, you won't get anything in the end but a formula and a lie. The atom? Why, the moment you discover the atom it will explode under your nose. The moment you discover the ether it will evaporate. The moment you get down to the real basis of anything, it will dissolve into a thousand problematic constituents. And the more problems you solve, the more will spring up with their fingers at their nose, making a fool of you.

There is only one clue to the universe. And that is the individual soul within the individual being. That outer universe of suns and moons and atoms is a secondary affair. It is the death-result of living individuals. There is a great polarity in life itself. Life itself is dual. And the duality is life and death. And death is not just shadow or mystery. It is the negative reality of life. It is what we call Matter and Force, among other things.

Life is individual, always was individual and always will be. Life consists of living individuals, and always did so consist, in the beginning of everything. There never was any universe, any cosmos, of which the first reality was anything but living, incorporate individuals. I don't say the individuals were exactly like you and me. And they were never wildly different.

And therefore it is time for the idealist and the scientist—they are one and the same, really—to stop his monkey-jargon about the atom and the origin of life and the mechanical clue to the universe. There isn't any such thing. I might as well say: "Then they took the cart, and rubbed it all over with grease. Then they sprayed it with white wine, and spun round the right wheel five hundred revolutions to the minute and the left wheel, in the opposite direction, seven hundred and seventy-seven revolutions to the minute. Then a burning torch was applied to each axle. And lo, the footboard of the cart began to swell, and suddenly as the cart groaned and writhed, the horse was born, and lay panting between the shafts." The whole scientific theory of the universe is not worth such a tale: that the cart conceived and gave birth to the horse.

I do not believe one-fifth of what science can tell me about the sun. I do not believe for one second that the moon is a dead world spelched off from our globe. I do not believe that the stars came flying off from the sun like drops of water when you spin your wet hanky. I have believed it for twenty years, because it seemed so ideally plausible. Now I don't accept any ideal plausibilities at all. I look at the moon and the stars, and I know I don't believe anything that I am told about them. Except that I like their names, Aldebaran and Cassiopeia, and so on.

I have tried, and even brought myself to believe in a clue to the outer universe. And in the process I have swallowed such a lot of jargon that I would rather listen now to a Negro witch-doctor than to Science. There is nothing in the world that is true except empiric discoveries which work in actual appliances. I know that the sun is hot. But I won't be told that the sun is a ball of blazing gas which spins round and fizzes. No, thank you.

At length, for *my* part, I know that life, and life only is the clue to the universe. And that the living individual is the clue to life. And that it always was so, and always will be so.

When the living individual dies, then is the realm of death established. Then you get Matter and Elements and atoms and forces and sun and moon and earth and stars and so forth. In short, the outer universe, the Cosmos. The Cosmos is nothing but the aggregate of the dead bodies and dead energies of by-gone individuals. The dead bodies decompose as we know into earth, air, and water, heat, and radiant energy and free electricity and innumerable other scientific facts. The dead souls likewise decompose—or else they don't decompose. But if they *do* decompose, then it is not into any elements of Matter and physical energy. They decompose into some psychic reality, and into some potential will. They re-enter into the living psyche of living individuals. The living soul partakes of the dead souls, as the living breast partakes of the outer air, and the blood partakes of the sun. The soul, the individuality, never resolves itself through death into physical constituents. The dead soul remains always soul, and always retains its individual quality. And it does not disappear, but re-enters into the soul of the living, of some living individual or individuals. And there it continues its part in life, as a death-witness and a life-agent. But it does not, ordinarily, have any separate existence there, but is incorporate in the living individual soul. But in some extraordinary cases, the dead soul may really act separately in a living individual.

How this all is, and what are the laws of the relation between life and death, the living and the dead, I don't know. But that this relation exists, and exists in a manner as I describe it, for my own part I know. And I am fully aware that once we direct our living attention this way, instead of to the absurdity of the atom, then we have a whole *living* universe of knowledge before us. The universe of life and death, of which we, whose business it is to live and to die, know nothing. Whilst concerning the universe of Force and Matter we pile up theories and make staggering and disastrous discoveries of machinery and poison-gas, all of which we were much better without.

It is life we have to live by, not machines and ideals. And life means nothing else, even, but the spontaneous living soul which is our central reality. The spontaneous, living, individual soul, this is the clue, and the only clue. All the rest is derived.

How it is contrived that the individual soul in the living sways the very sun in its centrality, I do not know. But it is so. It is the peculiar dynamic polarity of the living soul in every weed or bug or beast, each one separately and individually polarized with the great returning pole of the sun, that maintains the sun alive. For I take it that the sun is the great sympathetic centre of our in-animate universe. I take it that the sun breathes in the effluence of all that fades and dies. Across space fly the innumerable vibra-tions which are the basis of all matter. They fly, breathed out from the dying and the dead, from all that which is passing away, even in the living. These vibrations, these elements pass away across space, and are breathed back again. The sun itself is invis-ible as the soul. The sun itself is the soul of the inanimate uni-verse, the aggregate clue to the substantial death, if we may call it so. The sun is the great active pole of the sympathetic death-activity. To the sun fly the vibrations or the molecules in the great sympathy-mode of death, and in the sun they are renewed, they turn again as the great gift back again from the sympathetic death-centre towards life, towards the living. But it is not even

the dead which *really* sustain the sun. It is the dynamic relation
between the solar plexus of individuals and the sun's core, a perfect circuit. The sun is materially composed of all the effluence
of the dead. But the *quick* of the sun is polarized with the living,
the sun's quick is polarized in dynamic relation with the quick
of life in all living things, that is, with the solar plexus in mankind. A direct dynamic connection between my solar plexus and
the sun.

Likewise, as the sun is the great fiery, vivifying pole of the
inanimate universe, the moon is the other pole, cold and keen and
vivifying, corresponding in some way to a *voluntary* pole. We
live between the polarized circuit of sun and moon. And the
moon is polarized with the lumbar ganglion, primarily, in man.
Sun and moon are dynamically polarized to our actual tissue, they
affect this tissue all the time.

The moon is, as it were, the pole of our particular terrestrial
volition in the universe. What holds the earth swinging in space
is first the great dynamic attraction to the sun, and then counter-
posing assertion of independence, singleness, which is polarized
in the moon. The moon is the clue to our earth's individual identity, in the wide universe.

The moon is an immense magnetic centre. It is quite wrong
to say she is a dead snowy world with craters and so on. I should
say she is composed of some very intense element, like phosphorus or radium, some element or elements which have very
powerful chemical and kinetic activity, and magnetic activity,
affecting us through space.

It is not the sun which we see in heaven. It is the rushing
thither and the rushing thence of the vibrations expelled by death
from the body of life, and returned back again to the body of
life. Possibly even a dead soul makes its journey to the sun and
back, before we receive it again in our breast. Just as the breath
we breathe out flies to the sun and back, before we breathe it
in again. And as the water that evaporates rises right to the sun,
and returns here. What we see is the great golden rushing thither,
from the death exhalation, towards the sun, as a great cloud of
bees flying to swarm upon the invisible queen, circling round,

and loosing again. This is what we see of the sun. The centre is invisible forever.

And of the moon the same. The moon has her back to us forever. Not her face, as we like to think. The moon also pulls the water, as the sun does. But not in evaporation. The moon pulls by the magnetic force we call gravitation. Gravitation not being quite such a Newtonian simple apple as we are accustomed to find it, we are perhaps farther off from understanding the tides of the ocean than we were before the fruit of the tree fell to Sir Isaac's head. It is certainly not simple little-things-tumble-towards-big-things gravitation. In the moon's pull there is peculiar, quite special force exerted over those water-born substances, phosphorus, salt, and lime. The dynamic energy of salt water is something quite different from that of fresh water. And it is this dynamic energy which the sea gives off, and which connects it with the moon. And the moon is some strange coagulation of substance such as salt, phosphorus, soda. It certainly isn't a snowy cold world, like a world of our own gone cold. Nonsense. It is a globe of dynamic substance like radium or phosphorus, coagulated upon a certain vivid pole of energy, which pole of energy is directly polarized with our earth, in opposition with the sun.

The moon is born from the death of individuals. All things, in their oneing, their unification into the pure, universal oneness, evaporate and fly like an imitation breath towards the sun. Even the crumbling rocks breathe themselves off in this rocky death, to the sun of heaven, during the day.

But at the same time, during the night they breathe themselves off to the moon. If we come to think of it, light and dark are a question both of the third body, the intervening body, what we will call, by stretching a point, the individual. As we all know, apart from the existence of molecules of individual matter, there is neither light nor dark. A universe utterly without matter, we don't know whether it is light or dark. Even the pure space between the sun and moon, the blue space, we don't know whether, in itself, it is light or dark. We can say it is light, we can say it is dark. But light and dark are terms which apply only to ourselves, the third, the intermediate, the substantial, the individual.

If we come to think of it, light and dark only mean whether we have our face or our back towards the sun. If we have our face to the sun, then we establish the circuit of cosmic or universal or material or infinite sympathy. These four adjectives, cosmic, universal, material, and infinite are almost interchangeable, and apply, as we see, to that realm of the non-individual existence which we call the realm of the substantial death. It is the universe which has resulted from the death of individuals. And to this universe alone belongs the quality of infinity: to the universe of death. Living individuals have no infinity save in this relation to the total death-substance and death-being, the summed-up cosmos.

Light and dark, these great wonders, are relative to us alone. These are two vast poles of the cosmic energy and of material existence. These are the vast poles of cosmic sympathy, which we call the sun, and the other white pole of cosmic volition, which we call the moon. To the sun belong the great forces of heat and radiant energy, to the moon belong the great forces of magnetism and electricity, radium-energy, and so on. The sun is not, in any sense, a material body. It is an invariable intense pole of cosmic energy, and what we see are the particles of our terrestrial decomposition flying thither and returning, as fine grains of iron would fly to an intense magnet, or better, as the draught in a room veers towards the fire, attracted infallibly, as a moth towards a candle. The moth is drawn to the candle as the draught is drawn to the fire, in the absolute spell of the material polarity of fire. And air escapes again, hot and different, from the fire. So is the sun.

Fire, we say, is combustion. It is marvellous how science proceeds like witchcraft and alchemy, by means of an abracadabra which has no earthly sense. Pray, what is combustion? You can try and answer scientifically, till you are black in the face. All you can say is that it is *that which happens* when matter is raised to a certain temperature—and so forth and so forth. You might as well say, a word is that which happens when I open my mouth and squeeze my larnyx and make various tricks with my throat muscles. All these explanations are so senseless. They describe the apparatus, and think they have described the event.

Fire may be accompanied by combustion, but combustion is not necessarily accompanied by fire. All A is B, but all B is not A. And therefore fire, no matter how you jiggle, is not identical with combustion. Fire. FIRE. I insist on the absolute word. You may say that fire is a sum of various phenomena. I say it isn't. You might as well tell me a fly is a sum of wings and six legs and two bulging eyes. It is the fly which has the wings and legs, and not the legs and wings which somehow nab the fly into the middle of themselves. A fly is not a sum of various things. A fly is a fly, and the items of the sum are still fly.

So with fire. Fire is an absolute unity in itself. It is a dynamic polar principle. Establish a certain polarity between the moon-principle and the sun-principle, between the positive and negative, or sympathetic and volitional dynamism in any piece of matter, and you have fire, you have the sun-phenomenon. It is the sudden flare into the one mode, the sun mode, the material sympathetic mode. Correspondingly, establish an opposite polarity between the sun-principle and the water-principle, and you have decomposition into water, or towards watery dissolution.

There are two sheer dynamic principles in our universe, the sun-principle and the moon-principle. And these principles are known to us in immediate contact as fire and water. The sun is not fire. But the principle of fire is the sun-principle. That is, fire is the sudden swoop towards the sun, of matter which is suddenly sun-polarized. Fire is the sudden sun-assertion, the release towards the one pole only. It is the sudden revelation of the cosmic One Polarity, One Identity.

But there is another pole. There is the moon. And there is another absolute and visible principle, the principle of water. The moon is not water. But it is the soul of water, the invisible clue to all the waters.

So that we begin to realize our visible universe as a vast dual polarity between sun and moon. Two vast poles in space, invisible in themselves, but visible owing to the circuit which swoops between them, round them, the circuit of the universe, established at the cosmic poles of the sun and moon. This then is the infinite, the positive infinite of the positive pole, the sun-pole, negative infinite of the negative pole, the moon-pole. And between the two infinites all existence takes place.

But wait. Existence is truly a matter of propagation between the two infinites. But it needs a third presence. Sun-principle and moon-principle, embracing through the aeons, could never by themselves propagate one molecule of matter. The hailstone needs a grain of dust for its core. So does the universe. Midway between the two cosmic infinites lies the third, which is more than infinite. This is the Holy Ghost Life, individual life.

It is so easy to imagine that between them the two infinites of the cosmos propagated life. But one single moment of pause and silence, one single moment of gathering the whole soul into knowledge, will tell us that it is a falsity. It was the living individual soul which, dying, flung into space the two wings of the infinite, the two poles of the sun and the moon. The sun and the moon are the two eternal death-results of the death of individuals. Matter, all matter, is the Life-born. And what we know as inert matter, this is only the result of death in individuals, it is the dead bodies of individuals decomposed and resmelted between the hammer and anvil, fire and sand of the sun and the moon. When time began, the first individual died, the poles of the sun and moon were flung into space, and between the two, in a strange chaos and battle, the dead body was torn and melted and smelted, and rolled beneath the feet of the living. So the world was formed, always under the feet of the living.

And so we have a clue to gravitation. We, mankind, are all one family. In our individual bodies burns the positive quick of all things. But beneath our feet, in our own earth, lies the intense centre of our human, individual death, our grave. The earth has one centre, to which we are all polarized. The circuit of our life is balanced on the living soul within us, as the positive centre, and on the earth's dark centre, the centre of our abiding and eternal and substantial death, our great negative centre, away below. This is the circuit of our immediate individual existence. We stand upon our own grave, with our death-fire, the sun, on our right hand, and our death-damp, the moon, on our left.

The earth's centre is no accident. It is the great individual pole of us who die. It is the centre of the first dead body. It is the first germ-cell of death, which germ-cell threw out the great nuclei of the sun and the moon. To this centre of our earth we, as humans, are eternally polarized, as are our trees. Inevitably, we fall to earth. And the clue of us sinks to the earth's centre, the clue of our death, of our *weight*. And the earth flings us out as wings to the sun and moon: or as the death-germ dividing into two nuclei. So from the earth our radiance is flung to the sun, our marsh-fire to the moon, when we die.

We fall into the earth. But our rising was not from the earth. We rose from the earthless quick, the unfading life. And earth, sun, and moon are born only of our death. But it is only their polarized dynamic connection with us who live which sustains them all in their place and maintains them all in their own activities. The inanimate universe rests absolutely on the life-circuit of living creatures, is built upon the arch which spans the duality of living beings.

❦ XIV ❦

Sleep and Dreams

This is going rather far, for a book—nay, a booklet—on the child consciousness. But it can't be helped. Child-consciousness it is. And we have to roll away the stone of a scientific cosmos from the tomb-mouth of that imprisoned consciousness.

Now, dear reader, let us see where we are. First of all, we are ourselves—which is the refrain of all my chants. We are ourselves. We are living individuals. And as living individuals we are the one, pure clue to our own cosmos. To which cosmos living individuals *have always* been the clue, since time began, and *will always* be the clue, while time lasts.

I know it is not so fireworky as the sudden evolving of life, somewhere, somewhen, and somehow, out of force and matter with a pop. But that pop never popped, dear reader. The boot was on the other leg. And I wish I could mix a few more metaphors, like pops and legs and boots, just to annoy you.

Life never evolved, or evoluted, out of force and matter, dear reader. There is no such thing as evolution, anyhow. There is only development. Man was man in the very first plasm-speck which was his own individual origin, and is still his own individual origin. As for the origin, I don't know much about it. I only know there is but one origin, and that is the individual soul. The individual soul originated everything, and has itself no origin. So that time is a matter of living experience, nothing else, and eternity is just a mental trick. Of course every living speck, amoeba or newt, has its own individual soul.

And we sit on our own globe, dear reader, here individually located. Our own individual being is our own single reality. But the single reality of the individual being is dynamically and directly polarized to the earth's centre, which is the aggregate negative centre of all terrestrial existence. In short, the centre which in life we thrust away from, and towards which we fall, in death. For, our individual existence being positive, we must have a negative pole to thrust away from. And when our positive individual existence breaks, and we fall into death, our wonderful individual gravitation-centre succumbs to the earth's gravitation-centre.

So there we are, individuals, single, life-born, life-living, yet all the while poised and polarized to the aggregate centre of our substantial death, our earth's quick, powerful centre-clue.

There may be other individuals, alive, and having other worlds under their feet, polarized to their own globe's centre. But the very sacredness of my own individuality prevents my pronouncing about them, lest I, in attributing qualities to them, transgress against the pure individuality which is theirs, beyond me.

If, however, there be truly other people, with their own world under their feet, then I think it is fair to say that we all have our infinite identity in the sun. That in the rush and swirl of death we pass through fiery ways to the same sun. And from the sun, can the spores of souls pass to the various worlds? And to the worlds of the cosmos seed across space, through the wild beams of the sun? Is there seed of Mars in my veins? And is astrology not altogether nonsense?

But if the sun is the centre of our infinite oneing in death with all the other after-death souls of the cosmos: and in that great central station of travel, the sun, we meet and mingle and change trains for the stars: then ought we to assume that the moon is likewise a meeting-place of dead souls? The moon surely is a meeting-place of cold, dead, angry souls. But from our own globe only.

The moon is the centre of our terrestrial individuality in the cosmos. She is the declaration of our existence in separateness. Save for the intense white recoil of the moon, the earth would stagger towards the sun. The moon holds us to our own cosmic individuality, as a world individual in space. She is the fierce centre of retraction, of frictional withdrawal into separateness. She it is who sullenly stands with her back to us, and refuses to meet and mingle. She it is who burns white with the intense friction of her withdrawal into separation, that cold, proud white fire of furious, almost malignant apartness, the struggle into fierce, frictional separation. Her white fire is the frictional fire of the last strange, intense watery matter, as this matter fights its way out of combination and out of combustion with the sun-stuff. To the pure polarity of the moon fly the essential waters of our universe. Which essential waters, at the moon's clue, are only an intense invisible energy, a polarity of the moon.

There are only three great energies in the universal life, which is always individual and which yet sways all the physical forces as well as the vital energy; and then the two great dynamisms of the sun and the moon. To the dynamism of the sun belong heat, expansion-force, and all that range. To the dynamism of the moon the *essential* watery forces: not just gravitation, but electricity, magnetism, radium-energy, and so on.

The moon likewise is the pole of our night activities, as the sun is the pole of our day activities. Remember that the sun and moon are but great self-abandons which individual life has thrown out, to the right hand and to the left. When individual life dies, it flings itself on the right hand to the sun, on the left hand to the moon, in the dual polarity, and sinks to earth. When any man dies, his soul divides in death; as in life, in the first germ, it was united from two germs. It divides into two dark germs, flung asunder: the sun-germ and the moon-germ. Then the material body sinks to earth. And so we have the cosmic universe such as we know it.

What is the exact relationship between us and the death-realm of the afterwards we shall never know. But this relation is none the less active every moment of our lives. There is a pure polarity between life and death, between the living and the dead, between each living individual and the outer cosmos. Between each living individual and the earth's centre passes a never-ceasing circuit of magnetism. It is a circuit which in man travels up the right side, and down the left side of the body, to the earth's centre. It never ceases. But while we are awake it is entirely under the control and spell of the total consciousness, the individual consciousness, the soul, or self. When we sleep, however, then this individual consciousness of the soul is suspended for the time, and we lie completely within the circuit of the earth's magnetism, or gravitation, or both: the circuit of the earth's centrality. It is this circuit which is busy in all our tissue removing or arranging the dead body of our past day. For each time we lie down to sleep we have within us a body of death which dies with the day that is spent. And this body of death is removed or laid in line by the activities of the earth-circuit, the great active death-circuit, while we sleep.

As we sleep the current sweeps its own way through us, as the streets of a city are swept and flushed at night. It sweeps through our nerves and our blood, sweeping away the ash of our day's spent consciousness towards one form or other of excretion. This earth-current actively sweeping through us is really the death-activity busy in the service of life. It behooves us to know nothing of it. And as it sweeps it stimulates in the primary centres of consciousness vibrations which flash images upon the mind. Usually, in deep sleep, these images pass unrecorded; but as we pass towards the twilight of dawn and wakefulness, we begin to retain some impression, some record of the dream-images. Usually also the images that are accidentally swept into the mind in sleep are as disconnected and as unmeaning as the pieces of paper which the street-cleaners sweep into a bin from the city gutters at night. We should not think of taking all these papers, piecing them together, and making a marvellous book of them, prophetic of the future and pregnant with the past. We should not do so, although every rag of printed paper swept from the gutter would have some connection with the past day's event. But its significance, the significance of the words printed upon it is so small, that we relegate it into the limbo of the accidental and meaningless. There is no vital connection between the many torn bits of paper—only an accidental connection. Each bit of paper has reference to some actual event: a bus-ticket, an envelope, a tract, a pastry-shop bag, a newspaper, a hand-bill. But take them all together, bus-ticket, torn envelope, tract, paper-bag, piece of newspaper, and hand-bill, and they have no individual sequence, they belong more to the mechanical arrangements than to the vital consequence of our existence. And the same with most dreams. They are the heterogeneous odds and ends of images swept together accidentally by the besom of the night-current, and it is beneath our dignity to attach any real importance to them. It is always beneath our dignity to go degrading the integrity of the individual soul by cringing and scraping among the rag-tag of accident and of the inferior, mechanic coincidence and automatic event. Only those events are significant which derive from or apply to the soul in its full integrity. To go kowtowing before the facts of change, as gamblers and fortune-readers and fatalists do, is merely a perverting of the soul's proud integral priority, a rearing up of idiotic idols and fetishes.

Most dreams are purely insignificant, and it is the sign of a weak and paltry nature to pay any attention to them whatever. Only occasionally they matter. And this is only when something *threatens* us from the outer mechanical, or accidental *death*-world. When anything threatens us from the world of death, then a dream may become so vivid that it arouses the actual soul. And when a dream is so intense that it arouses the soul—then we must attend to it.

But we may have the most appalling nightmare because we eat pancakes for supper. Here again, we are threatened with an arrest of the mechanical flow of the system. This arrest becomes so serious that it affects the great organs of the heart and lungs, and these organs affect the primary conscious-centres.

Now we shall see that this is the direct reverse of real living consciousness. In living consciousness the primary affective centres control the great organs. But when sleep is on us, the reverse takes place. The great organs, being obstructed in their spontaneous-automatism, at last with violence arouse the active conscious-centres. And these flash images to the brain.

These nightmare images are very frequently purely mechanical: as of falling terribly downwards, or being enclosed in vaults. And such images are pure physical transcripts. The image of falling, of flying, of trying to run and not being able to lift the feet, of having to creep through terribly small passages, these are direct transcripts from the physical phenomena of circulation and digestion. It is the directly transcribed image of the heart which, impeded in its action by the gases of indigestion, is switched out of its established circuit of earth-polarity, and is as if suspended over a void, or plunging into a void: step by step, falling downstairs, maybe, according to the strangulation of the heart-beats. The same paralytic inability to lift the feet when one needs to run, in a dream, comes directly from the same impeded action of the heart, which is thrown off its balance by some material obstruction. Now the heart swings left and right in the pure circuit of the earth's polarity. Hinder this swing, force the heart over to the left, by inflation of gas from the stomach or by dead pressure upon the blood and nerves from any obstruction, and you get the sensation of being unable to lift the feet from earth: a gasping sensation. Or force the heart to overbalance towards the right, and you get the sensation of flying or of falling. The heart telegraphs its distress to the mind, and wakes us. The wakeful soul at once begins to deal with the obstruction, which was too much for the mechanical night-circuits. The same holds good of dreams of imprisonment, or of creeping through narrow passages. They are direct transfers from the squeezing of the blood through constricted arteries or heart chambers.

Most dreams are stimulated from the blood into the nerves and the nerve-centres. And the heart is the transmission station. For the blood has a unity and a consciousness of its own. It has a deeper, elemental consciousness of the mechanical or material world. In the blood we have the body of our most elemental consciousness, our almost material consciousness. And during sleep this material consciousness transfers itself into the nerves and to the brain. The transfer in wakefulness results in a feeling of pain or discomfort—as when we have indigestion, which is pure blood-discomfort. But in sleep the transfer is made through the dream-images which are mechanical phenomena like mirages.

Nightmares which have purely mechanical images may terrify us, give us a great shock, but the shock does not enter our souls. We are surprised, in the morning, to find that the bristling horror of the night seems now just nothing—dwindled to nothing. And this is because what was a purely material obstruction in the physical flow, temporary only, is indeed a nothingness to the living, integral soul. We are subject to such accidents—if we will eat pancakes for supper. And that is the end of it.

But there are other dreams which linger and haunt the soul. These are true soul-dreams. As we know, life consists of reactions and interrelations from the great centres of primary consciousness. I may start a chain of connection from one centre, which inevitably stimulates into activity the corresponding centre. For example, I may develop a profound and passional love for my mother in my days of adolescence. This starts, willy-nilly, the whole activity of adult love at the lower centres. But admission is made only of the upper, spiritual love, the love dynamically polarized at the upper centres. Nevertheless, whether the admission is made or not, once establish the circuit in the upper or spiritual centres of adult love, and you will get a corresponding activity in the lower, passional centres of adult love.

The activity at the lower centre, however, is denied in the daytime. There is a repression. Then the friction of the night-flow liberates the repressed psychic activity explosively. And then the image of the mother figures in passionate, disturbing, soul-rending dreams.

The Freudians point to this as evidence of a repressed incest desire. The Freudians are too simple. It is *always* wrong to accept a dream-meaning at its face value. Sleep is the time when we are given over to the automatic processes of the inanimate universe. Let us not forget this. Dreams are automatic in their nature. The psyche possesses remarkably few dynamic images. In the case of the boy who dreams of his mother, we have the aroused but unattached sex plunging in sleep, causing a sort of obstruction. We have the image of the mother, the dynamic emotional image. And the automatism of the dream-process immediately unites the sex-sensation to the great stock image, and produces an incest dream. But does this prove a repressed incest desire? On the contrary.

The truth is, every man has, the moment he awakes, a hatred of his dream, and a great desire to be free of the dream, free of the persistent mother-image or sister-image of the dream. It is a ghoul, it haunts his dreams, this image, with its hateful conclusions. And yet he cannot get free. As long as a man lives he may, in his dreams of passion or conflict, be haunted by the mother-image or sister-image, even when he knows that the cause of the disturbing dream is the wife. But even though the actual subject of the dream is the wife, still, over and over again, for years, the dream-process will persist in substituting the mother-image. It haunts and terrifies a man.

Why does the dream-process act so? For two reasons. First, the reason of simple automatic continuance. The mother-image was the first great emotional image to be introduced in the psyche. The dream-process mechanically reproduces its stock image the moment the intense sympathy-emotion is aroused. Again, the mother-image refers only to the upper plane. But the dream-process is mechanical in its logic. Because the mother-image refers to the great dynamic stress of the upper plane, therefore it refers to the great dynamic stress of the lower. This is a piece of sheer automatic logic. The living soul is *not* automatic, and automatic logic does not apply to it.

But for our second reason for the image. In becoming the object of great emotional stress for her son, the mother also becomes an object of poignancy, of anguish, of arrest, to her son. She arrests him from finding his proper fulfilment on the sensual plane. Now it is almost always the object of arrest which becomes impressed, as it were, upon the psyche. A man very rarely has an image of a person with whom he is livingly, vitally connected. He only has dream-images of the persons who, in some way, *oppose* his life-flow and his soul's freedom, and so become impressed upon his plasm as objects of resistance. Once a man is dynamically caught on the upper plane by mother or sister, then the dream-image of mother or sister will persist until the dynamic *rapport* between himself and his mother or sister is finally broken.

And the dream-image from the upper plane will be automatically applied to the disturbance of the lower plane.

Because—and this is very important—the dream-process *loves* its own automatism. It would force everything to an automatic-logical conclusion in the psyche. But the living, wakeful psyche is so flexible and sensitive, it has a horror of automatism. While the soul really lives, its deepest dread is perhaps the dread of automatism. For automatism in life is a forestalling of the death-process.

The living soul has its great fear. The living soul *fears* the automatically logical conclusion of incest. Hence the sleep-process invariably draws this conclusion. The dream-process, fiendishly, plays a triumph of automatism over us. But the dream-conclusion is almost invariably just the *reverse* of the soul's desire, in any distress-dream. Popular dream-telling understood this, and pronounced that you must read dreams backwards. Dream of a wedding, and it means a funeral. Wish your friend well, and fear his death, and you will dream of his funeral. Every desire has its corresponding fear that the desire shall not be fulfilled. It is *fear* which forms an arrest-point in the psyche, hence an image. So the dream automatically produces the fear-image as the desire-image. If you secretly wished your enemy dead, and feared he might flourish, the dream would present you with his wedding.

Of course this rule of inversion is too simple to hold good in all cases. Yet is is one of the most general rules for dreams, and applies most often to desire-and-fear dreams of a psychic nature.

So that an incest-dream would not prove an incest-desire in the living psyche. Rather the contrary, a living fear of the automatic conclusion: the soul's just dread of automatism. And though this may sound like casuistry, I believe it does explain a good deal of the dream-trick. That which is lovely to the automatic process is hateful to the spontaneous soul. The wakeful living soul fears automatism as it fears death: death being automatic.

It seems to me these are the first two dream-principles, and the two most important: the principle of automatism and the principle of inversion. They will not resolve everything for us, but they will help a great deal. We have to be *very* wary of giving way to dreams. It is really a sin against ourselves to prostitute the living spontaneous soul to the tyranny of dreams, or of chance, or fortune or luck, or any of the processes of the automatic sphere.

Then consider other dynamic dreams. First, the dream-image generally. Any *significant* dream-image is usually an image or a symbol of some arrest or scotch in the living spontaneous psyche. There is another principle. But if the image is a symbol, then the only safe way to explain the symbol is to proceed from the quality of emotion connected with the symbol.

For example, a man has a persistent passionate fear-dream about horses. He suddenly finds himself among great, physical horses, which may suddenly go wild. Their great bodies surge madly round him, they rear above him, threatening to destroy him. At any minute he may be trampled down.

Now a psychoanalyst will probably tell you off-hand that this is a father-complex dream. Certain symbols seem to be put into complex catalogues. But it is all too arbitrary.

Examining the emotional reference we find that the feeling is sensual, there is a great impression of the powerful, almost beautiful physical bodies of the horses, the nearness, the rounded haunches, the rearing. Is the dynamic passion in a horse the danger-passion? It is a great sensual reaction at the sacral ganglion, a reaction of intense, sensual, dominant volition. The horse which rears and kicks and neighs madly acts from the intensely powerful sacral ganglion. But this intense activity from the sacral ganglion is male: the sacral ganglion is at its highest intensity in the male. So that the horse-dream refers to some arrest in the deepest sensual activity in the male. The horse is presented as an object of terror, which means that to the man's automatic dream-soul, which loves automatism, the great sensual male activity is the greatest menace. The automatic pseudo-soul, which has got the sensual nature repressed, would like to keep it repressed. Whereas the greatest desire of the living spontaneous soul is that this very male sensual nature, represented as a menace, shall be actually accomplished in life. The spontaneous self is secretly yearning for the liberation and fulfilment of the deepest and most powerful sensual nature. There may be an element of father-complex. The horse may also refer to the powerful sensual being in the father. The dream may mean a love of the dreamer for the sensual male who is his father. But it has nothing to do with *incest*. The love is probably a just love.

The bull-dream is a curious reversal. In the bull the centres of power are in the breast and shoulders. The horns of the head are symbols of this vast power in the upper self. The woman's fear of the bull is a great terror of the dynamic *upper* centres in man. The bull's horns, instead of being phallic, represent the enormous potency of the upper centres. A woman whose most positive dynamism is in the breast and shoulders is fascinated by the bull. Her dream-fear of the bull and his horns which may run into her may be reversed to a significance of desire for connection, not from the centres of the lower, sensual self, but from the intense physical centres of the upper body: the phallus polarized from the upper centres, and directed towards the great breast centre of the woman. Her wakeful fear is terror of the great breast-and-shoulder, *upper* rage and power of man, which may pierce her defenseless lower self. The terror and the desire are near together —and go with an admiration of the slender, abstracted bull loins.

Other dream-fears, or strong dream-impressions, may be almost imageless. They may be a great terror, for example, of a purely geometric figure—a figure from pure geometry, or an example of pure mathematics. Or they may have no image, but only a sensation of smell, or of colour, or of sound.

These are the dream-fears of the soul which is falling out of human integrity into the purely mechanical mode. If we idealize ourselves sufficiently, the spontaneous centres do at last work only, or almost only, in the mechanical mode. They have no dynamic relation with another being. They cannot have. Their whole power of dynamic relationship is quenched. They act now in reference purely to the mechanical world, of force and matter, sensation and law. So that in dream-activity sensation or abstraction, abstract law or calculation occurs as the predominant or exclusive image. In the dream there may be a sensation of admiration or delight. The waking sensation is fear. Because the soul fears above all things its fall from individual integrity into the mechanic activity of the outer world, which is the automatic death-world.

And this is our danger today. We tend, through deliberate idealism or deliberate material purpose, to destroy the soul in its first nature of spontaneous, integral being, and to substitute the second nature, the automatic nature of the mechanical universe. For this purpose we stay up late at night, and we rise late in the morning.

To stay up late into the night is always bad. Let us be as ideal as we may, when the sun goes down the natural mode of life changes in us. The mind changes its activity. As the soul gradually goes passive, before yielding up its sway, the mind falls into its second phase of activity. It collects the results of the spent day into consciousness, lays down the honey of quiet thought, or the bitter-sweet honey of the gathered flower. It is the consciousness of that which is past. Evening is our time to read history and tragedy and romance—all of which are the utterance of that which is past, that which is over, that which is finished, is concluded: either sweetly concluded, or bitterly. Evening is the time for this.

But evening is the time also for revelry, for drink, for passion. Alcohol enters the blood and acts as the sun's rays act. It inflames into life, it liberates into energy and consciousness. But by a process of combustion. That life of the day which we have not lived, by means of sun-born alcohol we can now flare into sensation, consciousness, energy, and passion, and live it out. It is a liberation from the laws of idealism, a release from the restriction of control and fear. It is the blood bursting into consciousness. But naturally the course of the liberated consciousness may be in either direction: sharper mental action, greater fervour of spiritual emotion, or deeper sensuality. Nowadays the last is becoming much more unusual.

The active mind-consciousness of the night is a form of retrospection, or else it is a form of impulsive exclamation, direct from the blood, and unbalanced. Because the active physical consciousness of the night is the blood-consciousness, the most elemental form of consciousness. Vision is perhaps our highest form of *dynamic* upper consciousness. But our deepest lower consciousness is blood-consciousness.

And the dynamic lower centres are swayed from the blood. When the blood rousees into its night intensity, it naturally kindles first the lowest dynamic centres. It transfers its voice and its fire to the great hypogastric plexus, which governs, with the help of the sacral ganglion, the flow of urine through us, but which also voices the deep swaying of the blood in sex passion. Sex is our deepest form of consciousness. It is utterly non-ideal, non-mental. It is pure blood-consciousness. It is the basic consciousness of the blood, the nearest thing in us to pure material consciousness. It is the consciousness of the night, when the soul is *almost* asleep.

The blood-consciousness is the first and last knowledge of the living soul: the depths. It is the soul acting in part only, speaking with its first hoarse half-voice. And blood-consciousness cannot operate purely until the soul has put off all its manifold degrees and forms of upper consciousness. As the self falls back into quiescence, it draws itself from the brain, from the great nerve-centres, into the blood, where at last it will sleep. But as it draws and folds itself livingly in the blood, at the dark and powerful hour, it sends out its great call. For even the blood is alone and in part, and needs an answer. Like the waters of the Red Sea, the blood is divided in a dual polarity between the sexes. As the night falls and the consciousness sinks deeper, suddenly the blood is heard hoarsely calling. Suddenly the deep centres of the sexual consciousness rouse to their spontaneous activity. Suddenly there is a deep circuit established between me and the woman. Suddenly the sea of blood which is me heaves and rushes towards the sea of blood which is her. There is a moment of pure frictional crisis and contact of blood. And then all the blood in me ebbs back into its ways, transmuted, changed. And this is the profound basis of my renewal, my deep blood renewal.

And this has nothing to do with pretty faces or white skin or rosy breasts or any of the rest of the trappings of sexual love. These trappings belong to the day. Neither eyes nor hands nor mouth have anything to do with the final massive and dark collision of the blood in the sex crisis, when the strange flash of electric transmutation passes through the blood of the man and the blood of the woman. They fall apart and sleep in their transmutation.

But even in its profoundest, and most elemental movements, the soul is still individual. Even in its most material consciousness, it is still integral and individual. You would think the great blood-stream of mankind was one and homogeneous. And it is indeed more nearly one, more near to homogeneity than anything else within us. The blood-stream of mankind is almost homogeneous.

But it isn't homogeneous. In the first place, it is dual in a perfect dark dynamic polarity, the sexual polarity. No getting away from the fact that the blood of woman is dynamically polarized in opposition, or in difference to the blood of man. The crisis of their contact in sex connection is the moment of establishment of a new flashing circuit throughout the whole sea: the dark, burning red waters of our under-world rocking in a new dynamic rhythm in each of us. And then in the second place, the blood of an individual is his *own* blood. That is, it is individual. And though we have a potential dynamic sexual connection, we men, with almost every woman, yet the great outstanding fact of the individuality even of the blood makes us need a corresponding individuality in the woman we are to embrace. The more individual the man or woman, the more unsatisfactory is a non-individual connection: promiscuity. The more individual, the more does our blood cry out for its own specific answer, an individual woman, blood-polarized with us.

We have made the mistake of idealism again. We have thought that the woman who thinks and talks as we do will be the blood-answer. And we force it to be so. To our disaster. The woman who thinks and talks as we do is almost sure to have no dynamic blood-polarity with us. The dynamic blood-polarity would make her different from me, and not like me in her thought mode. Blood-sympathy is so much deeper than thought-mode, that it may result in very different expression, verbally.

We have made the mistake of turning life inside out: of dragging the day-self into the night, and spreading the night-self over into the day. We have made love and sex a matter of seeing and hearing and of day-conscious manipulation. We have made men and women come together on the grounds of this superficial likeness and commonalty—their mental and upper sympathetic consciousness. And so we have forced the blood to submission. Which means we force it into disintegration.

We have too much light in the night, and too much sleep in the day. It is an evil thing for us to prolong as we do the mental, visual, ideal consciousness far into the night when the hour has come for this upper consciousness to fade, for the blood alone to know and to act. By provoking the reaction of the great blood-stress, the sex-reaction, from the upper, outer mental consciousness and mental lasciviousness of conscious purpose, we thereby destroy the very blood in our bodies. We prevent it from having its own dynamic sway. We prevent it from coming to its own dynamic crisis and connection, from finding its own fundamental being. No matter how we work our sex, from the upper or outer consciousness, we don't achieve anything but the falsification and impoverishment of our own blood-life. We have no choice. Either we must withdraw from interference or slowly deteriorate.

We have made a corresponding mistake in sleeping on into the day. Once the sun rises our constitution changes. Once the sun is well up our sleep—supposing our life fairly normal—is no longer truly sleep. When the sun comes up the centres of active dynamic upper consciousness begin to wake. The blood changes its vibration and even its chemical constitution. And then we too ought to wake. We do ourselves great damage by sleeping too long into the day. The half-hour's sleep after midday meal is a readjustment. But the long hours of morning sleep are just a damage. We submit our now active centres of upper consciousness to the dominion of the blood-automatic flow. We chain ourselves down in our morning sleep. We transmute the morning's blood-strength into false dreams and into an ever-increasing force of inertia. And naturally, in the same line of inertia we persist from bad to worse.

With the result that our chained-down, active nerve-centres are half-shattered before we arise. We never become newly day-conscious, because we have subjected our powerful centres of day-consciousness to be trampled and wasted into dreams and inertia by the heavy flow of the blood-automatism in the morning sleeps. Then we arise with a feeling of the monotony and autom-atism of life. There is no good, glad refreshing. We feel tired to start with. And so we protract our day-consciousness on into the night, when we *do* at last begin to come awake, and we tell our-selves we must sleep, sleep, sleep in the morning and the day-time. It is better to sleep only six hours than to prolong sleep on and on when the sun has risen. Every man and woman should be forced out of bed soon after the sun has risen: particularly the nervous ones. And forced into physical activity. Soon after dawn the vast majority of people should be hard at work. If not, they will soon be nervously diseased.

❧   X V   ❧

The Lower Self

So it comes about that the moon is the planet of our nights, as the sun of our days. And this is not just accidental, or even mechanical. The influence of the moon upon the tides and upon us is not just an accident in phenomena. It is the result of the creation of the universe by life itself. It was life itself which threw the moon apart on the one hand, the sun on the other. And it is life itself which keeps the dynamic-vital relation constant between the moon and the living individuals of the globe. The moon is as dependent upon the life of individuals, for her continued existence, as each single individual is dependent upon the moon.

The same with the sun. The sun sets and has his perfect polarity in the life-circuit established between him and all living individuals. Break that circuit, and the sun breaks. Without man, beasts, butterflies, trees, toads, the sun would gutter out like a spent lamp. It is the life-emission from individuals which feeds his burning and establishes his sun-heart in its powerful equilibrium.

The same with the moon. She lives from us, primarily, and we from her. Everything is a question of relativity. Not only is every force relative to other force or forces, but every existence is relative to other existences. Not only does the life of man depend on man, beast, and herb, but on the sun and moon, and the stars. And in another manner, the existence of the moon depends absolutely on the life of herb, beast, and man. The existence of the moon depends upon the life of individuals, that which alone is original. Without the life of individuals the moon would fall asunder. And the moon particularly, because she is polarized dynamically to this, our own earth. We do not know what far-off life breathes between the stars and the sun. But our life alone supports the moon. Just as the moon is the pole of our single terrestrial individuality.

Therefore we must know that between the moon and each individual being exists a vital dynamic flow. The life of individuals depends directly upon the moon, just as the moon depends directly upon the life of individuals.

But in what way does the life of individuals depend directly upon the moon?

The moon is the mother of darkness. She is the clue to the active darkness. And we, below the waist, we have our being in darkness. Below the waist we are sightless. When, in the daytime, our life is polarized upwards, towards the open, sun-wakened eyes and the mind which sees in vision, then the powerful dynamic centres of the lower body act in subservience, in their negative polarity. And then we flow upwards, we go forth seeking the universe, in vision, speech, and thought—we go forth to see all things, to hear all things, to know all things by acquaintance and by knowledge. One flood of dynamic flow are we, upwards polarized, in our tallness and our wide-eyed spirit seeking to bring all the universe into the range of our conscious individuality, and eager always to make new worlds, out of this old world, to bud new green tips on the tree of life. Just as a tree would die if it were not making new green tips upon all its vast old world of a body, so the whole universe would perish if man and beast and herb were not always putting forth a newness: the toad taking a vivider color, spreading his hands a little more gently, developing a more *rusé* intelligence, the birds adding a new note to their speech and song, a new sharp swerve to their flight, a new nicety to their nests; and man, making new worlds, new civilizations. If it were not for this striving into new creation on the part of living individuals, the universe would go dead, gradually, gradually and fall asunder. Like a tree that ceases to put forth new green tips, and to advance out a little further.

But each new tip arises out of the apparent death of the old, the preceding one. Old leaves have got to fall, old forms must die. And if men must at certain periods fall into death in millions, why, so must the leaves fall every single autumn. And dead leaves make good mould. And so dead men. Even dead men's souls.

So if death has to be the goal for a great number, then let it be so. If America must invent this poison-gas, let her. When death is our goal of goals we shall invent the means of death, let our professions of benevolence be what they will.

But this time, it seems to me, we have consciously and responsibly to carry ourselves through the winter-period, the period of death and denudation: that is, some of us have, some *nation* even must. For there are not now, as in the Roman times, any great reservoirs of energetic barbaric life. Goths, Gauls, Germans, Slavs, Tartars. The world is very full of people, but all fixed in civilizations of their own, and they all have all our vices, all our mechanisms, and all our means of destruction. This time, the leading civilization cannot die out as Greece, Rome, Persia died. It must suffer a great collapse, maybe. But it must carry through all the collapse the living clue to the next civilization. It's no good thinking we can leave it to China or Japan or India or Africa— any of the great swarms.

And here we are, we don't look much like carrying through to a new era. What have we got that will carry through? The latest craze is Mr. Einstein's Relativity Theory. Curious that everybody catches fire at the word Relativity. There must be something in the mere suggestion, which we have been waiting for. But what? As far as I can see, Relativity means, for the common amateur mind, that there is no one absolute force in the physical universe, to which all other forces may be referred. There is no one single absolute central principle governing the world. The great cosmic forces or mechanical principles can only be known in their relation to one another, and can only exist in their relation to one another. But, says Einstein, this relation between the mechanical forces is constant, and may be expressed by a mathematical formula: which mathematical formula may be used to equate all mechanical forces of the universe.

I hope that is not scientifically all wrong. It is what I understand of the Einstein theory. What I doubt is the equation formula. It seems to me, also, that the velocity of light through space is the *deus ex machina* in Einstein's physics. Somebody will some day put salt on the tail of light as it travels through space, and then its simple velocity will split up into something complex, and the Relativity formula will fall to bits. But I am a confirmed outsider, so I'll hold my tongue.

All I know is that people have got the word Relativity into their heads, and catch-words always refer to some latent idea or conception in the popular mind. It has taken a Jew to knock the last center-pin out of our ideally spinning universe. The Jewish intelligence for centuries has been picking holes in our ideal system—scientific and sociological. Very good thing for us. Now Mr. Einstein, we are glad to say, has pulled out the very axle pin. At least that is how the vulgar mind understands it. The equation formula doesn't count. So now, the universe, according to the popular mind, can wobble about without being pinned down. Really, an anarchical conclusion. But the Jewish mind insidiously drives us to anarchical conclusions. We are glad to be driven from false, automatic fixities, anyhow. And once we are driven right on to nihilism we may find a way through.

So, there is nothing absolute left in the universe. Nothing. Lord Haldane says pure knowledge is absolute. As far as it goes, no doubt. But pure knowledge is only such a tiny bit of the universe, and always relative to the thing known and to the knower.

I feel inclined to Relativity myself. I think there is no one absolute principle in the universe. I think everything is relative. But I also feel, most strongly, that in itself each individual living creature is absolute: in its own being. And that all things in the universe are just relative to the individual living creature. And that individual living creatures are relative to each other.

And what about a goal? There is no final goal. But every step taken has its own little relative goal. So what about the next step?

Well, first and foremost, that every individual creature shall come to its own particular and individual fullness of being. Very nice, very pretty—but *how?* Well, through a living dynamic relation to other creatures. Very nice again, pretty little adjectives. But what *sort* of a living dynamic relation? Well, *not* the relation of love, that's one thing, nor of brotherhood, nor equality. The next relation has got to be a relationship of men towards men in a spirit of unfathomable trust and responsibility, service and leadership, obedience and pure authority. Men have got to choose their leaders, and obey them to the death. And it must be a system of culminating aristocracy, society tapering like a pyramid to the supreme leader.

All of which sounds very distasteful at the moment. But upon all the vital lessons we have learned during our era of love and spirit and democracy we can found our new order.

We wanted to be all of a piece. And we couldn't bring it off. Because we just *aren't* all of a piece. We wanted first to have nothing but nice day-time selves, awfully nice and kind and refined. But it didn't work. Because whether we want it or not, we've got night-time selves. And the most spiritual woman ever born or made has to perform her natural functions just like anybody else. We must *always* keep in line with this fact.

Well, then, we have night-time selves. And the night-self is the very basis of the dynamic self. The blood-consciousness and the blood-passion is the very source and origin of us. Not that we can *stay* at the source. Nor even make a *goal* of the source, as Freud does. The business of living is to travel away from the source. But you must start every single day fresh from the source. You must rise every day afresh out of the dark sea of the blood.

When you go to sleep at night, you have to say: "Here dies the man I am and know myself to be." And when you rise in the morning you have to say: "Here rises an unknown quantity which is still myself."

The self which rises naked every morning out of the dark sleep of the passionate, hoarsely-calling blood: this is the unit for the next society. And the polarizing of the passionate blood in the individual towards life, and towards leader, this must be the dynamic of the next civilization. The intense, passionate yearning of the soul towards the soul of a stronger, greater individual, and the passionate blood-belief in the fulfilment of this yearning will give men the next motive for life.

We have to sink back into the darkness and the elemental consciousness of the blood. And from this rise again. But there is no rising until the bath of darkness and extinction is accomplished.

As social units, as civilized men we have to do what we do as physical organisms. Every day, the sun sets from the sky, and darkness falls, and every day, when this happens, the tide of life turns in us. Instead of flowing upwards and outwards towards mental consciousness and activity, it turns back, to flow downwards. Downwards towards the digestion processes, downwards further to the great sexual conjunctions, downwards to sleep.

This is the soul now retreating, back from the outer life of day, back to the origins. And so, it stays its hour at the first great sensual stations, the solar plexus and the lumbar ganglion. But the tide ebbs on, down to the immense, almost inhuman passionate darkness of sex, the strange and moon-like intensity of the hypogastric plexus and the sacral ganglion, then deep, deeper, past the last great station of the darkest psyche, down to the earth's center. Then we sleep.

And the moon is the tide-turner. The moon is the great cosmic pole which calls us back, back out of our day-self, back through the moonlit darknesses of the sensual planes, to sleep. It is the moon that sways the blood, and sways us back into the extinction of the blood. And as the soul retreats back into the sea of its own darkness, the mind, stage by stage, enjoys the mental consciousness that belongs to this retreat back into the sensual deeps; and then it goes extinguished. There is sleep.

And so we resolve back towards our elementals. We dissolve back, out of the upper consciousness, out of mind and sight and speech, back, down into the deep and massive, swaying consciousness of the dark, living blood. At the last hour of sex I am no more than a powerful wave of mounting blood. Which seeks to surge and join with the answering sea in the other individual. When the sea of individual blood which I am at that hour heaves and finds its pure contact with the sea of individual blood which is the woman at that hour, then each of us enters into the wholeness of our deeper infinitude, our profound fullness of being, in the ocean of our oneness and our consciousness.

This is under the spell of the moon, of sea-born Aphrodite, mother and bitter goddess. For I am carried away from my sunny day-self into this other tremendous self, where knowledge will not save me, but where I must obey as the sea obeys the tides. Yet however much I go, I know that I am all the while myself, in my going.

This then is the duality of my day and my night being: a duality so bitter to an adolescent. For the adolescent thinks with shame and terror of his night. He would wish to have no night-self. But it is Moloch, and he cannot escape it.

The tree is born of its roots and its leaves. And we of our days and our nights. Without the night-consummation we are trees without roots.

And the night-consummation takes place under the spell of the moon. It is one pure motion of meeting and oneing. But even so, it is a circuit, not a straight line. One pure motion of meeting and oneing, until the flash breaks forth, when the two are one. And this, this flashing moment of the ignition of two seas of blood, this is the moment of begetting. But the begetting of a child is less than the begetting of the man and the woman. Woman is begotten of man at that moment, into her greater self: and man is begotten of woman. This is the main. And that which cannot be fulfilled, perfected in the two individuals, that which cannot take fire into individual life, this trickles down and is the seed of a new life, destined ultimately to fulfil that which the parents could not fulfil. So it is forever.

Sex then is a polarization of the individual blood in man towards the individual blood in woman. It is more, also. But in its prime functional reality it is this. And sex union means bringing into connection the dynamic poles of sex in man and woman.

In sex we have our basic, most elemental being. Here we have our most elemental contact. It is from the hypogastric plexus and the sacral ganglion that the dark forces of manhood and womanhood sparkle. From the dark plexus of sympathy run out the acute, intense sympathetic vibrations direct to the corresponding pole. Or so it should be, in genuine passionate love. There is no mental interference. There is even no interference of the upper centres. Love is supposed to be blind. Though modern love wears strong spectacles.

But love is really blind. Without sight or scent or hearing the powerful magnetic current vibrates from the hypogastric plexus in the female, vibrating onto the air like some intense wireless message. And there is immediate response from the sacral ganglion in some male. And then sight and day-consciousness begin to fade. In the lower animals apparently any male can receive the vibration of any female: and if need be, even across long distances of space. But the higher the development the more individual the attunement. Every wireless station can only receive those messages which are in its own vibration key. So with sex in specialized individuals. From the powerful dynamic centre the female sends out her dark summons, the intense dark vibration of sex. And according to her nature, she receives her responses from the males. The male enters the magnetic field of the female. He vibrates helplessly in response. There is established at once a dynamic circuit, more or less powerful. It would seem as if, while ever life remains free and wild and independent, the sex-circuit, while it lasts, is omnipotent. There is one electric flow which encompasses one male and one female, or one male and one particular group of females all polarized in the same key of vibration.

This circuit of vital sex magnetism, at first loose and wide, gradually closes and becomes more powerful, contracts and grows more intense, until the two individuals arrive into contact. And even then the pulse and flow of attraction and recoil varies. In free wild life, each touch brings about an intense recoil, and each recoil causes an intense sympathetic attraction. So goes on the strange battle of desire, until the consummation is reached.

It is the precise parallel of what happens in a thunder-storm, when the dynamic forces of the moon and the sun come into collison. The result is threefold: first, the electric flash, then the birth of pure water, new water.

So it is in sex relation. There is a threefold result. First, the flash of pure sensation and of real electricity. Then there is the birth of an entirely new state of blood in each partner. And then there is the liberation.

But the main thing, as in the thunder-storm, is the absolute renewal of the atmosphere: in this case, the blood. It would no doubt be found that the electro-dynamic condition of the white and red corpuscles of the blood was quite different after sex union, and that the chemical composition of the fluid of the blood was quite changed.

And in this renewal lies the great magic of sex. The life of an individual goes on apparently the same from day to day. But as a matter of fact there is an inevitable electric accumulation in the nerves and the blood, an accumulation which weighs there and broods there with intolerable pressure. And the only possible means of relief and renewal is in pure passional interchange. There is and must be a pure passional interchange from the upper self, as when men unite in some great creative or religious or constructive activity, or as when they fight each other to the death. The great goal of creative or constructive activity, or of heroic victory in fight, *must* always be the goal of the day-time self. But the very possibility of such a goal arises out of the vivid dynamism of the conscious blood. And the blood in an individual finds its great renewal in a perfected sex circuit.

A perfected sex circuit and a successful sex union. And there can be no successful sex union unless the greater hope of purposive constructive activity fires the soul of the man all the time: or the hope of passionate, purposive *destructive* activity: the two amount religiously to the same thing, within the individual. Sex as an end in itself is a disaster: a vice. But an ideal purpose which has no roots in the deep sea of passionate sex is a greater disaster still. And now we have only these two things: sex as a fatal goal, which is the essential theme of modern tragedy: or ideal purpose as a deadly parasite. Sex passion as a goal in itself always leads to tragedy. There must be the great purposive inspiration always present. But the automatic ideal-purpose is not even a tragedy, it is a slow humiliation and sterility.

The great thing is to keep the sexes pure. And by pure we don't mean an ideal sterile innocence and similarity between boy and girl. We mean pure maleness in a man, pure femaleness in a woman. Woman is really polarized downwards, towards the centre of the earth. Her deep positivity is in the downward flow, the moon-pull. And man is polarized upwards, towards the sun and the day's activity. Women and men are dynamically different, in everything. Even in the mind, where we seem to meet, we are really utter strangers. We may speak the same verbal language, men and women: as Turk and German might both speak Latin. But *whatever* a man says, his meaning is something quite different and changed when it passes through a woman's ears. And though you reverse the sexual polarity, the flow between the sexes, still the difference is the same. The *apparent* mutual understanding, in companionship between a man and a woman, is always an illusion, and always breaks down in the end.

Woman can polarize her consciousness upwards. She can obtain a hand even over her sex receptivity. She can divert even the electric spasm of coition into her upper consciousness: it was the trick which the snake and the apple between them taught her. The snake, whose consciousness is *only* dynamic, and non-cerebral. The snake, who has no mental life, but only an intensely vivid dynamic mind, he envied the human race its mental consciousness. And he knew, this intensely wise snake, that the one way to make humanity pay more than the price of mental consciousness was to pervert woman into mentality: to stimulate her into the upper flow of consciousness.

For the true polarity of consciousness in woman is downwards. Her deepest consciousness is in the loins and belly. Even when perverted, it is so. The great flow of female consciousness is downwards, down to the weight of the loins and round the circuit of the feet. Pervert this, and make a false flow upwards, to the breast and head, and you get a race of "intelligent" women, delightful companions, tricky courtesans, clever prostitutes, noble idealists, devoted friends, interesting mistresses, efficient workers, brilliant managers, women as good as men at all the manly tricks: and better, because they are so very headlong once they go in for men's tricks. But then, after a while, pop it all goes. The moment woman has got man's ideals and tricks drilled into her, the moment she is competent in the manly world—there's an end of it. She's had enough. She's had more than enough. She hates the thing she has embraced. She becomes absolutely perverse, and her one end is to prostitute herself and her ideals to sex. Which is her business at the present moment.

We bruise the serpent's head: his flat and brainless head. But his revenge of bruising our heel is a good one. The heels, through which the powerful downward circuit flows: these are bruised in us, numbed with a horrible neurotic numbness. The dark strong flow that polarizes us to the earth's centre is hampered, broken. We become flimsy fungoid beings, with no roots and no hold in the earth, like mushrooms. The serpent has bruised our heel till we limp. The lame gods, the enslaved gods, the toiling limpers moaning for the woman. You don't find the sun and moon playing at pals in the sky. Their beams cross the great gulf which is between them.

So with man and woman. They must stand clear again. They must fight their way out of their self-consciousness: there is nothing else. Or, rather, each must fight the other out of self-consciousness. Instead of this leprous forbearance which we are taught to practise in our intimate relationships, there should be the most intense open antagonism. If your wife flirts with other men, and you don't like it, say so before them all, before wife and man and all, say you won't have it. If she seems to you false, in any circumstance, tell her so, angrily, furiously, and stop her. Never mind about being justified. If you hate anything she does, turn on her in a fury. Harry her, and make her life a hell, so long as the real hot rage is in you. Don't silently hate her, or silently forbear. It is such a dirty trick, so mean and ungenerous. If you feel a burning rage, turn on her and give it to her, and *never* repent. It'll probably hurt you much more than it hurts her. But never repent for your real hot rages, whether they're "justifiable" or not. If you care one sweet straw for the woman, and if she makes you that you can't bear any more, give it to her, and if your heart weeps tears of blood afterwards, tell her you're thankful she's got it for once, and you wish she had it worse.

The same with wives and their husbands. If a woman's husband gets on her nerves, she should fly at him. If she thinks him too sweet and smarmy with other people, she should let him have it to his nose, straight out. She should lead him a dog's life, and never swallow her bile.

With wife or husband, you should never swallow your bile. It makes you go all wrong inside. Always let fly, tooth and nail, and never repent, no matter what sort of a figure you make.

We have a vice of love, of softness and sweetness and smarminess and intimacy and promiscuous kindness and all that sort of thing. We think it's so awfully nice of us to be like that, in ourselves. But in our wives or our husbands it gets on our nerves horribly. Yet we think it oughtn't to, so we swallow our spleen.

We shouldn't. When Jesus said, "If thine eye offend thee, pluck it out," he was beside the point. The eye doesn't really offend us. We are rather fond of our own squint eye. It only offends the person who cares for us. And it's up to this person to pluck it out.

This holds particularly good of the love and intimacy vice. It'll never offend us in ourselves. While it will be gall and wormwood to our wife or husband. And it is on this promiscuous love and intimacy and kindness and sweetness, all a vice, that our self-consciousness really rests. If we are battered out of this, we shall be battered out of self-consciousness.

And so, men, drive your wives, beat them out of their self-consciousness and their soft smarminess and good, lovely idea of themselves. Absolutely tear their lovely opinion of themselves to tatters, and make them look a holy ridiculous sight in their own eyes. Wives, do the same to your husbands.

But fight for your life, men. Fight your wife out of her own self-conscious preoccupation with herself. Batter her out of it till she's stunned. Drive her back into her own true mode. Rip all her nice superimposed modern-woman and wonderful-creature garb off her. Reduce her once more to a naked Eve, and send the apple flying.

Make her yield to her own real unconscious self, and absolutely stamp on the self that she's got in her head. Drive her forcibly back, back into her own true unconscious.

And then you've got a harder thing still to do. Stop her from looking on you as her "lover." Cure her of that, if you haven't cured her before. Put the fear of the Lord into her that way. And make her know she's got to believe in you again, and in the deep purpose you stand for. But before you can do that, you've got to *stand* for some deep purpose. It's no good faking one up. You won't take a woman in, not really. Even when she *chooses* to be taken in, for prettiness' sake, it won't do you any good.

But combat her. Combat her in her sexual pertinacity, and in her secret glory or arrogance in the sexual goal. Combat her in her cock-sure belief that she "knows" and that she is "right." Take it all out of her. Make her yield once more to the male leadership: if you've got anywhere to lead to. If you haven't, best leave the woman alone; she has *one* goal of her own, anyhow, and it's better than your nullity and emptiness.

You've got to take a new resolution into your soul, and break off from the old way. You've got to know that you're a man, and being a man means you must go on alone, ahead of the woman, to break a way through the old world into the new. And you've got to be alone. And you've got to start off ahead. And if you don't know which direction to take, look round for the man your heart will point out to you. And follow—and never look back. Because if Lot's wife, looking back, was turned to a pillar of salt, these miserable men, forever looking back to their women for guidance, they are miserable pillars of half-rotten tears.

You'll have to fight to make a woman believe in you as a real man, a real pioneer. No man is a man unless to his woman he is a pioneer. You'll have to fight still harder to make her yield her goal to yours: her night goal to your day goal. The moon, the planet of women, sways us back from our day-self, sways us back from our real social unison, sways us back, like a retreating tide, in a friction of criticism and separation and social disintegration.

That is woman's inevitable mode, let her words be what they will. Her goal is the deep, sensual individualism of secrecy and night-exclusiveness, hostile, with guarded doors. And you'll have to fight very hard to make a woman yield her goal to yours, to make her, in her own soul, *believe* in your goal as the goal beyond, in her goal as the way by which you go. She'll never believe until you have your soul filled with a profound and absolutely inalterable purpose, that will yield to nothing, least of all to her. She'll never believe until, in your soul, you are cut off and gone ahead, into the dark.

She may of course already love you, and love you for yourself. But the love will be a nest of scorpions unless it is overshadowed by a little fear or awe of your further purpose, a living *belief* in your going beyond her, into futurity.

But when once a woman *does* believe in her man, in the pioneer which he is, the pioneer who goes on ahead beyond her, into the darkness in front, and who may be lost to her forever in this darkness; when once she knows the pain and beauty of this belief, knows that the loneliness of waiting and following is inevitable, that it must be so; ah, then, how wonderful it is! How wonderful it is to come back to her, at evening, as she sits half in fear and waits! How good it is to come home to her! How good it is then when the night falls! How richly the evening passes! And then, for her, at last, all that she has lost during the day, to have it again between her arms, all that she has missed, to have it poured out for her, and a richness and a wonder she had never expected. It is her hour, her goal. That's what it is to have a wife.

Ah, how good it is to come home to your wife when she *believes* in you and submits to your purpose that is beyond her. Then, how wonderful this nightfall is! How rich you feel, tired, with all the burden of the day in your veins, turning home! Then you too turn to your other goal: to the splendour of darkness between her arms. And you know the goal is there for you: how rich that feeling is. And you feel an unfathomable gratitude to the woman who loves you and believes in your purpose and receives you into the magnificent dark gratification of her embrace That's what it is to have a wife.

But no man ever had a wife unless he served a great predominant purpose. Otherwise, he has a lover, a mistress. No matter how much she may be married to him, unless his days have a living purpose, constructive or destructive, but a purpose beyond her and all she stands for; unless his days have this purpose, and his soul is really committed to his purpose, she will not be a wife, she will be only a mistress and he will be her lover.

If the man has no purpose for his days, then to the woman alone remains the goal of her nights: the great sex goal. And this goal is no goal, but always cries for the something beyond: for the rising in the morning and the going forth beyond, the man disappearing ahead into the distance of futurity, that which his purpose stands for, the future. The sex goal needs, absolutely needs, this further departure. And if there *be* no further departure, no great way of belief on ahead: and if sex is the starting point and the goal as well: then sex becomes like the bottomless pit, insatiable. It demands at last the departure into death, the only available beyond. Like Carmen, or like Anna Karenina. When sex is the starting point and the returning point both, then the only issue is death. Which is plain as a pike-staff in *Carmen* or *Anna Karenina*, and is the theme of almost *all* modern tragedy. Our one hackneyed, hackneyed theme. Ecstasies and agonies of love, and final passion of death. Death is the only pure, beautiful conclusion of a great passion. Lovers, pure lovers should say, "Let it be so."

And one is always tempted to say, "Let it be so." But no, let it be not so. Only I say this, let it be a great passion and then death, rather than a false or faked purpose. Tolstoi said "No" to the passion and the death conclusion. And then drew into the dreary issue of a false conclusion. His books were better than his life. Better the woman's goal, sex and death, than some *false* goal of man's.

Better Anna Karenina and Vronsky a thousand times than Natasha and that porpoise of a Pierre. This pretty, slightly sordid couple tried so hard to kid themselves that the porpoise Pierre was puffing with great purpose. Better Vronsky than Tolstoi himself, in my mind. Better Vronsky's final statement: "As a soldier I am still some good. As a man I am a ruin"—better that than Tolstoi and Tolstoi-ism and that beastly peasant blouse the old man wore.

Better passion and death than any more of these "isms." No more of the old purpose done up in aspic. Better passion and death.

But still—we *might* live, mightn't we?

For heaven's sake answer plainly, "No," if you feel like it. No good temporizing.

Epilogue

"*Tutti i salmi finiscono in gloria.*"

All the psalms wind up with the Gloria. "As it was in the beginning, is now, and ever shall be, World without end. Amen."

Well, then, Amen.

I hope you say Amen! along with me, dear little reader: if there be any dear little reader who has got so far. If not, I say Amen! all by myself. But don't you think the show is all over. I've got another volume up my sleeve, and after a year or two years, when I have shaken it down my sleeve, I shall bring it and lay it at the foot of your Liberty statue, oh Columbia, as I do this one.

I suppose Columbia means the States. "Hail Columbia!" I suppose, etymologically, it is a nest of turtle-doves, Lat. *columba*, a dove. Coo me softly, then, Columbia; don't roar me like the sucking doves of the critics of my *Psychoanalysis and the Unconscious*.

And when I lay this little book at the foot of the Liberty statue, that brawny lady is not to look down her nose and bawl: "Do you see any green in my eye?" Of course I don't, dear lady. I only see the reflection of that torch—or is it a carrot?—which you are holding up to light the way into New York harbour. Well, many an ass has strayed across the uneasy paddock of the Atlantic to nibble your carrot, dear lady. And I must say, you can keep on slicing off nice little carrot-slices of guineas and doubloons for an extraordinarily inexhaustible long time. And innumerable asses can collect themselves nice little heaps of golden carrot-slices, and then lift up their heads and brag over them with fairly pandemoniac yells of gratification. Of course I don't see any green in your eye, dear Libertas, unless it is the smallest glint from the carrot-tips. The gleam in your eye is golden, oh Columbia!

Nevertheless, and in spite of all this, up trots this here little ass and makes you a nice present of this pretty book. You needn't sniff, and glance at your carrot-sceptre, lady Liberty. You needn't throw down the thinnest carrot-paring you can pare off, and then say: "Why should I pay for this tripe, this wordy mass of rather revolting nonsense!" You can't pay for it, darling. If I didn't make you a present of it you could never buy it. So don't shake your carrot-sceptre and feel supercilious. Here's a gift for you, Missis. You can look in its mouth, too. Mind it doesn't bite you. No, you needn't bother to put your carrot behind your back, nobody wants to snatch it.

How do you do, Columbia! Look, I brought you a posy: this nice little posy of words and wisdom which I made for you in the woods of Ebersteinburg, on the borders of the Black Forest, near Baden-Baden, in Germany, in this summer of scanty grace but nice weather. I made it specially for you—Whitman, for whom I have an immense regard, says "These States." I suppose I ought to say: "Those States." If the publisher would let me, I'd dedicate this book to you, to "Those States." Because I wrote this book entirely for you, Columbia. You may not take it as a compliment. You may even smell a tiny bit of Schwarzwald sap in it, and be finally disgusted. I admit that trees ought to think twice before they flourish in such a disgraced place as the Fatherland. "*Chi va coi zoppi, all' anno zoppica.*" But you've not only to gather ye rosebuds while ye may, but *where* ye may. And so, as I said before, the Black Forest, etc.

I know, Columbia, dear Libertas, you'll take my posy and put your carrot aside for a minute, and smile, and say: "I'm sure, Mr. Lawrence, it is a *long* time since I had such a perfectly beautiful bunch of ideas brought me." And I shall blush and look sheepish and say: "So glad you think so. I believe you'll find they'll keep fresh quite a long time, if you put them in water." Whereupon you, Columbia, with real American gallantry: "Oh, they'll keep for*ever*, Mr. Lawrence. They *couldn't* be so cruel as to go and die, such perfectly lovely-coloured ideas. Lovely! Thank you ever, ever so much."

Just think of it, Columbia, how pleased we shall be with one another: and how much nicer it will be than if you snorted "High-falutin' Nonsense"—or "Wordy mass of repulsive rubbish."

"When they were busy making Italy, and were just going to put it in the oven to bake: that is, when Garibaldi and Vittorio Emmanuele had won their victories at Caserta, Naples prepared to give them a triumphant entry. So there sat the little king in his carriage: he had short legs and huge swagger moustaches and a very big bump of philoprogeniture. The town was all done up, in spite of the rain. And down either side of the wide street were hasty statues of large, well-fleshed ladies, each one holding up a forefinger. We don't know what the king thought. But the staff held their breath. The king's appetite for strapping ladies was more than notorious, and naturally it looked as if Naples had done it on purpose.

As a matter of fact, the forefinger meant *Italia Una!* "Italy shall be one." Ask Don Sturzo.

Now you see how risky statues are. How many nice little asses and poets trot over the Atlantic and catch sight of Liberty holding up this carrot of desire at arm's length, and fairly hear her say, as one does to one's pug dog, with a lump of sugar: "Beg! Beg!" and "Jump! Jump, then!" And each little ass and poodle begins to beg and to jump, and there's a rare game round about Liberty, zap, zap, zapperty-zap!

Do lower the carrot, gentle Liberty, and let us talk nicely and sensibly. I don't like you as a *carotaia*, precious.

Talking about the moon, it is thrilling to read the announcements of Professor Pickering of Harvard, that it's almost a dead cert that there's life on our satellite. It is almost as certain that there's life on the moon as it is certain there is life on Mars. The professor bases his assertions on photographs—hundreds of photographs—of a crater with a circumference of thirty-seven miles. I'm not satisfied. I demand to know the yards, feet, and inches. You don't come it over me with the triteness of these round numbers.

"Hundreds of photographic reproductions have proved irrefutably the springing up at dawn, with an unbelievable rapidity, of vast fields of foliage which come into blossom just as rapidly [sic!] and which disappear in a maximum period of eleven days." Again I'm not satisfied. I want to know if they're cabbages, cress, mustard, or marigolds or dandelions or daisies. Fields of foliage, mark you. And *blossom!* Come now, if you can get so far, Professor Pickering, you might have a shrewd guess as to whether the blossoms are good to eat, or if they're purely for ornament.

I am only waiting at last for an airplane to land on one of these fields of foliage and find a donkey grazing peacefully. Hee-haw!

"The plates moreover show that great blizzards, snow-storms, and volcanic eruptions are also frequent." So no doubt the blossoms are edelweiss.

"We find," says the professor, "a living world at our very doors where life in some respects resembles that of Mars." All I can say is: "Pray come in, Mr. Moony. And how is your cousin Signor Martian?"

Now I'm sure Professor Pickering's photographs and observations are really wonderful. But his *explanations!* Come now, Columbia, where is your High-falutin' Nonsense trumpet? Vast fields of foliage which spring up at dawn (!!!) and come into blossom just as quickly (!!!!) are rather too flowery even for my flowery soul. But there, truth is stranger than fiction.

I'll bet my moon against the Professor's, anyhow.

So long, Columbia. *A rivedérci.*